HPBooks'
Guide to GM Muscle Cars

1964–1973

HPBooks'
Guide to GM Muscle Cars
1964–1973

Published by HPBooks, a division of Price Stern Sloan, Inc.
11150 Olympic Boulevard, Suite 650
Los Angeles, California 90064

10 9 8 7 6 5 4 3 2 1
First Printing

Cover Photos: Courtesy of *Musclecar Review Magazine.*

Library of Congress Cataloging-in-Publication Data

HPBooks' guide to GM muscle cars, 1964-1973
    p. cm.
ISBN: 1-55788-003-4 (pbk. : alk. paper)
  1. General Motors automobiles. 2. Muscle cars. I. Title.
II. Title: Guide to GM muscle cars, 1964-1973.
TL215.G4B66 1990   90-41342
629.222—dc20   CIP

Notice: The information in this book is true and complete to the best of our knowledge. All recommendations are made without any guarantees on the part of Price Stern Sloan. The publisher disclaims all liability incurred in connection with the use of this information.

This book is printed on acid-free paper.

How to use this Guide

HPBooks' *Guide to GM Muscle Cars* is divided into four sections: Chevrolet, Pontiac, Buick and Oldsmobile. Each section is broken down into year-by-year chapters that contain a number of subsections. The first is a brief description of notable facts about that particular division such as design changes, production statistics, new model introductions, engine development and details of the division's overall development that occured during that year. This is followed by a description of the particular muscle car(s) covered in the chapter on a per model basis.

VIN Numbers, which stands for *Vehicle Identification Number,* explains the division's numbering system. Each automobile has an individual VIN number that identifies it. The VIN numbers can be found in the following places:

> 1965-1967: On the left front door hinge pillar post
> 1968-1973: On the left hand side of the instrument panel

Production Totals lists the units of a particular model and certain optional packages produced in a model year. If optional packages are listed, the percentage of optional units of the model's overall production is given. For example, in 1969 there were 26,357 Oldsmobile 4-4-2s built and 1,389 were equipped with the W30 option—which is 5% of the 4-4-2s built that model year. Please note that *production* figures, the number of vehicles recorded by the factory as they rolled off the assembly line, are not necessarily the same as *sales* figures, which are the numbers of vehicles recorded by dealers as having actually been sold.

Drivetrain Data lists specifications on the standard and optional engines available on the muscle cars covered in that chapter. If two or more models use the same engine, the information is not repeated, but the column is labeled with both of those models. From 1964-1971, the horsepower figures are *gross*; after 1971 these ratings are in *net* terms. The following is an explanation of the abbreviations used in the *Drivetrain Data* section:

Cyl:	cylinder
Bore (in):	bore (in inches)
Stroke (in):	stroke (in inches)
CID:	cubic inches displaced
Carbs:	carburetor (2- or 4-barrel)
Make:	make of carburetor
Model:	model of carburetor
Comp:	compression ratio
Max BHP:	maximum brake horsepower
@ RPM	at number of revolutions per minute
Torque ft-lb:	brake torque (in foot-pounds)
@ RPM:	at number of revolutions per minute

Transmissions lists the standard and optional transmission for a particular model and/or model with an optional engine. Under *Rear Axle Ratios,* the standard and optional ratios are listed. If a particular ratio is available only on a particular transmission, that transmission is enclosed in parenthesis next to that ratio. When a rear axle ratio has no transmission listed, it is available for all transmissions available on that particular model.

Exterior Data lists major specifications for the models covered in that chapter. Weight is given in terms of shipping weight, not curbside weight. The specifications are given for each model style. Each column is clearly labled as to model and style. All specifications are for that model. If the option is not specified in the column heading, the shipping weight is for the model without the option. Unfortunately, many shipping weights for models with option packages are unavailable.

Factory Base Price Data lists the Factory A.D.P. (Advertised Delivery Price) including standard equipment *only.* It includes a provision for recovery of federal excise tax and suggested delivery handling. It does not include transportation or state and local taxes.

Popular Factory Options is divided into three sections: *Interior, Exterior* and *Miscellaneous*. Prices for these options were not always available.

All of this information is compiled from data supplied by original factory sales literature, *Automotive News Yearly Journal* and the National Automobile Dealers Association (NADA).

DOBBS PUBLISHING GROUP

Many of the photos that appear in this book were supplied by Dobbs Publishing Group, publishers of the automotive enthusiast magazines:

Musclecar Review
Mustang Monthly
Corvette Fever
Super Ford
Mopar Muscle
Chevy Action

Their cooperation and donation of material is gratefully acknowledged. For subscription information, contact: Dobbs Publishing Group, 3816 Industry Blvd., Lakeland, FL 33811. (813) 644-0449.

CONTENTS

Chevrolet Muscle Cars
1964–1973

Chevrolet in the Muscle Car Era

Chevrolet has long had the atmosphere of a company unto itself. A view not entirely unreasonable, especially in the 1950s and 1960s when Chevy was regularly selling nearly one out of every three cars in America. During these two decades, Chevrolet was larger than all of the other GM divisions *combined* — larger even than Ford Motor Company or Chrysler Corporation — a reality reflected not only in sales but in personnel, facilities and financial resources within the corporation.

The joke around Pontiac in those days was that there were more Chevy engineers lost in the halls at Chevy engineering than were employed on the entire Pontiac engineering staff! Because of its size and domination of the marketplace, government anti-trust busters were taking a long, hard look at Chevy during this period and there was recurrent speculation that the Justice Department would file suit to break up General Motors and make Chevy an independent car company.

Nothing ever came of the anti-trust talk — and it all seems a little silly today with GM struggling to hang on to a combined 35% market share — but Chevrolet was a genuine colossus in the industry for decades. In fact, Chevrolet once owned GM! When GM founder William C. Durant was forced out in 1911, he bankrolled Chevrolet and used that little company's stock to plot a successful take-over of giant GM. Later, GM was reorganized and Chevrolet assumed its now-traditional role as a GM division. Eventually,

Durant was forced out again, but the stories of GM and Chevrolet are inextricably intertwined in ways few modern observers can imagine.

Another fact modern observers would have trouble comprehending is that Chevy never had much interest in high performance until comparatively recent times. After Ford introduced its long-awaited four-cylinder Model A in 1928, Chevy one-upped its rival with a spanking new inline six, the engine that was to become famous as the "stovebolt" six.

Ford, not to be out-done, upped the ante again in 1932 with its famous flathead V-8, whose manufacturing was masterminded by Charles "Cast Iron Charlie" Sorensen. The V-8 did not do all that much for Ford sales — during the economically depressed years of the 1930s, low-priced car buyers resisted eight-cylinder cars because they valued economy above all else — but it clearly gave Ford the performance lead in the low-priced field for more than 20 years, while Chevy sold the most cars.

When peacetime returned, it quickly became obvious that the nation was in a prosperous, expansionist mood and, by the early 1950s, performance was beginning to exert significant appeal in the marketplace. Chevrolet began to worry that, due to the sedateness of its cars, it was slowly losing its customers to Ford.

Thomas H. Keating was general manager of the division during this period. He had been sales manager in the late 1940s and had a strong nose for marketing trends. The 1953

Corvette was Chevrolet's initial effort to respond to America's growing desire for exciting transportation. The decision to build a modern, overhead-valve V-8 was the second.

Oldsmobile and Cadillac had introduced modern V-8s in 1949. Buick followed in 1953. Only Chevrolet and Pontiac were hold-outs, and Pontiac had been hard at work on a V-8 since the end of the war. But when Ford announced its intentions to build its own overhead-valve V-8 for the 1954 model year, the program at Chevy became urgent.

Edward N. Cole signed on as chief engineer in May 1952, and it was under his direction that the V-8 program was rushed through. In 1955, Chevy — like Pontiac — announced its first V-8, a 265 cubic-inch unit. Unlike Pontiac, the Chevy engine had numerous early problems stemming from its rushed development. Still, the problems were quickly fixed and never seriously dampened the enthusiasm of Chevy buyers or the performance-inclined who suddenly found themselves looking at Chevys in a whole new light.

Ed Cole was one of the finest engineers in the business and there was never any question of the soundness of his new power plant. In fact, it was so good it is still with us: The current GM 5.0 liter and 5.7 liter V-8s are direct descendants of that 1955 Chevy engine! Along the way, it has done loyal service for every GM nameplate including Cadillac, where it is presently listed as an option on the rear-drive Brougham. The performance possibilities with the new engine were known early on and a variety of applications (authorized and otherwise) began to appear almost immediately.

The performance pace quickened when Ed Cole was promoted to the general manager's office in 1956. Chevy began to invest substantial resources in racing. Then, the bottom fell out in 1957 when GM upper management, in league with the Automobile Manufacturer's Association, handed down its infamous ban on factory-sponsored racing.

Chevrolet was too far along the high performance road to consider quitting entirely, though. Fuel injection had appeared as a factory option on the Corvette 283 cube V-8 in 1957 and soon made it into other Chevy models. Chevy claimed this was the first production engine ever to deliver one horsepower per cubic inch, although the honor probably goes to the 1956 Chrysler 300-B (if fitted with the optional engine). Engine development continued under the talented direction of Harry F. Barr, who had replaced Cole as chief engineer in 1956, and Chevy continued to wage a low-key, behind-the-scenes performance war with Ford throughout the late 1950s and early 1960s.

The first model other than the Corvette to be specifically marketed as a high performance model was the Impala Super Sport announced in mid-year 1961, which also coincided with the arrival of Semon E. "Bunkie" Knudsen as general manager (fresh from a rousing engagement at Pontiac). Only 127 of the 1961 Super Sports were built with Chevy's new big-block 409 cubic-inch engine, essentially a bored and stroked 348 truck engine. Engineering minds behind it included John Rausch, Howard Kerl and Don McPherson. This same team later produced the fabulous 427 "Z-11" engine.

The 409 was an eye-opener. There had been performance sedans before, but this was performance in neon lights. A stock 409, rated at 409 hp, came with special heads and valves, larger ports, solid-lifter camshaft and a dual-quad aluminum intake manifold. Hayden Profitt won the Stock Eliminator honors at the 1962 NHRA Indy Nationals with a 409, turning in a 113.92 mph quarter-mile in 12.33 seconds. Dan Gurney even competed successfully in Europe with one.

The Z-11 was a 409 bored out to 427 cubic inches. Liberal use of aluminum reduced the weight of the 427 by as much as 233 pounds over a stock Chevy V-8. The powerplant featured special heads, intake manifold, pistons and a host of body modifications, including aluminum hood, front fenders and bumper, as well as the expected numerous tweakings to the chassis. The Z-11 was rated at 430 hp, but probably delivered more like 500.

Despite the power on tap, the Impala Super Sport never set any sales records. The first Super Sport to achieve wide appeal was the Chevelle SS of 1965. This car, a direct response to the fabulously successful Pontiac GTO first announced as a mid-year 1964 option, featured a light performance version of the new Chevy 396 cube powerplant, normally rated at 325 hp.

The hydraulically cammed Z-16 option version of the 396 rated at 375 hp was supplied to a mere 201 Chevelle 396s, but they were screamers. By 1970, Chevy was putting the big block 454 into the Chevelle Super Sport.

Despite the GM anti-racing edict, Chevrolet would supply special engines under-the-counter in this period for Chevelle racing applications. These included L-78 327s rated at 375 hp, and the L-72 Corvette engine. This latter powerplant was a big-block 427 rated at 425 hp, and at least 50 Chevelle's must have been built with them because the option qualified for NHRA competition.

The 1967 model year saw the introduction of the Camaro. The SS was available with the 375 hp 396 engine, although very few were so equipped. There were even a few 427 conversions done privately. Super Sport (SS) and Rally Sport (RS) editions were listed in the catalogue, but another one that really got the enthusiast's juices flowing was the original Z-28.

The Z-28 was built so that it could qualify for SCCA Trans-Am competition, and came with a 302 cubic-inch, solid-lifter engine rated at 290 hp. The 302 engine was produced by putting a 283 crank in a 327 block. Corvette heads were borrowed, while over-size valves and a tuned aluminum manifold added to the excitement. The factory even built approximately 50 Camaros with the 427 big-block engine for NHRA competition.

The Monte Carlo was announced for the 1970 model year as a Chevy competitor to the highly successful down-sized 1969 Pontiac Grand Prix. A Super Sport version was available with a big-block 454 engine, but was more suited for high speed, long-distance cruising than for flat out quarter-mile drag racing. Nonetheless, the 1970 Monte Carlo SS 454 is the most sought-after Monte Carlo today.

The second generation Camaro was also introduced about midway through the 1970 model year. High performance was on the beginning of a long downhill slide by the time it arrived, however, and this series never had the opportunity to establish itself the way the 1967-69 series did. There were a few fabulous Camaro non-factory conversions in the 1970-1973 era, though. Baldwin Chevrolet in Long Island, for example, offered a Phase III Camaro fitted with a 454 big-block performance engine.

For the most part, however, the hottest performing Chevys — and the hottest collectibles today — date from the 1960s. It just wasn't the same after the insurance companies and the government got into the act.

Chevrolet wasted no time in bringing out a performance version of the new-for -'64 Chevelle. Despite the GTO's big-block power, a 300-hp 327 was the top engine. Supercar status was just a year away. Courtesy Musclecar Review Magazine.

1964 Chevrolet

In a sluggish year for the car industry overall, Chevrolet sales were down slightly but the division still recorded a respectable 2,114,691 units. This was the year that the Chevelle SS would be first offered. It was powered by Chevrolet's tried and true 283 small-block V-8 which delivered a sedate 230 hp. Later in the year, the Chevelle SS would be available with the more potent 327 cid engine, but the Chevelle SS would need an even bigger V-8 before it could truly be considered a muscle car. The SS option was also continued from the year before on the Chevy II Nova, but it too lacked the sort of powertrain that would make it a genuine muscle car contender. The Impala SS, on the other hand, continued to offer the required kind of power and performance.

FULL SIZE

Big-block 409 power was available across the full-size line.

Most buyers were interested in the top-level Impala SS. But drag racers, budget-minded street performance enthusiasts and those wanting serious power in a tow vehicle could order the fabulous 409 in a humble Biscayne or Bel Air, complete with full vinyl bench seats and rubber floor mats. These lighter bodies offered lower cost and a higher power-to-weight ratio.

The Impala SS finally came into its own in 1964. For the first time it was offered as a separate series, not merely an option. The SS differed externally from the rest of the Impalas in a number of ways. On the SS a distinctive bright trim ran along the upper edge of the concave sculptured side, and patterned body trim accents and the rear cove panel were silver. The familiar "SS" letters were placed behind "Impala" on the rear quarter panel and on the rear cove panel and appeared on the wheel covers. The interior of the SS was the most lavish offered yet. Full carpeting and all-vinyl bucket seats were standard and a refined center console carried the transmission. The final touch consisted of a unique swirl patterned trim decorating the instrument panel. The Super Sport was offered on four models — as a convertible or Sport coupe in both the six-cylinder and V-8 form. The 409

Super Sport was the right name. Decorated in SS trim, the '64 Malibu SS was a big hit in its debut year, racking up 76,860 sales in hardtop and convertible form. Courtesy Musclecar Review Magazine.

continued to be the most powerful engine offered, but it was little changed from the year before. Four-speed manual transmission was required on the 400 hp and 425 hp engines because of the extensive torque of the 409. After three years of an almost open field in the muscle car market, in 1964 the SS faced increasingly tough competition. With the introduction of such cars as the GTO and the mid-year Mustang, Chevrolet realized that it would have to start grabbing for the youth performance car market.

VIN NUMBERS

Vehicle Identification Number: 4( )( )( )( )( )100001
Explanation:
First digit: Last digit of model year = 4
Second to third digit: Model number
    Impala SS V-8 = 14
Fourth to fifth digit: Body number
    Sports Coupe = 47
    Convertible = 67
Sixth digit: Letter indicating assembly plant
Last six digits: Sequential production number

PRODUCTION TOTALS

Model	Total Units	Percent
Impala SS	185,325	
409 cid*	8,684	5

*Though most 409's were equipped with the SS option, it is not known exactly how many were so equipped.

DRIVETRAIN DATA

	Full Size 409 (Opt.)	Full Size 409 (Opt.)	Full Size 409 (Opt.)
Cyl:	V-8	V-8	V-8
Bore (in):	4.31	4.31	4.31
Stroke (in):	3.5	3.5	3.5
CID:	409	409	409
Carbs.:	1 4-bbl	1 4-bbl	2 4-bbl
Make:	Rochester	Rochester	Rochester
Model:	4MV	4MV	4MV
Comp.:	10.0:1	11.0:1	11.0:1
Max. BHP:	340	400	425
@ RPM:	5000	5800	6000
Torque ft-lb:	420	425	425
@ RPM:	3200	3600	4200

TRANSMISSIONS

Impala SS 409 (340 hp)
Std: 3-speed Synchro-Mesh Manual
Opt: 4-speed Synchro-Mesh Floor-Mounted Manual,
2-speed Powerglide Console-Mounted Automatic

Impala SS 409 (400 hp, 425 hp)
Std: 3-speed Synchro-Mesh Manual
Opt: 4-speed Synchro-Mesh Console-Mounted Manual

REAR AXLE RATIOS

Impala SS 409
Std: 3.36
Opt: 2.56, 2.20, 4.11, 4.56

EXTERIOR DATA

Impala

	Sports Coupe	Convertible
Length (in):	209.9	209.9
Width (in):	78.1	78.1
Height (in):	56.2	56.2
Wheelbase (in):	119	119
Weight (lb):	3450	3555

FACTORY BASE PRICE DATA

| Impala SS 409 cid, 400 hp | $ 3375 | $ 3624 |
| Impala SS 409 cid, 425 hp | 3431 | 3680 |

POPULAR FACTORY OPTIONS

Interior: Driver seat belt, $10; Pair of front seat belts, $19; Comfort and convenience group, $31; Six-way power seat, $97; Power windows, $102; Manual radio, $48; Push-button radio, $57; Pushbutton radio with antenna and rear speaker, $70; Deluxe steering wheel, $4; Tachometer, $48.

Exterior: Tinted glass, $38; Tinted windshield glass only, $22; Grille guard, $19; Passenger car rear bumper guard, $10; Two-tone paint, $16; Vinyl roof, $75; Wheel discs, $18; Wire wheel discs, $25; Two-speed electric washers and wipers, $17.

Miscellaneous: Deluxe air conditioning, including heater, $364; Cool Pack air conditioning, $317; Heavy-duty brakes with metallic facings, $38; Posi-Traction differential, $43; Four-speed transmission, $237; Power brakes, $43; Power steering, $102.

If your dealer was well connected and your bank account could stand it, $1501.05 would buy you one of 201 Z16 Chevelles built in '65. Performance was incredible even through the open 3.31:1 rear end. Courtesy Musclecar Review Magazine.

1965 Chevrolet

Chevrolet came out with an "all new line-up" in 1965, in the hopes of revitalizing the division after a not too successful 1964. For the car industry as a hole, 1965 was a very good year with over nine million units sold. Chevrolet's production would follow suit with a total of 2,587,490 units produced. The Caprice made its debut on the option list for the Impala in 1965. Unlike the SS, it came only as a V-8. Chevrolet confirmed rumors that had abounded early in the year about the return of the "Daytona Mystery Engine" of 1963 with the mid-year introduction of the Mark IV. This engine, which quickly drew raves, was a 396 cid V-8 based on the famous Mark II engine. It employed the "porcupine" head configuration and had an output of 325 hp at the low end and 425 hp at the high end.

CHEVELLE MALIBU SS 396

Though the Chevelle SS had been introduced first in 1964, it was not until 1965 that it received the powertrain that would make it a real muscle car. During 1964 and for most of 1965, Chevrolet had been watching enviously as Pontiac's GTO swept the nation. Buick and Oldsmobile jumped on the muscle car bandwagon with the introduction of Buick Gran Sport and the Olds 4-4-2. Chevrolet needed to match its sporty looking Chevelle SS with a big-block engine that would truly make it competitive in the muscle car market. Though a new 327 cid, 350-hp engine had been introduced early in 1965, it was not enough to compete with Pontiac's 389 cid engine or the 400 cid Olds and Buick engines. Not to be out-gunned, Chevrolet introduced the 396 cid engine in mid-year. With an output of 375 hp, the highest of any intermediate-size car, this engine propelled the Chevelle SS into the forefront of the muscle car market. Due to the late introduction of this engine, only a limited amount (201 to be exact) of Chevelle SSs were so equipped. The 396 could be identified by the special "SS 396" deck emblem high on the right side. Additionally the Malibu SS emblems, which were on the rear quarter panels, were moved for the 396 to the front fenders, just behind the wheel house openings. The rear deck cove had a cleaner look with the use of standard Chevelle taillight lenses and a unique blacked-out panel that covered the lower half of the cove area. *Mechanix Illustrated* measured the SS's 0 to 60 time at 6.1 seconds and its top speed at 137 mph.

Built on the heavy-duty convertible frame, the Z16 was different than any other Malibu SS. The Malibu SS emblem was moved to the front fender and 7.75 x 14 inch Gold Line tires were standard equipment. Courtesy Musclecar Review Magazine.

FULL SIZE 396/409

The Impala was completely redesigned for 1965. New, rounder lines were employed and a more streamlined look replaced the boxiness of earlier Impalas. Curved glass side windows helped achieve this look. Bel Air and Biscayne continued as low line cars. In February, the 409 was phased out and subsequent big-block cars carried the new Mark IV 396 V-8. Both 409 and 396 engines were available in any full size Chevrolet, including station wagons. The Impala SS continued as a separate series. It was distinguished from the other Impalas by the removal of the rocker trip and the addition of the "Super Sport" identification script behind the front wheel housing. The "SS" monogram was placed on the front grille and on the right of the rear black insert trim bank as well as on the wheel caps. The Impala SS was even more luxurious than the year before. All-vinyl bucket seats were again standard, but a new instrument panel with oil, temperature and amp gauges replaced the more Spartan panel of 1964. Much to the disappointment of car enthusiasts, the 425-hp dual four-barrel version of the 409 cid engine was dropped. But just as things looked down for high-performance fans, in February, Chevrolet introduced

the 396 to replace the 409. Though Chevrolet claimed the 396 was an all-new design, racing fans knew better. It was a direct descendant of the "Daytona Mystery Engine." This engine was the first of a new generation of V-8s for passenger cars given the family name "Turbo-Jet" by Chevrolet. Most likely, Chevrolet had originally intended to place this engine in the mid-size Chevelle. Because of GM's prohibition of engines larger than 400 cid in intermediate-size cars, it was only bored to 396 cubic inches. With the introduction of this engine came the new automatic transmission, Turbo Hydra-matic 350.

VIN NUMBERS

Vehicle Identification Number: 1( )( )( )( )5( )100001
Explanation:
First digit: GM line number: 1 = Chevrolet
Second digit: Series number: 3 = Chevelle
Second digit: Series number: 6 = Impala
Third digit: Model/engine number:
    Chevelle Malibu SS V-8 = 8
    Impala SS V-8 = 6

(con't. after next page)

The heart of the Z16 was RPO L37, a hydraulic-cammed 396, pounding out 375-hp at 5600 rpm. Exhaust manifolds were specific to the Z16 to adapt the engine to the chassis. Courtesy Musclecar Review Magazine.

Taillights and rear end were unique to the Z16 model. Courtesy Musclecar Review Magazine.

Chevrolet's venerable 409 came to the end of it's road in February 1965, handing the baton of performance to the new MK IV big-block initially available as a 396. This Impala SS also carries optional wire wheel covers. Courtesy Musclecar Review Magazine.

The '65 Impala has been called the best car ever made. Decked out in SS trim, the Impala SS had less brightwork on the body than a regular Impala thanks to the deletion of lower rocker mouldings. Courtesy Musclecar Review Magazine.

This handsome SS convertible, one of 27,842, was delivered with a 325-hp 396 and two-speed Powerglide, the only year for that drive-train combination. Courtesy Musclecar Review Magazine.

VIN NUMBERS *(con't.)*

Fourth & fifth digit: Body type number:
  Convertible = 67
  Hardtop = 37
Sixth digit: Last digit of model year = 5
Seventh symbol: Letter indicating assembly plant
Eighth to thirteenth digit:
Sequential production number starting with 100001

PRODUCTION TOTALS

Model	Total Units	Percent
Chevelle Malibu SS	72,500	
396 opt.	201	.28
Impala SS V-8	239,500	

DRIVETRAIN DATA

	Chevelle SS 396 (Opt.)	Full Size 396 (Opt.)	Full Size 396 (Opt.)
Cyl:	V-8	V-8	V-8
Bore (in):	4.094	4.094	4.094
Stroke (in):	3.76	3.76	3.76
CID:	396	396	396
Carbs.:	1 4-bbl	1 4-bbl	1 4-bbl
Make:	Holley	Rochester	Rochester
Model:	4150	4MV	4MV
Comp.:	11.0:1	10.25:1	11.0:1
Max. BHP:	375	325	425
@ RPM:	5600	4800	6400
Torque ft-lb:	420	410	415
@ RPM:	3600	3200	4000

	Full Size (Opt.)	Full Size (Opt.)
Cyl:	V-8	V-8
Bore (in):	4.31	4.31
Stroke (in):	3.5	3.5
CID:	409	409
Carbs.:	1 4-bbl	1 4-bbl
Make:	Rochester	Rochester
Model:	4MV	4MV
Comp.:	10.0:1	11.0:1
Max. BHP:	340	400
@ RPM:	5000	5800
Torque ft-lb:	420	425
@ RPM:	3200	3600

TRANSMISSIONS

Chevelle SS 396, Full Size
Std: 3-speed Synchro-Mesh Column-Mounted Manual
Opt: 4-speed Synchro-Mesh Floor-Mounted Manual,
3-speed Turbo Hydra-matic Column-Mounted Automatic,
2-speed Powerglide Console-Mounted Automatic

Full Size 409 (340 hp)
Std: 3-speed Synchro-Mesh Manual
Opt: 4-speed Synchro-Mesh Floor-Mounted Manual,
2-speed Powerglide Console-Mounted Automatic

Sleepers are among the most interesting musclecars. This non-SS Chevelle has a 350-hp L79 327, one of 6,021 Chevelles (3% of production) so equipped that year. Courtesy Musclecar Review Magazine.

TRANSMISSIONS *(con't.)*
Full Size 409 (400 hp)
Std: 3-speed Synchro-Mesh Manual
Opt: 4-speed Synchro-Mesh Floor-Mounted Manual

REAR AXLE RATIOS
Chevelle SS 396
Std: 3.36 (man), 3.31 (2-sp auto), 2.20 (3-sp auto)
Opt: 4.88

Full Size 409
Std: 3.36 (man), 3.31 (auto)
Opt: 2.56, 2.20, 4.11, 4.56

Full Size 409 (400 hp)
Std: 3.36
Opt: 4.10, 4.56, 4.88

EXTERIOR DATA
Chevelle SS

	Hardtop	Convertible
Length (in):	196.6	196.6
Width (in):	74.6	74.6
Height (in):	52.8	52.9
Wheelbase (in):	115	115
Weight (lb):	3115	3210

Impala SS

	Hardtop	Convertible
Length (in):	213	213
Width (in):	79.6	79.6
Height (in):	54.1	54.1
Wheelbase (in):	119	119
Weight (lb):	3570	3645

FACTORY BASE PRICE DATA

Model	Hardtop	Convertible
Chevelle Malibu SS 396 cid	$ 4091	$ 4297
Impala SS*	2886	3146
Impala SS 409 cid, 340 hp	3128	3388
Impala SS 409 cid, 400 hp	3206	3460

*Prices for optional 396 engine are unavailable

POPULAR FACTORY OPTIONS
Interior: Deluxe front seat belts with retractors, $8; Power windows, $102; Manual radio, $50; Pushbutton radio, $59; AM/FM pushbutton radio, $137; Pushbutton radio with rear speaker, $72 (Chevelle, not available on convertible); Sport styled steering wheel, $32; Comfort-tilt steering wheel, $43; Tachometer, $48 (Chevelle).

Exterior: Tinted glass, $38; Tinted windshield glass only, $22; Rear bumper guards, $10; Front bumper guards, $10 (Chevelle), $16 (Impala); Wire wheel design wheel covers, $57; Electric two-speed windshield wipers with washer, $17.

Miscellaneous: Power brakes, $43; Power steering, $86 (Chevelle), $96 (Impala); Four-season air conditioning (not available with 409, 400 hp engine), $363; Rear window defroster, $22; Heater/defroster deletion, $72 credit; Tri-volume horn, $14; Posi-Traction differential, $38; Power top on convertible, $54 (Chevelle); Powerglide transmission, $199; Four-speed manual transmission $188 (Chevelle), $237 (Impala); Turbo Hydra-matic transmission.

The luxurious Caprice debuted in '65 also, but it wasn't necessarily a barge. As a full-sized passenger car, every big-block engine was available all the way up to the spine-tingling L78 396/425-hp. Courtesy Musclecar Review Magazine.

After being little more than a publicity device thanks to low production in '65, Chevelle SS 396 caught on like wildfire in 1966, selling 72,272 units. Courtesy Musclecar Review Magazine.

1966 *Chevrolet*

After 1965's sales surge, it was no surprise that both industry-wide and Chevy sales were down slightly. Chevrolet's calendar year sales dropped to 2,202,806. Though muscle car sales continued to rise as more big block engines were offered, the Impala SS's sales suffered greatly. In mid-1965 the luxurious full-size Caprice had been introduced and by 1966 it had established itself as Chevrolet's luxury leader eroding the Impala Super Sport's prestige as Chevrolet's flagship line. The Caprice had even been elevated to the status of a separate series in recognition of its popularity. Furthermore, there were fewer distinctions between the Impala and the SS, which was becoming little more than a mild cosmetic package to the Impala. In 1966 the Chevelle SS's name was changed to "Chevelle SS 396" in order to reflect its only available engine, the 396. All other intermediate-size vehicles were prohibited from using this engine, with the exception of the El Camino, which was both passenger car and pickup.

CHEVELLE *SS 396*

In addition to receiving a new name, the 1966 Chevelle also got an all-new look. A new bumper and the "SS 396" emblem dramatically centered in the all black grille gave this car its distinctive air. The Sports Coupe featured a roofline with a "tunneled" recessed rear window between the sailing roof side panels. Two simulated air scoops on the hood, which would become a distinctive SS feature, were introduced this year. The shock absorbers were recalculated and stronger springs and special ball joints were added. Bucket seats and special wheel covers were extra-cost options this year, but interiors remained all-vinyl. On the outside, the SS was quite plain, especially with the standard red-line tires and small hub caps. Its no-frills, all-business look was leading the way to the unadorned pure performance muscle car that would become the mainstay of the later part of the muscle car era. The standard 396 engine was rated at 325 hp and the optional engine produced 360 hp. This was 15 hp less than the most powerful motor of 1965, and the drop was definitely noticeable. Chevrolet, realizing that this could be a big tactical mistake, introduced the 375-hp 396 in mid-1966. But very few 396s were equipped with this engine. Though Chevelle

Loading your Chevelle with options was as easy as checking off boxes on the order sheet. This one has wood grained steering wheel, tachometer, tilt column, AM/FM radio with multiplex, four-speed, console and bucket seats. Courtesy Musclecar Review Magazine.

production increased in 1966, the SS's production was down slightly due to the hot competition in the market.

EL CAMINO 396

Chevrolet advertised this half car, half pickup vehicle as the one which "Likes to work, loves to play." When it was equipped with the 396, the playing could be especially fun. Though the El Camino, when equipped with this powertrain, could certainly be considered a Super Sport, Chevrolet withheld this designation for a couple of years. The 396 was available on both the regular El Camino and the El Camino Custom. Standard equipment included specially calibrated high rate springs and double-acting shocks at each wheel. The interior was all-vinyl and bucket seats and special consoles were available. The Synchro-Mesh three-speed transmission was standard, but a four-speed wide- or close-ratio transmission or the two-speed Powerglide automatic could be ordered.

IMPALA SS 396/427

The Impala SS was mildly revised from the previous year. The six round taillight units that had been an Impala trademark since 1958 were dropped. New large rectangular lamps divided into three segments replaced them. The front was made cleaner and given a more massive appearance. Super Sport emblems were placed on the grille and above the right taillight. For the first time, the side trim of the Super Sports was the same as that of the Impala. The Mark IV 396 engine remained virtually unchanged from the previous year, but a larger 427 cid version of the Mark IV was introduced this year. Its standard output was rated at 390 hp, while the "special performance" version was pegged at 425 hp with its solid-lifters, four-barrel with aluminum manifold and heavy-duty four-bolt main block. This engine was available with a special-performance, extra-rugged, extra-noisy, four-speed manual transmission, called the "rock-crusher." The Impala SS's sales were down by more than 50% in 1966 to 119,312. The Caprice was attracting the Impala SS's luxury car buyers and the mid-size big-block cars were having an impact on the SS's performance car buyers.

Since it went down the same assembly line, product planners saw no reason to restrict drivetrain choices. Any Chevelle engine was also available in the El Camino. The high-performance 396 made for white-knuckle driving in snow. Courtesy Musclecar Review Magazine.

VIN NUMBERS

Vehicle Identification Number: 1( )( )( )( )6( )100001
Explanation:
First digit: GM line number: 1 = Chevrolet
Second digit: Series number: 3 = Chevelle*
Second digit: Series number: 6 = Impala
Third digit: Model/engine number:
   Chevelle Malibu SS V-8 = 8
   El Camino = 4
   El Camino Custom = 6
   Impala SS V-8 = 8
Fourth & fifth digit: Body type number:
   Convertible = 67
   Hardtop (Chevelle SS) = 17
   Hardtop (Impala SS) = 37
   Sedan Pickup = 80
Sixth digit: Last digit of model year = 6
Seventh symbol: Letter indicating assembly plant
Eighth to thirteenth digit:
Sequential production number starting with 100001
*El Camino is listed under the Chevelle series

PRODUCTION TOTALS

Model	Total Units	Percent
Chevelle Malibu SS	72,272	
El Camino	35,119	
Impala SS V-8	119,314	

DRIVETRAIN DATA

	Chevelle SS (Std.) El Camino Impala SS 396 (Opt.)	Chevelle SS El Camino 396 (Opt.)	Chevelle SS 396 (Opt.)
Cyl:	V-8	V-8	V-8
Bore (in):	4.094	4.094	4.094
Stroke (in):	3.76	3.76	3.76
CID:	396	396	396
Carbs.:	1 4-bbl	1 4-bbl	1 4-bbl
Make:	Rochester	Holley	Carter
Model:	4MV	4160	4MV

(con't. next page)

Stripped down full-size cars like this 427/425-hp Biscayne were terrors on the street, offering fantastic horsepower per buck and unbelievable power-to-weight ratios. Courtesy Musclecar Review Magazine.

DRIVETRAIN DATA *(con't.)*

	Chevelle SS *(Std.)* El Camino Impala SS 396 *(Opt.)*	Chevelle SS El Camino 396 *(Opt.)*	Chevelle SS 396 *(Opt.)*
Comp.:	10.25	10.25	11
Max. BHP:	325	360	375
@ RPM:	4800	5200	5600
Torque ft-lb:	410	420	415
@ RPM:	3200	3600	3600

	Impala SS 427 *(Opt.)*	Impala SS 427 *(Opt.)*
Cyl:	V-8	V-8
Bore (in):	4.31	4.31
Stroke (in):	3.5	3.5
CID:	427	427
Carbs.:	1 4-bbl	1 4-bbl
Make:	Rochester	Rochester
Model:	4MV	4MV

Comp.:	10.0:1	11.0:1
Max. BHP:	390	425
@ RPM:	5200	5600
Torque ft-lb:	470	460
@ RPM:	3600	4000

TRANSMISSIONS

Chevelle SS 396
Std: 3-speed Synchro-Mesh Column-Mounted Manual
Opt: 4-speed Synchro-Mesh Floor-Mounted Manual, 2-speed Powerglide Column-Mounted Automatic

El Camino 396 (325 hp)
Std: 3-speed Synchro-Mesh Column-Mounted Manual
Opt: 4-speed Synchro-Mesh Wide-Range Floor-Mounted Manual, 2-speed Powerglide Automatic

El Camino 396 (360 hp)
Std: 3-speed Synchro-Mesh Column-Mounted Manual
Opt: 4-speed Synchro-Mesh Wide-Range Floor-Mounted Manual, 4-speed Close-Ratio Manual, 2-speed Powerglide Automatic

(con't. next page)

Biscaynes were sleepers. This interior could have been a taxicab or grandma's grocery-getter. Courtesy Musclecar Review Magazine.

The 396 was quickly making a name for itself in L35 (325-hp), L34 (360-hp) or L78 (375-hp) versions. Courtesy Musclecar Review Magazine.

TRANSMISSIONS *(con't.)*
Impala SS 396
Std: 3-speed Synchro-Mesh Manual
Opt: 4-speed Synchro-Mesh Floor-Mounted Manual, 2-speed Powerglide Console-Mounted Automatic, 3-speed Turbo Hydra-matic Automatic

Impala SS 427 (390 hp)
Std: 3-speed Synchro-Mesh Manual
Opt: 4-speed Synchro-Mesh Floor-Mounted Manual, 3-speed Turbo Hydra-matic Automatic

Impala SS 427 (425 hp)
Std: 3-speed Synchro-Mesh Manual
Opt: 4-speed Close-Ratio Synchro-Mesh Floor-Mounted Manual, 4-speed Synchro-Mesh Floor-Mounted Manual

REAR AXLE RATIOS
Chevelle SS 396
Std: 3.07
Opt: 3.73

El Camino 396 (325 hp)
Std: 3.31
Opt: 3.55, 3.73, 4.10

El Camino 396 (360 hp)
Std: 3.73
Opt: 3.31, 3.55, 4.10, 4.56, 4.88

Impala SS 427 (360 hp)
Std: 3.36 (man), 3.31 (auto)
Opt: 2.56, 2.20, 4.11, 4.56

Impala SS 427 (400 hp)
Std: 3.36
Opt: 4.10, 4.56, 4.88

EXTERIOR DATA
Chevelle

	SS Hardtop	SS Convertible	El Camino
Length (in):	197	197	194
Width (in):	75	75	NA
Height (in):	51.9	52.8	NA
Wheelbase (in):	115	115	115
Weight (lb):	3375	3470	2930

Impala

	Hardtop	Convertible
Length (in):	213.2	213.2
Width (in):	79.6	79.6
Height (in):	54.4	53.3
Wheelbase (in):	119	119
Weight (lb):	3585	3630

FACTORY BASE PRICE DATA

Model	Hardtop	Convert.	Pickup	Custom
Chevelle SS 396	$ 2776	$ 2984		
El Camino*			$ 2318	$ 2930
Impala SS 396	3105	3357		
Impala SS 427, 390 hp	3363	3515		
Impala SS 427, 425 hp	NA	NA		

*Prices for optional 396 engine are unavailable

POPULAR FACTORY OPTIONS

Interior: Strato-ease front seat headrests, $53 (Impala); Special instrumentation, $79 (Impala); Manual radio, $50; AM/FM pushbutton radio with front antenna, $134; AM/FM pushbutton stereo radio with front antenna, $239; AM/FM pushbutton radio with front antenna and rear speaker, $147; AM pushbutton radio with front antenna, $57; AM pushbutton radio with front antenna and rear speaker, $71; Front and rear Custom Deluxe color matched seat belts with front retractors, $8; Four-way power drivers seat, $70; Comfort-Tilt steering wheel, $42 (Impala); Sport-styled steering wheel, $32; Tilt-telescopic steering wheel (Impala); Tachometer, $48; Power windows, $100.

Exterior: Power rear antenna, $28 (Impala); Power windows, $102; Soft Ray tinted glass, $37; Soft-Ray tinted windshield glass only, $21; Front bumper guards, $16 (Impala), $10 (Chevelle); Rear bumper guards, $16 (Impala), $10 (Chevelle); Vinyl roof cover, $79; Mag style wheel covers, $53 (Impala); Wire wheel covers, $75 (Chevelle); Simulated wire wheel covers, $56 (Impala).

Miscellaneous: Power brakes, $42; Power steering, $95 (Impala), $86 (Chevelle); Power top, $54 (convertibles only); Four-Season comfort air conditioning, $364; Rear window defroster, $22; Emergency road kit; Heater/defroster deletion , $71 credit; Tri-volume horn, $14 (Impala); High volume horn, $14 (Chevelle); Spare wheel lock; Traffic hazard warning system; Posi-Traction differential, $38; Powerglide transmission, $199; Four-speed manual transmission, $188; Turbo Hydra-matic transmission, $226 (Impala).

This was the hot ticket for maximum muscle in '66, the L72 425-hp 427. Its credentials included four-bolt block, solid lifter cam, 11.0:1 compression, big port and valve heads, aluminum intake and a 780 cfm Holley carb. Smart people didn't mess with it. Courtesy Musclecar Review Magazine.

1967 brought a graceful new look to the Impala SS. Still hotter than a firecracker with the L72 425-hp 427, this was brute force in a beautiful body. Courtesy Musclecar Review Magazine.

1967 Chevrolet

Industry-wide sales slipped badly in 1967 from their previous highs. Chevrolet was not immune from the downturn as their sales dropped to 1,900,049. On the positive side, Chevrolet introduced its answer to the popular Ford Mustang, in the form of the Camaro. Rumors had sprung up in 1966 that Chevrolet would soon make such a move and in April, 1966 Chevrolet confirmed that it planned to introduce a ponycar code-named the Panther. Just before its public introduction September 29, 1966, the Panther was renamed the "Camaro." Chevrolet's public relations department let it be known that "Camaro" had a meaning. They maintained that in French "camaro" meant "comrade, pal, buddy, friend." Some linguists took exception to this asserting that "camaro" was not in their French dictionaries, but in their Spanish ones and referred to a type of shrimp, not exactly the best name for a muscle car. Chevrolet countered these linguists by issuing a press release with a photocopy of an old French dictionary, giving the "comrade, pal, buddy, friend" definition.

The Camaro's design was extensively aided by the use of computer technology in analyzing the handling, aerodynamics, the design parameters and even the volume of the gas tank. Its marketing strategy was taken from the Mustang's building-block concept of selling. If you bought a new Camaro in 1967, you had over 80 factory options and over 40 dealer accessories to choose from. You could, in effect, build your own version of the Camaro. One option, which soon would become famous, was the Regular Production Option (RPO) Z-28; but unless you were a real car enthusiast, you would not have known about the Z-28 option. Most Chevrolet salesmen didn't know about it and none of the sales literature mentioned or illustrated it. To get a Z-28, you had to order the base Camaro, the Z-28 option, mandatory front disc brakes with power assist and the Muncie four-speed manual transmission, but you could not order the SS package, automatic transmission, air conditioning or the convertible. The engine that came with this option was the 302 cid V-8. Its compression ratio was 11:1 and its listed horsepower was 290, but that was purely an arbitrary number. When tested by many car magazines, its horsepower was closer to 360. Only 602 Z-28s were built in 1967.

Stacking options got you an RS/SS, a dressed up Camaro packing a 295-hp punch. Courtesy Musclecar Review

The Camaro SS came with a 350 cid V-8 engine exclusive to and introduced on the Camaro.

Camaro RS/SS

When the Camaro was initially announced, the Super Sport option package was available with only one engine, the 350 cid V-8. This engine was a modified version of Chevrolet's long-time standard 327 cid small-block engine. But shortly after the Camaro's introduction, a second engine was offered with the SS equipment, the L35, 325-hp 396. The Rally Sport (RS) option could be ordered in combination with the Super Sport option and, in that case, its trim work would supplant the Super Sport trim. The SS 350's engine, which was a Camaro exclusive, came with a single-snorkel air cleaner, fitted with a chromed cover plate carrying an engine identification sticker and dual exhausts with resonators. The second engine, introduced later in the year, was the 375-hp version of the 396. Simulated air-intakes on the hood, a blacked-out grille with the "SS 350" or "396" emblem centered on it and a distinctive "bumble-bee striping" encircling the frontal grille intake set the SS apart from the other Camaros. Other identification included the "SS" monogram on the front fenders, the fuel filler cap, and on the horn button cap. The RS option, which was purely a trim option, included full-width black grilles with hidden headlamps covered by electrically operated doors. The parking lamps were moved to the valance panel beneath the grille opening and all-red taillamp lenses with black-striped bezels replaced the conventional Camaro units. The "RS" monogram replaced the "SS" monogram when both options were ordered together.

Chevelle SS 396

The Chevelle SS underwent few changes in 1967. The simulated hood air scoops now sported a new horizontal louver and horizontal chrome bars softened the solid black grille of the 1966 SS. Taillights were wrapped around the fender caps and the "Super Sport" script was displayed on the rear fender. The 396 engine came in two forms this year: the 325-hp version and a 35- hp version, downgraded 10 hp from the year before. The 375-hp 396 was not offered in the sales literature in 1967, but was quietly installed in a few 1967 Chevelle SSs. (The drivetrain figures for this engine are listed below, but since it was not officially offered, other data is unavailable.) For the first time, the Turbo Hydra-matic 350 transmission was offered on the Chevelle SS. The Chevelle SS's production was down that year. Only 63,006 units were produced, down by 12.8 % or 9,266 units from the year before.

El Camino 396

The El Camino continued in 1967 with few changes from the year before. The grille was new, but that was not unusual since almost every year the El Camino received a new grille. The front bumper was also new and the side trim was moved up the side panels from the lower body molding. The tailgate was trimmed with an attractive vinyl, wood-grained strip and new taillights. A vinyl roof was made available for the first time on the El Camino. Interiors were all-vinyl and the Custom pickup had more trim detail and textured vinyl seats. Air-adjustable shock absorbers were introduced on the El Camino; they could be inflated or deflated to provide proper support depending on the load. The performance suspension was required for those El Camino's equipped with the 396 engine. The 396 could be had in two different versions, one with an output of 325 hp and the other with an output of 350 hp.

Impala SS 396/427

Impala SS's sales continued to plummet. It was becoming increasingly apparent that there was little room in the

"El Camino" meant "the road," which is where Chevrolet felt it best exhibited its "dual-personality" as car and pickup.

Chevrolet stable for this kind of luxury and performance car. The Caprice was attracting those who wanted a full-sized luxurious car and the Chevelle SS and the Camaro satisfied those who wanted true performance. The Impala SS lost more of its distinguishing characteristics and looked more like the standard Impala than ever before. The major difference in appearance between the SS and the Impala was a black-accented lower body sill and bright fender moldings on the SS. The SS could be equipped with the 427 cid, 385-hp engine. In that case it carried special exterior identification in the form of grille and rear deck emblems and a special "427" emblem on the front fender. "Eyebrow" special accent stripes on the upper body molding were also available. The 396 engine was still available on the Impala, but only in the 325-hp form. A host of new safety and convenience items were introduced that year, including a dual master cylinder brake system, an energy-absorbing steering column and an ignition switch illuminated by a light-carrying plastic tube. This illuminated switch was the first example of fiber optics technology to appear in a Chevrolet.

VIN NUMBERS

Vehicle Identification Number: 1( )( )( )( )7( )100001
Explanation:
First digit: GM line number: 1 = Chevrolet
Second digit: Series number: 2 = Camaro
Second digit: Series number: 3 = Chevelle*
Second digit: Series number: 6 = Impala
Third digit: Model/engine number:
   Camaro V-8 = 4
   Chevelle SS V-8 = 8
   El Camino = 4
   El Camino Custom = 6
   Impala SS V-8 = 8

Fourth & fifth digit: Body type number:
   Convertible = 67
   Hardtop (Camaro, Impala SS) = 37
   Hardtop (Chevelle SS) = 17
   Sedan Pickup = 80
Sixth digit: Last digit of model year = 7
Seventh symbol: Letter indicating assembly plant
Eigth to thirteenth digit:
Sequential production number starting with 100001
*El Camino is listed under the Chevelle series

PRODUCTION TOTALS

Model	Total Units	Percent
Camaro	220,917	
Camaro RS	64,842	29
Camaro SS	34,411	15.6
Chevelle SS 396	63,006	
El Camino	34,830	
Impala SS V-8	75,600	
Impala SS 427	2,124	2.8

DRIVETRAIN DATA

	Camaro SS 350 (Std.)	Chevelle SS (Std.) Camaro SS (Opt.) Impala SS 396 (Opt.)	Chevelle SS (Opt.) El Camino 396 (Opt.)
Cyl:	V-8	V-8	V-8
Bore (in):	4.0	4.094	4.094
Stroke (in):	3.48	3.76	3.76
CID:	350	396	396
Carbs.:	1 4-bbl	1 4-bbl	1 4-bbl
Make:	Rochester	Rochester	Holley
Model:	4MV	4MV	4160
Comp.:	10.25	10.25	10.25
Max. BHP:	295	325	350
@ RPM:	4800	4800	5200
Torque ft-lb:	380	410	415
@ RPM:	3200	3200	3400

	Chevelle Chevy II	Chevelle SS Camaro SS 396 (Opt.)	Impala SS 427 (Opt.)
Cyl:	V-8	V-8	V-8
Bore (in):	4.001	4.094	4.31
Stroke (in):	3.25	3.76	3.5
CID:	327	396	427

(con't. next page)

Camaro burst out of the starting gate in '67 eager to make up ground lost to Ford's Mustang. By dropping in the beefy 396, the Camaro could run circles around 390 Mustangs. Courtesy Musclecar Review Magazine.

By 1967, Chevelle was an all-American favorite. No small-blocks were offered in Super Sport Chevelles, only 396s. Courtesy Musclecar Review Magazine.

DRIVETRAIN DATA *(con't.)*

	Chevelle Chevy II	Chevelle SS Camaro SS 396 *(Opt.)*	Impala SS 427 *(Opt.)*
Carbs.:	1 4-bbl	1 4-bbl	1 4-bbl
Make:	Holley	Rochester	Rochester
Model:		4MV	4MV
Comp.:	11.0:1	11.0:1	10.25:1
Max. BHP:	350	375	385
@ RPM:	5800	5600	5200
Torque ft-lb:	360	415	460
@ RPM:	3600	3600	3400

TRANSMISSIONS

Camaro RS/SS
Std: 3-speed Fully Synchronized Floor-Mounted Manual
Opt: 4-speed Fully Synchronized Floor-Mounted Manual, 2-speed Powerglide Column-Mounted Automatic

Chevelle SS 396 (325 hp)
Std: 3-speed Special Fully Synchronized Floor-Mounted Manual
Opt: 4-speed Fully Synchronized Floor-Mounted Manual, 2-speed Powerglide Column-Mounted Automatic, 3-speed Turbo Hydra-matic Automatic

Chevelle SS 396 (350 hp)
Std: 3-speed Special Fully Synchronized Floor-Mounted Manual
Opt: 4-speed Fully Synchronized Floor-Mounted Manual, 4-speed Fully Synchronized Floor-Mounted Manual, 2-speed Powerglide Column-Mounted Automatic, 3-speed Turbo Hydra-matic Automatic

El Camino 396 (325 hp)
Std: 3-speed Fully Synchronized Column-Mounted Manual
Opt: 4-speed Fully Synchronized Wide-Range Floor-Mounted Manual, 2-speed Powerglide Automatic, 3-speed Turbo Hydra-matic Automatic

El Camino 396 (350 hp)
Std: 3-speed Fully Synchronized Column-Mounted Manual
Opt: 4-speed Fully Synchronized Wide-Range Floor-Mounted Manual, 4-speed Close-Ratio Manual Transmission, 2-speed Powerglide Automatic, 3-speed Turbo Hydra-matic Automatic

Impala SS 396
Std: 3-speed Fully Synchronized Manual
Opt: 4-speed Fully Synchronized Floor-Mounted Manual, 2-speed Powerglide Console-Mounted Automatic, 3-speed Turbo Hydra-matic Automatic 350

Impala SS 427 (425 hp)
Std: 3-speed Fully Synchronized Manual
Opt: 4-speed Fully Synchronized Floor-Mounted Manual, 3-speed Turbo Hydra-matic Automatic 350

Chevrolet gave Camaro full rein, with the same engine options as the larger Chevelle. Even convertibles were built with big-block power. Courtesy Musclecar Review Magazine.

Advertising was playing up the RS and SS Camaro and being hush-hush about the sizzling Z/28. As a result, only 602 were built for the '67 model year. Hood and trunk stripes were the only visual Z/28 identification. Courtesy Musclecar Review Magazine.

REAR AXLE RATIOS

Camaro RS/SS
Std: 3.31
Opt: 3.07, 3.55, 3.73, 4.10, 4.56, 4.88

Chevelle SS 396 (325 hp)
Std: 3.31 (man), 3.07 (2-sp auto), 2.73 (3-sp auto)
Opt: 3.07, 3.55, 3.73, 4.10, 2.73 (2-sp auto), 3.31

Chevelle SS 396 (350 hp)
Std: 3.55 (man), 3.31 (2-sp auto), 3.07 (3-sp auto)
Opt: 3.31, 3.73, 4.10, 3.07 (2-sp auto), 3.55, 2.73, 4.56, 4.88

El Camino 396 (325 hp)
Std: 3.31 (man), 3.07 (2-sp auto), 2.73 (3-sp auto)
Opt: 3.07, 3.55, 3.73, 4.10, 2.73 (2-sp auto), 3.31

El Camino 396 (350 hp)
Std: 3.55 (man), 3.31 (2-sp auto), 3.07 (3-sp auto)
Opt: 3.31, 3.73, 4.10, 3.07 (2-sp auto), 4.56, 4.88, 2.73

Impala SS 396/427
Std: 3.36 (man), 2.73 (auto)
Opt: 3.07, 3.55, 3.73, 3.31

EXTERIOR DATA

Camaro

	Hardtop	Convertible
Length (in):	184.7	184.7
Width (in):	72.5	72.5

	Hardtop	Convertible
Height (in):	51.4	51.4
Wheelbase (in):	108	108
Weight (lb):	2920	3180

Chevelle

	SS Hardtop	SS Convertible	El Camino
Length (in):	197	197	194
Width (in):	75	75	NA
Height (in):	51.9	52.8	NA
Wheelbase (in):	115	115	115
Weight (lb):	3415	3495	3100

Impala SS

	Hardtop	Convertible
Length (in):	213.2	213.2
Width (in):	79.9	79.6
Height (in):	54.5	55.3
Wheelbase (in):	119	119
Weight (lb):	3615	3650

FACTORY BASE PRICE DATA

Model	Hardtop	Convert.	Pickup	Custom
Camaro SS	$ 2783	$ 3020		
Chevelle SS 396	2825	3033		
El Camino 396			$ 2597	$ 2575
Impala SS 396	3161	3410		
Impala SS 427	3319	3568		

NOTE: Rally Sport option available with Camaro for an additional cost of $132.

POPULAR FACTORY OPTIONS

Interior: Custom Deluxe front and rear seat belts, $6; Front shoulder belts, $23; Head rests, $53; Special instrumentation, $79; Special instrument panel, $18 (Chevelle); Color keyed floor mats, $11 (Impala, Chevelle); Six-way power seat, not available with bucket seats, $95 (Impala); Bucket seats, $111 (Chevelle); Four-way power seats, $70; Folding rear seat, $32 (Camaro); Strato-back front seat, $26 (Camaro); Power windows, $100; Pushbutton radio with front antenna, $57; Pushbutton AM/FM radio with front antenna, $134 (Impala); Pushbutton radio with rear speaker, $71 (Chevelle, Camaro); Pushbutton AM/FM radio with front antenna and rear speaker, $147 (Impala); AM/FM stereo radio with front antenna, $239 (Impala); Rear seat speaker, $13; Speed warning indicator, $11; Comfort-lift steering wheel, $42 (Impala, Camaro); Sport styled steering wheel, $32; Stereo tape system with four speakers, $129; Tachometer, $47 (Chevelle).

Exterior: Rear manual antenna, not available with AM/FM radio, $10; Tinted glass, $37 (Impala), $31 (Chevelle, Camaro); Tinted windshield glass only, $21; Rear bumper guards, $16 (Impala), $13 (Chevelle), $10 (Camaro); Front bumper guards, $16 (Impala), $13 (Chevelle, Camaro); Left outside remote control mirror, $10; Rear power antenna, $28 (Impala); Vinyl roof, $74-$79; Rear fender skirts, $26 (Impala); Mag style wheel covers, $53 (Impala); Wheel covers, $21 (Chevelle); Simulated wire wheel covers, $56 (Impala, Chevelle), $74 (Camaro).

Miscellaneous: Power brakes, $42; Power steering, $95 (Impala), $84 (Chevelle, Camaro); Four-Season air conditioning, $356; Comforton air conditioning, $435 (Impala); Rear window defroster, $21; Door edge guards, $3; Heater and defroster deletion, $71 credit (Impala, Chevelle), $32 credit (Camaro); Tri-volume horn, $14; Automatic superlift level control, $79 (Impala); Speed and cruise control, $50; Posi-Traction differential, $38; Four-speed manual transmission, $184 (Impala, Camaro), $106 (Chevelle); Powerglide automatic transmission, $195; Turbo Hydra-matic automatic transmission, $226 (Impala), $231 (Chevelle).

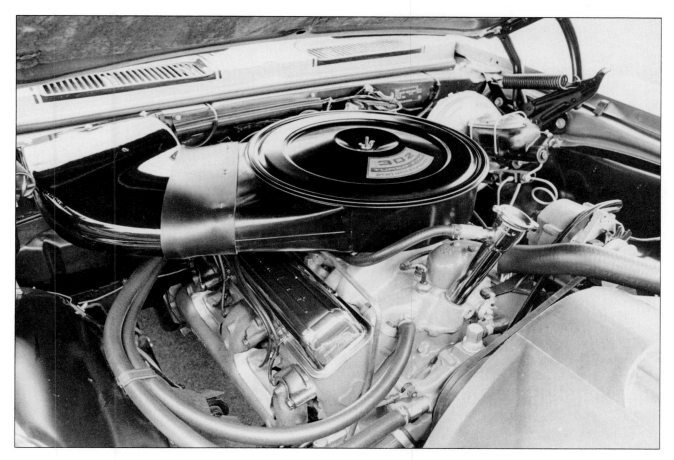

The Z/28 was the only Camaro to use the potent 290-hp 302, shown here with the seldom seen cowl plenum assembly, which carried no RPO number. Courtesy Musclecar Review Magazine.

This 1968 Z-28 was equipped with the Rally Sport option and a tack-on fiberglass rear spoiler. The total cost of a Z-28 equipped so was $3519.73. If you ordered the twin 4-barrel manifold with dual Holley 600-cfm carbs, the price would have gone up by $500.

1968 Chevrolet

Chevrolet and the rest of the auto industry rebounded from the disappointing sales of the previous year. In 1968 Chevrolet's sales were up by 5% to 2,148,091. The Nova SS, which had been around since 1963, had yet to receive a big-block engine that would make it a true muscle car. Finally, in 1968, the Nova SS was given the option of having the 396 Mark IV power it. The El Camino, which had been available previously with the 396 engine, was finally given its due in the form of a name change. It was officially called the "SS 396." Also, for the first time, the Z-28 was advertised by Chevrolet.

Camaro RS/SS/Z-28

Very few cosmetic changes were made to the Camaro in 1968. The grille used argent accenting creating a more horizontal look. The vent windows were dropped and flow-through ventilation took their place. Side marker lights were mounted just behind the front and just ahead of the

rear bumpers. On the inside, new multi-leaf rear springs replaced the single-leaf units on the previous year's models and the rear shock absorbers were now staggered. These changes significantly reduced the axle tramp problem that had afflicted high performance Camaros of 1967. This year the Camaro SS was available with the 396 cid engine with 325-hp, 350-hp and 375-hp. The Camaro SS was identifiable by its emblems on the wheelhouse, centered in the grille and on the fuel cap. The SS 396s additionally had eight-grid chromed hood inserts on their raised center hoods, while SS 350s kept the 1967 trim. The RS package again had the concealed headlamps behind a special grille. When combined with the SS, the RS script could be found over the SS insignia on the front fenders. The Z-28 carried the same restrictions this year as it had the year before: no convertible, no automatic transmission and no air conditioning. A four-speed transmission and front disc brakes with power assist were still required to be bought with the Z-28 option. The same 302 cid engine was standard, with Chevrolet giving the same underrated figure for its horsepower. The Z-28 was a bit easier to identify this year with "Z/28" or "302" emblems mounted on the front fenders.

Camaro sales continued to climb, thanks in part to the Z-28, which had been extremely successful in Trans-Am sedan racing, where it outperformed most other ponycars, including the Mustang. In fact, as Camaro sales rose, Mustang sales dropped.

CHEVELLE SS 396

The Chevelle SS underwent major styling changes in 1968. The wheelbase was shortened by a full three inches. The hood was stretched out and its deck was shortened. The recessed rear window was converted into what was almost a pure fastback. The rear side windows were given a "vee" design which emphasized the power motif of the body's lines. Finally, the most dramatic change was the rakish front end with its over-hanging hood and bold swept-back lines of the front fenders. A black band swept from the headlights to the rear bumper and was further accented by a bright trim at its top edge. The "SS 396" identification could be found on the rear deck and "396" was placed on the front fenders. Simulated twin-domed hood scoops were placed on the rear edge of the hood. Both the 325 and 350-hp versions of the 396 were again available. *World Car* measured their top speed at 118 and 120 mph respectively. The 375-hp version was available if you knew enough to ask, but orders for cars equipped with this engine could take three or more months to process. Possibly up to 2,000 of these SSs were built.

EL CAMINO SS 396

The El Camino shared the Chevelle's 1968 restyling, using the sedan and wagon 116-inch wheelbase. The SS 396 was added as a separate model to the standard and Custom models. Though for the last few years the El Camino could be bought with almost all the SS equipment available to the Chevelle, this title had, until now, been refused to the El Camino. The new El Camino sported a longer hood, "vee" rear side windows, a recessed rear window like the Chevelle's and a rakish front end. The tailgate of the SS had a narrow band of black which framed the SS 396 emblem. The front fenders sported the new "396" emblem. Simulated twin-domed hood scoops were included with louvered ports located at the rear edge of the hood. The grille was accented in black and featured the "396" emblem. The interior of the El Camino could be customized to provide almost any level of comfort the driver desired. The standard engine for the 396 was the 325-hp version; the 350 could also be ordered and reportedly, the 375 V-8 was a little known option. El Camino SS sales were just over 5,000 units. This would be the last year separate figures were available for the El Camino until 1974; in the interim El Camino sales would be included in Chevelle sales.

IMPALA SS 396/427

The Impala SS was clearly coming to the end of its trail. Due to poor sales figures in 1967, the Impala SS was classified in 1968 as an option, the first time since 1963. As Chevrolet sales rebounded in 1968, Impala SS sales continued their downward descent. Of the 710,900 Impalas produced, only 38,210 were equipped with the SS option, down by over 40% from the year before. The SS option was available on three models: the Sport Coupe (hardtop coupe), the Custom Coupe and the convertible. It was identifiable by the black-accented grille with SS nameplates centered on it and the SS insignia on the front fenders and rear deck lid. Strato-bucket seats with a center console and head restraints came with the SS package. The engines were carryovers from the previous year. The 427 was continued despite lackluster sales the previous year and although it would do little better this year, it would last through 1969 before being phased out.

1968 Camaros equipped with the Rally Sport option had a thin molding in the groove along the rocker panel.

The 1968 Impala SS Convertible came with strato-bucket seats, a center console and head restraints.

This Z-28 was equipped with the Rally Sport option; many other performance options were also available.

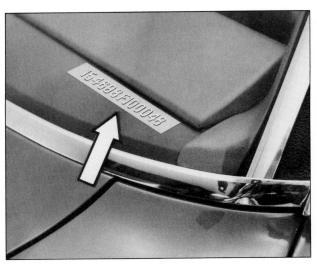

In 1968 VIN plates were moved from the left front door hinge pillar post to the top left side of the instrument panel.

Nova SS

For the first time, the Chevy II Nova could be ordered with Chevrolet's big-block engines. The Nova received a new body, which would last for eleven model years, to support this big powertrain. The 1968 Nova was rather unassuming in its basic form. It came in either a two- or four-door version. It was designed with the Camaro concurrently and with a great deal of the same technology as the first Camaro. Thus it shared with the Camaro many of the elements that made the Camaro such a great performance car, including many of the special speed and handling parts. The Nova SS came with the same standard engine as the Camaro SS (which had heretofore been a Camaro exclusive). But late in the model year, Chevrolet released a few hundred Nova SS's equipped with the 396/375-hp V-8 and some with the 350-hp version. This car was only identifiable on sight by the small "396" number placed in the front side-marker lamp bezels. The Nova SS was, in hot rodder's slang, a "sleeper." Its bite was a whole lot worse than its bark. It looked rather innocent. If a Nova SS equipped with the 396/375 hp pulled up beside you at a red light, you would barely give it a second glance. But, when the light turned green, you would hear the sound of the big, solid-lifter-cam engine and then see the smoke left behind as the SS went over the horizon. *Car and Driver* recorded its 0 to 60 time at just 5.9 seconds and its standing quarter-mile at 101.1 mph in only 14.5 seconds. The SS decoration was mild; the grille was black-accented, the rear deck panel was black-filled, a special hood with a pair of bright-metal simulated air intakes was used and the "SS" monogram was placed on the front and rear. If you wanted a little more élan in your Nova, many external options were available. Despite these new developments in the Nova, sales were not very good.

VIN NUMBERS

Vehicle Identification Number: 1( )( )( )( )8( )100001

Explanation:

First digit: GM line number: 1 = Chevrolet
Second digit: Series number: 2 = Camaro
Second digit: Series number: 3 = Chevelle*
Second digit: Series number: 6 = Impala
Second digit: Series number: 1 = Chevy II Nova
Third digit: Model/engine number:
    Camaro V-8 = 4
    Chevelle SS V-8 = 8
    El Camino = 4
    El Camino Custom = 6
    Impala V-8 = 4
    Chevy Nova V-8 = 4
Fourth & fifth digit: Body type number:
    Convertible = 67
    Coupe = 27
    Hardtop (Camaro, Chevelle SS) = 37
    Custom Coupe (Impala) = 47
    Sports Coupe (Impala) = 87
    Sedan Pickup = 80
Sixth digit: Last digit of model year = 8
Seventh symbol: Letter indicating assembly plant
Eighth to thirteenth digit:
Sequential production number starting with 100001
*El Camino is listed under the Chevelle series

PRODUCTION TOTALS

Model	Total Units	Percent
Camaro	235,151	
Camaro RS opt.	40,977	17.4
Camaro SS opt.	27,884	11.9

(con't. next page)

PRODUCTION TOTALS (con't.)

Camaro Z-28 opt.	7,199	3.1
Chevelle SS 396	57,600*	
El Camino	41,791	
El Camino SS opt.	5,190	12.4
Impala V-8	699,500	
Impala SS opt.	38,210	5.7
SS 427 opt.	1,778	4.7
Nova V-8	53,400	
Nova SS opt.	5,571	10.4
396 cid, 350 hp opt.	234	4.2
396 cid, 375 hp opt.	667	11.9

*57,600 cars were produced according to industry statistics, but other statistics, released by Chevrolet, indicate production of 62,785 units. This may be due to either an error in industry statistics or possibly some cars were produced with the Super Sport equipment but without the 396 engine.

DRIVETRAIN DATA

	Camaro Z-28 (Std.)	Camaro SS 350 (Std.)	Chevelle SS El Camino SS (Std.) Camaro SS Impala SS 396 (Opt.)
Cyl:	V-8	V-8	V-8
Bore (in):	4.0	4.0	4.094
Stroke (in):	3.0	3.48	3.76
CID:	302	350	396
Carbs.:	1 4-bbl	1 4-bbl	1 4-bbl
Make:	Holley	Rochester	Rochester
Model:	800-cfm	4MV	4MV
Comp.:	11.0:1	10.25:1	10.25:1
Max. BHP:	290	295	325
@ RPM:	5800	4800	4800
Torque ft-lb:	290	380	410
@ RPM:	4200	3200	3200

	Camaro SS El Camino SS Chevelle SS Nova SS 396 (Opt.)	Camaro SS El Camino SS Chevelle SS Nova SS 396 (Opt.)	Impala SS 427 (Opt.)
Cyl:	V-8	V-8	V-8
Bore (in):	4.094	4.094	4.31
Stroke (in):	3.76	3.76	3.5
CID:	396	396	427
Carbs.:	1 4-bbl	1 4-bbl	1 4-bbl
Make:	Rochester	Rochester	Rochester
Model:	4MV	4MV	4MV
Comp.:	10.25:1	11.0:1	10.25:1
Max. BHP:	350	375	385
@ RPM:	5200	5600	5200
Torque ft-lb:	415	415	460
@ RPM:	3200	3600	3400

TRANSMISSIONS

Camaro RS/SS 350
Std: 3-speed Fully Synchronized Floor-Mounted Manual
Opt: 3-speed Special Fully Synchronized Floor-Mounted Manual, 4-speed Fully Synchronized Floor-Mounted Manual, 2-speed Powerglide Console- or Column-Mounted Automatic

Camaro RS/SS 396
Std: 3-speed Special Fully Synchronized Floor-Mounted Manual
Opt: 4-speed Fully Synchronized Floor-Mounted Manual, 3-speed Turbo Hydra-matic Column- or Floor-Mounted Automatic

Camaro Z-28
Std: 4-speed Muncie Fully Synchronized Floor-Mounted Manual
Opt: 4-speed Close-Ratio Muncie Floor-Mounted Manual

Chevelle SS 396 (325 hp)
Std: 3-speed Special Fully Synchronized Floor-Mounted Manual
Opt: 4-speed Fully Synchronized Floor-Mounted Manual

Chevelle SS 396 (350 hp)
Std: 3-speed Special Fully Synchronized Floor-Mounted Manual
Opt: 4-speed Fully Synchronized Floor-Mounted Manual, 2-speed Powerglide Column-Mounted Automatic, 3-speed Turbo Hydra-matic Automatic

El Camino 396 SS
Std: 3-speed Fully Synchronized Column-Mounted Manual
Opt: 3-speed Heavy-Duty Column-Mounted Manual, 4-speed Fully Synchronized Wide-Range Floor-Mounted Manual, 4-speed Fully Synchronized Close-Ratio Floor-Mounted Manual, 2-speed Powerglide Automatic, 3-speed Turbo Hydra-matic Automatic

Impala SS 396
Std: 3-speed Special Fully Synchronized Manual
Opt: 4-speed Fully Synchronized Floor-Mounted Manual, 2-speed Powerglide Console-Mounted Automatic, 3-speed Turbo Hydra-matic Automatic

(con't. next page)

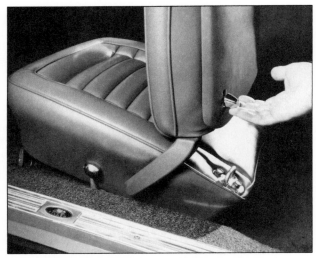

Improved safety features on the 1968 Chevelle included a bucket seat safety lock and energy absorbing seat backs.

TRANSMISSIONS *(con't.)*
Impala SS 427
Std: 3-speed Special Fully Synchronized Manual
Opt: 4-speed Fully Synchronized Floor-Mounted Manual, 3-speed Turbo Hydra-matic Automatic

Nova SS
Std: 3-speed Fully Synchronized Column-Mounted Manual
Opt: 3-speed Special Fully Synchronized Floor-Mounted Manual, 4-speed Fully Synchronized Floor-Mounted Manual, 2-speed Powerglide Column-Mounted Automatic

---

REAR AXLE RATIOS
Camaro RS/SS 350
Std: 3.31 (man), 3.07 (auto)
Opt: 3.07, 3.55, 3.73, 4.10 (4-sp man), 4.56 (4-sp man), 4.88 (4-sp man), 2.73 (auto)

Camaro RS/SS 396 (325 hp)
Std: 3.07 (man), 2.73 (auto)
Opt: 2.73 (man), 3.07, 3.31 (man), 2.56 (auto)

Camaro RS/SS 396 (350 hp)
Std: 3.31 (man), 3.07 (auto)
Opt: 2.73 (auto), 3.31 (auto), 3.07, 3.55 (man), 4.88 (man)

Camaro RS/SS 396 (375 hp)
Std: 3.55
Opt: 3.31, 3.73, 4.88

Camaro Z-28
Std: 3.73
Opt: 3.07, 3.31, 3.55, 4.10, 4.56, 4.88

Chevelle SS 396 (325 hp)
Std: 3.31 (man), 3.07 (2-sp auto), 2.73 (3-sp auto)
Opt: 3.07 (man, 3-sp auto), 3.55 (man, 2-sp auto), 3.73 (man, 2-sp auto), 4.10 (man, 2-sp auto), 2.73 (2-sp auto), 3.31 (2-sp auto, 3-sp auto), 2.56 (3-sp auto)

Chevelle SS 396 (350 hp)
Std: 3.55 (man), 3.31 (2-sp auto), 3.07 (3-sp auto)
Opt: 3.31 (man, 3-sp auto), 3.73 (man, 2-sp auto), 4.10 (man, 2-sp auto), 3.07 (2-sp auto, 4-sp man), 3.55 (2-sp auto), 2.73 (3-sp auto), 4.56 (4-sp man), 4.88 (4-sp man)

El Camino SS
Std: 3.31
Opt: NA

Impala SS 396/427
Std: NA
Opt: NA

Nova SS 396
Std: NA
Opt: NA

EXTERIOR DATA
Camaro

	Hardtop	Convertible
Length (in):	185	185
Width (in):	73	73
Height (in):	51.4	51.4
Wheelbase (in):	108	108
Weight (lb):	2985	3245

Chevelle

	SS Hardtop	SS Convert.	El Camino
Length (in):	197.1	197.1	NA
Width (in):	75.7	75.7	NA
Height (in):	52.7	53.2	NA
Wheelbase (in):	112	112	116
Weight (lb):	3415	3495	3210

Impala

	Custom Coupe	Sports Coupe	Convert.
Length (in):	214.7	214.7	214.7
Width (in):	79.6	79.6	79.6
Height (in):	55.8	55.8	55.8
Wheelbase (in):	119	119	119
Weight (lb):	3623	3628	3677

(con't. next page)

EXTERIOR DATA (con't.)
Nova SS

	Coupe
Length (in):	183.3
Width (in):	72.4
Height (in):	52.6
Wheelbase (in):	111
Weight (lb):	2850

FACTORY BASE PRICE DATA

Model	Coupe	Hardtop	Convert.
Camaro SS 350	$ —	$ 2905	$ 3119
Camaro SS 396, 325 hp	—	2957	3171
Camaro SS 396, 350 hp	—	3063	3277
Camaro SS 396, 370 hp	—	3194	3408
Camaro Z-28*	—	3379	—
Chevelle SS 396, 325 hp	—	2899	3102
Chevelle SS 396, 350 hp	—	3004	3207
Chevelle SS 396, 375 hp	—	3136	3339
Impala SS 396	3147†	3200††	3376
Impala SS 427	3326†	3379††	3555
Nova SS 396, 375 hp	2995	—	—

Model	Pickup	Custom Pickup
El Camino 396	$ 3057	$ 3138

*The Z-28 price was determined by adding the base price of the Camaro ($2694), the Z-28 option ($400) and the two mandatory options: front disc brakes with vacuum assist, $100, and four-speed manual transmission, $185.
†Custom Coupe
††Sports Coupe
NOTE: Rally Sport option available with Camaro for an additional cost of $105.

POPULAR FACTORY OPTIONS

Interior: Electric clock, $16; Center console including electric clock, $50 (Chevelle, Nova); Head rests, $53 (Impala); Light monitoring system, $26 (Chevelle, Camaro); Special instrumentation including ammeter, oil pressure, temperature gauges and tachometer, $95; Six way power seat, $95 (Impala); Four way power lefthand bucket seat, $70 (Impala); Power steering, $95 (Impala, Chevelle), $84 (Nova, Camaro); Power convertible top, $53 (Chevelle, Camaro); Power windows, $100 (Impala, Chevelle, Camaro); Pushbutton AM radio with antenna, $61; Pushbutton AM/FM radio with front antenna, $134; AM/FM radio and stereo, $239; Rear speaker, $13 (Impala, Chevelle); Stereo tape system with four speakers, $133; Strato-bucket seats, $110 (Chevelle); Cloth Strato-back seats, $105 (Impala); Strato-back seats, bucket style, $158 (Impala);

Rear folding seat, $42 (Camaro); Speed warning indicator, $11 (Impala, Chevelle, Camaro); Deluxe steering wheel, $4 (Impala); Comfort-Tilt steering wheel, $42 (Impala, Chevelle, Camaro); Sport steering wheel, $32.

Exterior: Tinted glass, $40 (Impala), $35 (Chevelle), $31 (Nova, Camaro); Tinted windshield glass only, $25 (Impala, Chevelle, Camaro), $21 (Nova); Remote control lefthand mirror, $10 (Impala, Chevelle, Nova); Power rear antenna, $29 (Impala); Rear manual antenna, $10 (Impala, Camaro); Vinyl roof, $90 (Impala), $84 (Chevelle), $74 (Nova, Camaro); Rear fender skirts, $26 (Impala); Wheel covers, $21 (Impala, Camaro), $6 (Chevelle); Mag-style wheel covers, $53 (Impala), $21 (Chevelle), $73 (Nova, Camaro); Simulated wire wheel covers, $56 (Impala), $73 (Chevelle, Nova, Camaro); Mag spoke wheel covers, $53 (Impala), $73 (Chevelle, Camaro), $32 (Nova); Rally wheels, $21 (Impala); Custom exterior group, $69 (Nova); Rallye wheels with special hub caps and trim rings, $32 (Chevelle, Camaro); Hidden windshield wipers, $19 (Chevelle).

Miscellaneous: Four Season air conditioning, $369 (Impala, not with 425 hp engine), $360 (Chevelle, Camaro), $348 (Nova); Comfortron automatic temperature control air conditioning, $448 (Impala, not with 425 hp engine); Posi-Traction differential, $42; Heavy-duty battery, $7 (Chevelle); Economy or performance rear axle, $2 (Chevelle); Heavy-duty clutch, $11 (Impala, Chevelle), $5 (Nova); Rear window defroster, $21 (Impala, Chevelle, Camaro); Dual exhausts, $27; Temperature controlled fan, $16 (Chevelle); Power drum brakes, $42; Power disc front brakes, $100 (Chevelle, Nova, Camaro); Power disc brakes, $121 (Impala); Power door lock system, $45 (Impala); Heavy-duty radiator, $13 (Impala, Camaro); Superlift shock absorbers, $42 (Impala, Chevelle); Automatic level control type shock absorbers, $89 (Impala); Cruise Master speed control, $52 (Impala, Chevelle, Camaro); Special rear springs, includes rear bumper guards, $20 (Camaro); Special steering with quick response, $16 (Camaro); Front and rear special-purpose suspension, $21 (Impala); Powerglide transmission, $195 (Impala, Chevelle, Camaro), $184 (Nova); Wide-range four-speed manual transmission $237 (Chevelle); Close-Ratio four-speed manual transmission, $185 (Impala, Chevelle, Camaro), $79 (Nova); Close-Ratio four-speed heavy-duty manual transmission, $311 (Camaro); Wide-Ratio four-speed manual transmission, $184 (Impala, Chevelle, Camaro); Turbo Hydra-matic transmission, $227 (Impala, Chevelle, Camaro).

As the industry grew towards louder graphics, sleepers like the 427 Biscayne became even less conspicuous, though just as dangerous. *Courtesy Musclecar Review Magazine.*

Chevelle SS 396 had a classic muscle car interior featuring bucket seats and headrests, center console and three-spoke steering wheel. Many memories were made here. *Courtesy Musclecar Review Magazine.*

The 1969 Z-28 was almost identical to the previous year's model. The major external difference was the addition of a cowl-induction hood with a rear-facing scoop. Rear wheel disc brakes, which had been a service option in '68, became a regular production option.

1969 Chevrolet

Overall industry sales fell in 1969. Chevrolet was not exempt from this downward turn; sales fell to 1,999,256. General Motors appointed John DeLorean general manager of Chevrolet in the hopes of revitalizing it. Over the last few years, Chevrolet had been steadily losing its market share and it was hoped that DeLorean would do for Chevrolet what he had done for Pontiac as general manager. There were many name and designation changes in 1969. The Chevelle Malibu SS and the El Camino SS both lost their designations as separate models. The SS was relegated to the option list. The "II" in the Chevy II Nova was dropped and was formally called the Chevy Nova. On the Camaro front, Chevrolet began advertising the Z-28 in its sales literature as well as in high-performance magazines. The Z-28 won the Trans-Am championship for the second year in a row, greatly increasing the popularity of the Camaro. The Camaro also won *Car and Driver's* 1969 poll as the year's best sporty car. While sales of many of the muscle cars were down, Camaro sales continued to rise.

CAMARO RS/SS/Z-28

The first of Camaro's sheet metal changes came in 1969. It was still basically the same car as the 1967 and 68 models, but it looked considerably different. The grille became deeper set and bolder. The taillamps were longer and thinner, segmented in three angled sections. Pressed-in hashmarks were placed just ahead of the rear-wheel cut-outs. The biggest change, though, was the inclusion of a heavy "eyebrow" crease which rose from the front and over the top of the wheel well and then extended along the beltline to the front of the rear wheel well. A matching brow went over the rear wheel well and extended to the rear of the quarter panel. According to the designer, Henry Haga, these brows were derived from the Mercedes 300-SL gullwing, which had very pronounced brows above each wheel cutout. Non-functional louvers adorned the rear quarter panels, ahead of the wheel wells. Endura rubber bumpers were available for the first time on the Camaro as was a ram air induction system for the SS. There were actually two types of ram air systems. First, there was a new special hood with a rear-facing inlet and cold-air duct underneath the hood. Second, there was the dealer-installed cowl plenum ram air kit that came with a special air cleaner and adapter. This system could be set up by blocking off the ventilator section of the cowl, installing this kit and connecting the new chamber to the air cleaner by a rubber sleeve. No special hood was needed. The Rally Sport option continued to be popular. It included a special grille with concealed headlights with washers, chrome wheel well moldings, drip rails and bright accents for the simulated louvers. Pinstripes decorated the "eyebrows" and the rocker panels were blacked-out. The "RS" emblems were placed on the horn ring and between the taillights. Chrome "Rally Sport" insignia were mounted on the front fenders. The SS's standard engine continued to be the 350, but this year's version had a slightly higher horsepower rating of 300. The 396/325-hp engine was optional and the higher output 427s could be ordered through the Central Office as COPO 9561 and 9562. The Z-28 option included a special handling suspension, twin wide stripes on the hood and trunk lid, a "Z-28" emblem on the grille and "302" emblems on the front fenders. Power-assisted front disc brakes and a four-speed manual transmission were still mandatory. The 302 engine continued to power the Z-28 with the slight modification of four-bolt main bearing caps fitted on the engine, although this would be the last year for this engine. A cold air, rear-facing scoop could be ordered to improve engine breathing. Because of the development delays of an all-new Camaro, the 1969 Camaros were continued well into the 1970 model year.

CHEVELLE MALIBU SS 396

The SS reverted to the option list in 1969 after three short years of being a distinct model. For the first time in Chevelle's history, the SS equipment became an option package for certain Chevelle models, rather than just a distinct series feature. It was available on all coupe and convertible Chevelles. The SS option included a twin-domed hood, the "SS" monogram on the front and rear wheel well moldings and sport wheels. The "SS 396" emblem was placed just ahead of the doors. The 396/325-hp and 350-hp engines were available in 1969. Though the 375 hp version was never listed in the sales literature, it has been reported that 500 or so Malibu's were equipped with this powertrain. The SS 396 did better as an option than it had done as a model. Just over 86,000 Malibus were equipped with this option, which was to be the all time high for Chevelle SS production.

EL CAMINO SS 396

After the big styling change in the previous year, the El Camino was basically a carryover in 1969. The biggest

The RS option included headlamps hidden behind a ribbed door. If the doors didn't open, the lamps could still be seen.

Included in the 1969 Camaro SS package were sport striping, rally wheels, a cowl-induction hood and a body color bumper.

Chevrolet claimed that the SS was "All-muscle, all-car, without a tacky piece of gingerbread anywhere."

In 1969, Camaro hit the bullseye, selling like never before thanks to a great styling and plenty of engine options. One engine not on the list was the L72 427/425-hp. Though available as a regular production option for full size cars, the L72 427 was installed in Camaros only through the COPO program. COPO Camaros bore no external badges hinting at the potential within-—the ultimate sleeper. Courtesy Musclecar Review Magazine.

news for the El Camino was a change in the designation of the SS. The El Camino SS, as a separate model, was no longer; the SS could now be had as an option on the El Camino. Exterior changes were basically limited to a new grille and front bumper and rear back-up lights now located on the tailgate. The SS equipment for the El Camino was the same as that for the Malibu. Engine availability was unchanged from the year before—the 396/325 hp and the 396/350 hp. Separate production figures are unavailable for the El Camino since they were included in Chevelle figures.

IMPALA SS 427

Due to poor sales in 1968, Chevrolet canceled the Super Sport option for its big cars, with one exception: the SS 427, which was continued for this final year. Only 2,455 Impalas equipped with the SS 427 were sold in 1969; it was apparent that this was a car without a market. The 427 engine remained virtually unchanged from the year before. The SS option consisted of SS emblems on the black-accented grille, front fenders, rear deck and on the steering wheel. The Impala received a new body in 1969. It featured

new pontoon-bulge fender lines which created an impression of bulk. Vent windows were removed for good and were replaced by "full door glass" window styling. Despite the Impala Super Sport's dismal last few years, total production of the Impala SS was impressive; since its inception, 918,000 SSs were manufactured.

NOVA SS

The Chevy Nova body style was also carried over from 1968, when it had a major body style change. The SS 396 continued to be a trim/engine option. The "SS" emblem was still on the front and rear, but the "Super Sport" lettering on the trailing edge of the lower front fender was moved. Four simulated fender louvers located just in front of the door were added to the SS equipment. (One commentator suggested that their purpose was "to take in simulated air!") The standard engine for the SS continued to be the 350 V-8 used by the Camaro SS. The 396/350-hp V-8 and the 375-hp version were available but were not listed in the sales literature for the Nova SS. The previous year's introduction of the big-block engine finally paid off for Nova SS with a production increase of more than 200%.

With the factory finally installing the mighty L72 427 through the COPO program, Don Yenko, a leading performance Chevrolet dealer from Canonsburg, Pennsylvania, no longer had to swap engines to create his legendary Yenko Camaros. ·Courtesy Musclecar Review Magazine.

Option Z27 was the Super Sport equipment. Though a 300-hp 350 was the base SS Camaro engine, three 396s were offered: the L35 396/325-hp, L34 396/350-hp and the brutal L78 396/ 375-hp, also available with the L89 aluminum heads. Courtesy Musclecar Review Magazine.

VIN NUMBERS

Vehicle Identification Number: 1( )( )( )( )9( )100001

Explanation:

First digit: GM line number: 1 = Chevrolet
Second digit: Series number: 2 = Camaro
Second digit: Series number: 3 = Chevelle*
Second digit: Series number: 6 = Impala
Second digit: Series number: 1 = Chevy Nova
Third digit: Model/engine number:
   Camaro V-8 = 4
   Chevelle Malibu V-8 = 6
   El Camino = 4
   El Camino Custom = 6
   Impala V-8 = 4
   Chevy Nova V-8 = 4
Fourth & fifth digit: Body type number:
   Convertible = 67
   Coupe = 27
Fourth & fifth digit: Body type number:
   Hardtop (Sports Coupe) = 37
   Custom Coupe (Impala) = 47
   Sedan Pickup = 80
Sixth digit: Last digit of model year = 9
Seventh symbol: Letter indicating assembly plant
Eighth to thirteenth digit:
Sequential production number starting with 100001
*El Camino is listed under the Chevelle series

PRODUCTION TOTALS

Model	Total Units	Percent
Camaro*	243,115	
Camaro SS opt.	33,980	14
Camaro RS opt.	37,773	15.5
Camaro Z-28 opt.	19,014	7.8
Chevelle Malibu	439,611	
Chevelle SS opt.	86,307	19.6
El Camino	NA	
El Camino SS opt.	NA	
Impala	777,000	
Impala SS 427 opt.	2,425**	0.31
Nova	251,903	
Nova SS opt.	17,654	7.0
396/375 hp	5,262	30
396/350 hp	1,947	11

*Production continued into 1970 due to the late introduction of 1970 model
**Estimates vary from 2,425 to 2,455

DRIVETRAIN DATA

	Camaro Z-28 (Std.)	Camaro SS 350 (Std.)
Cyl:	V-8	V-8
Bore (in):	4.002	4.00
Stroke (in):	3.005	3.48
CID:	302	350
Carbs.:	1 4-bbl	1 4-bbl
Make:	Holley	Rochester
Model:	800-cfm	4MV
Comp.:	11.0:1	10.25.0:1
Max. BHP:	290	300
@ RPM:	5800	4800
Torque ft-lb:	290	380
@ RPM:	4200	3200

(con't. next page)

DRIVETRAIN DATA *(con't.)*

	Camaro SS (Opt.) Chevelle SS El Camino SS 396 (Std.)	Impala SS COPO Chevelle 9562 COPO Camaro 9561
Cyl:	V-8	V-8
Bore (in):	4.094	4.251
Stroke (in):	3.76	3.76
CID:	396	427
Carbs.:	1 4-bbl	1 4-bbl
Make:	Rochester	Holley
Model:	4MV	800-cfm
Comp.:	10.25.01	11.0:1
Max. BHP:	325	425
@ RPM:	4800	5600
Torque ft-lb:	410	460
@ RPM:	3200	4000

	Camaro SS Chevelle SS El Camino SS Nova SS 396 (Opt.)	Camaro SS Chevelle SS Nova SS 396 (Opt.)
Cyl.:	V-8	V-8
Bore (in):	4.094	4.094
Stroke (in):	3.76	3.76
CID:	396	396
Carbs:	1 4-bbl	1 4-bbl
Make:	Rochester	Rochester
Model:	4MV	4MV
Comp.:	10.25	11
Max. BHP:	350	375
@ RPM:	5200	5600
Torque ft-lb:	415	415
@ RPM:	3400	3600

	Impala SS 427 (Std.)	COPO Camaro 9560 (Opt.)
Cyl.:	V-8	V-8
Bore (in):	4.251	4.251
Stroke (in):	3.76	3.76
CID:	427	427
Carbs:	1 4-bbl	1 4-bbl
Make:	Rochester	Holley
Model:	4MV	850-cfm
Comp.:	10.25	12.0:1
Max. BHP:	390	430
@ RPM:	5400	5200
Torque ft-lb:	460	450
@ RPM:	3600	4400

The 396 and 350 emblems looked alike, but experienced cruisers knew to look twice before engaging an SS Camaro in a street duel. Courtesy Musclecar Review Magazine

Bucket seats were standard on the '69 Camaro. The Hurst shifter indicates the presence of a four-speed transmission. Courtesy Musclecar Review Magazine.

TRANSMISSIONS

Camaro SS
Std: 3-speed Special Floor-Mounted Manual
Opt: 4-speed Muncie Floor-Mounted Manual,
2-speed Powerglide Column or Console-Mounted
Automatic, 3-speed Turbo Hydra-matic Column or
Floor-Mounted Automatic

Camaro Z-28
Std: 4-speed Muncie Fully Synchronized
Floor-Mounted Manual
Opt: 4-speed Close-Ratio Muncie Floor-Mounted Manual

Chevelle Malibu SS 396 (325 hp)
Std: 3-speed Special Floor-Mounted Manual
Opt: 4-speed Muncie Floor-Mounted Manual,
3-speed Turbo Hydra-matic Column or
Floor-Mounted Automatic

Chevelle SS 396 (350 hp)
Std: 3-speed Special Floor-Mounted Manual
Opt: 4-speed Wide-Ratio Muncie Floor-Mounted Manual,
4-speed Close-Ratio Muncie Floor-Mounted Manual,
3-speed Turbo Hydra-matic Column or
Floor-Mounted Automatic

El Camino SS 396
Std: 3-speed Fully Synchronized
Column-Mounted Manual
Opt: 3-speed Heavy-Duty Column-Mounted Manual,
4-speed Fully Synchronized Wide-Range Floor-
Mounted Manual, 4-speed Fully Synchronized
Close-Ratio Floor-Mounted Manual, 2-speed Powerglide
Automatic, 3-speed Turbo Hydra-matic Automatic

SS Camaros (34,932 built) got side stripes, emblems and these great looking 14 x 7 inch wheels. Courtesy Musclecar Review Magazine.

This is the Z87 Custom interior which included door panel armrests, door pulls, carpeted lowers, wood-grained instrument panel accents, steering wheel, pedal trim, glove box light, body insulation and trunk mat. Price for these upscale appointments was $110.60. The houndstooth upholstery, in vogue at the time, was a separate option. Courtesy Musclecar Review Magazine.

A versatile lineup helped Camaro to its strongest year to date, selling a total of 243,085 units. This is the SS 350, for the performance enthusiast who wanted more cubes than the Z/28's 302 cubic inches. Courtesy Musclecar Review Magazine.

TRANSMISSIONS *(con't.)*

Impala SS 427
Std: 3-speed Special Column-Mounted Manual
Opt: 4-speed Wide-Ratio Muncie Floor-Mounted Manual,
4-speed Close-Ratio Muncie Floor-Mounted Manual,
3-speed Turbo Hydra-matic Column or
Console-Mounted Automatic

Nova SS
Std: 3-speed Special Floor-Mounted Manual
Opt: 4-speed Muncie Floor-Mounted Manual
(available with console), 2-speed Powerglide Column
or Console-Mounted Automatic, 3-speed Turbo
Hydra-matic Column or Console-Mounted Automatic

REAR AXLE RATIOS
Camaro SS (350 cid)
Std: 3.31 (man), 3.08 (auto)
Opt: 3.07 (man), 3.08 (auto), 2.73 (auto), 3.55, 3.36 (auto),
3.73 (man), 4.10 (4-sp man)

Camaro SS (396 cid, 325 hp)
Std: 3.07
Opt: 2.73, 3.31 (man), 2.56 (auto)

Camaro Z-28
Std: 3.73
Opt: 3.55, 4.10, 3.07, 3.31

Chevelle Malibu SS 396 (325 hp)
Std: 3.31 (3-sp man, auto), 3.55 (4-sp man)
Opt: 3.07 (man), 3.31, 3.55 (3-sp man), 3.73 (man),
4.10 (man), 2.73 (auto)

Chevelle Malibu SS 396 (350 hp)
Std: 3.55
Opt: 3.31, 3.73, 4.10 (man), 3.07 (auto)

El Camino SS 396
Std: 3.31
Opt: NA

REAR AXLE RATIOS   *(continued)*
Impala SS 427
Std: 3.31 (man), 2.73 (auto)
Opt: 3.55 (man), 3.07, 2.29 (auto), 3.73 (man)

Nova SS
Std: 3.31 (man), 3.08 (auto)
Opt: 3.55, 3.07 (man), 2.73 (auto), 3.36 (auto)

EXTERIOR DATA
Camaro

	Hardtop	Convertible
Length (in):	186	186
Width (in):	74	74
Height (in):	51.1	51.1
Wheelbase (in):	108	108
Weight (lb):	3050	3295

(con't. next page)

Chevelle was having a great year too, selling over half a million. This is the rarest of Chevelles, the L72 427/425-hp COPO Chevelle. Built on the non-SS Malibu body, its existence was debated just a few years ago. At least 50 were built. Courtesy Musclecar Review Magazine.

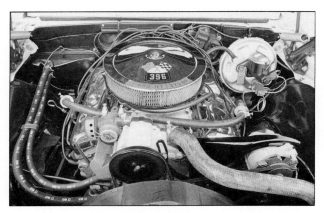

This is the incredible L78 396/375-hp. Production was 4,889 in hardtop and convertible Camaros. Courtesy Musclecar Review Magazine.

EXTERIOR DATA *(con't.)*
Chevelle

	Malibu SS Hardtop	Malibu SS Convertible	El Camino
Length (in):	196.9	196.9	NA
Width (in):	76	76	NA
Height (in):	53.5	53.5	NA
Wheelbase (in):	112	112	116
Weight (lb):	3230	3300	3248

Impala

	Sports Coupe	Custom Coupe	Convertible
Length (in):	215.9	215.9	215.9
Width (in):	79.8	79.8	79.8
Height (in):	55.9	55.9	55.9
Wheelbase (in):	119	119	119
Weight (lb):	3775	3800	3835

Nova SS

	Coupe
Length (in):	189.4
Width (in):	72.4
Height (in):	52.5
Wheelbase (in):	111
Weight (lb):	3033

FACTORY BASE PRICE DATA

Model	Coupe	Hardtop	Convertible
Camaro SS*	$ —	$ 3346	$ 3591
Camaro SS opt.	3398	3643	
Camaro Z-28**	3508		
Chevelle SS	NA	NA	
Impala SS 427	3455†	3507††	3683
Nova SS††	2685	—	—

Model	Pickup	Custom Pickup
El Camino SS	$ 3012	$ 3093

*After May 1, 1969 the hardtop was $3362, the convertible was $3607.
**After May 1, 1969 the hardtop was $3557, the convertible was $3802.
†Custom Coupe
††Sports Coupe
NOTE: Rally Sport option available with Camaro for an additional cost of $132.

POPULAR FACTORY OPTIONS
Interior: Custom DeLuxe shoulder belts, $12-$17; Electric clock, $16; Console with courtesy light, $54; Special instrumentation, $95 (Chevelle,Camaro); Light monitoring system, $26; AM pushbutton radio, $61; AM/FM pushbutton radio, $134; AM/FM stereo radio, $239; Folding rear seat, $42 (Camaro); Six Way power seat, $100; Strato Bucket seat, $121 (Chevelle); Comfort-Tilt steering column, $45; Sport styled steering wheel, $35 (Camaro, Chevelle, Impala).

Exterior: Special front bumper, $42 (Camaro); Adjustable roof rack, $53; Two-tone paint, $23 (Chevelle, Impala, Nova), $32 (Camaro, includes roof molding); Rear manual antenna, $10-$11; Vinyl roof, $79-$89;

(con't. next page)

POPULAR FACTORY OPTIONS *(con't.)*

SS 396 fender accent striping, $26 (Chevelle); Front accent or sport striping, $25 (Camaro); Power convertible top, $53 (Chevelle, Camaro); Headlight washer, $16; Hide-Away wipers, $19; Full wheel covers, $21; Mag-spoke wheel covers, $74; Mag-styled wheel covers, $74; Simulated wire wheels, $74; Special wheel covers, $79.

Miscellaneous: Four-Season air-conditioning, $363-$384; Comfortron air-conditioning, $463; Power drum brakes, $42; Power front disc brakes, $64; Heavy-duty clutch, $48-$53; Electro-Clear rear defroster, $33; Power door locks, $45; Automatic level control, $90; Speed and cruise control (automatic required), $58; Power steering, $90-$105; Special steering with Quick-Response feature, $16 (Camaro, power steering required with air-conditioner or 396 cid V-8); Liquid tire chain, $23; Power trunk opener, $15 (Impala).

After May 1, 1969: Electro-Clear rear defroster, $47; Special ducted hood with performance package, $79 (Camaro); Front and rear spoiler without performance package, $33 (Camaro); Special rear springs, includes rear bumper guards, $20 (Camaro).

Chevrolet didn't limit their thumping performance engines to Super Sports. This 427 Biscayne is representative of the unsung sleepers that walked softly but carried a big stick.

Thanks to the lifting of the corporate ban against displacement exceeding 400 cubic inches in A-body intermediates, Chevrolet cut loose in '70, offering two 454s in the Chevelle SS, the 360-hp LS5 and the blockbuster 450-hp LS6. Courtesy Musclecar Review Magazine.

1970 Chevrolet

Chevrolet sales continued to decline in 1970, but a 65 day strike certainly bears some of the blame for the lower production figures. Nearly 1.5 million cars were produced in 1970. This year was to be the last year of unrestrained catering to the muscle car market. It would also be a peak year for performance cars, with some of the largest big-block engines entering the market. This was the year that General Motors would rescind its policy against engines larger than 400 cid being placed in A-body cars. Chevrolet's first larger-than-400 engine was to be a real kicker. The 454 cid engine, another motor derived from the Mark IV, burst onto the mid-sized high-performance car scene. It came in two versions, one with a relatively calm output of 375-hp and the other with a truly potent official output of 450-hp. (The same engine in the Corvette was rated at 460-hp and that figure was probably a bit conservative.) The 454 was available on the Monte Carlo, Impala, Chevelle and El Camino. Chevrolet made its entry into the personal-luxury

market with the new Monte Carlo. Designed to compete with such cars as the Ford Thunderbird and the Buick Riviera, the Monte Carlo was a long-hooded "personal car." It was essentially a four-passenger model with distinctive styling and a luxury interior. One of the most exciting events of 1970 was the mid-year unveiling of the new Camaro. The Camaro's new European-inspired styling was well received. In fact, the Camaro would use the same basic body until 1982.

CAMARO RS/SS/Z-28

The all-new Camaro was brought out in mid-1970 to a somewhat uncertain future. The ponycar market had been declining steadily since 1969. In 1967, ponycars had captured 13% of the total U.S. new-car sales; in 1969 this figure declined to 9.2%. In its May 1970 issue *Car & Driver* ominously predicted that the restyled Camaro would soon wither and die from lack of sales. They prophesized that this new car would end up costing General Motors millions of dollars due to their lack of foresight into the declining ponycar market. Fortunately, the Camaro proved them wrong. The new Camaro was two inches longer than the year before. Glass area was increased by 10% and the doors were five inches longer than before. The body was much better insulated and quieter than previously. Engine availability was somewhat altered. The Camaro SS still came with the 350 engine, and the 396s, now only available in their 350 and 375-hp form, were optional. The 454/450 hp engine was originally slated as an optional engine for the Camaro, but somehow never made it. The 396s were actually not 396s. The bore had been increased so that this engine actually displaced 402 cubic inches. (This change was made after January 1970.) It is not known why Chevrolet increased the displacement nor why they chose not to change the name, although fear of rising insurance premiums could have been a factor. The Rally Sport option included a free-standing grille and twin bumperettes as well as a split bumper, a color-matched Endura rubber grille frame with a rubber central strip, parking lamps on the catwalk between the headlights and grille, hidden wipers and RS fender identification. The RS could be ordered on its own or with the SS or Z-28 option. The SS package included a special black grille, hidden wipers, power brakes, bright engine trim, white-letter tires and chromed dual exhaust tips; additionally, the SS 396 came with black-painted trunk panels and a special suspension. The Z-28 came with an all-new 350 cid engine, that had not been used by any Camaro before. This engine was essentially the same as the LT-1 350 introduced in the Corvette that year, but Chevrolet had rated its output at 360 hp — 10 hp lower than the Corvettes. The new engine received much praise. According to many writers, engineers and Camaro owners, it was by far superior to the 302. It was more tractable, more reliable, less temperamental and generally out-performed the 302. This year the Z-28 came with front disc brakes, front and rear anti-roll bars and a new front suspension. A one-piece, low-profile rear spoiler was also included in the package.

CHEVELLE MALIBU SS 396/454

A new "vee'd" front end, a bold "SS" grille emblem, functional hoodpins, five-spoke Rally wheels and a cowl air-induction scoop (optional), gave the SS a muscle look to match the ultra-high performance engines available. A new sporty instrument panel designed just for the Super Sport was also added. Round gauges were used and, if you ordered special instruments, they were housed in two round bezels flanking the speedometer. Additionally, a black steering wheel and column were used. The Chevelle SS's 396 V-8 engine availability remained the same as the year before, with the exception of the 325-hp version, which was dropped from the 396 line-up. But the 396 was not a 396 after January since Chevrolet had enlarged this engine to displace 402 cubic inches. The 454 was available on the Chevelle in both versions, though of course, one had to know enough to ask for the 450-hp LS-6 version. Performance of the Chevelle with the 450-hp 454 V-8 was spectacular. *Hot Rod* clocked the quarter-mile at 108.17 mph in 13.44 seconds. Many consider 1970 to be the pinnacle year for the Chevelle SS, both in terms of looks and performance. But it would also be the Chevelle SS's last year of glory. Skyrocketing insurance rates (which *Car and Driver* said could sometimes be higher than car payments) and federal concern over safety and pollution would steadily emasculate the Chevelle over the next few years.

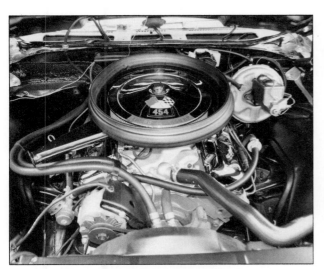

This is the engine many regard as the pinnacle of the muscle car movement, the LS6 454. It was available with either this cowl induction breather, an open element breather or a dual snorkel unit. Note the deep groove large diameter alternator pulley. Courtesy Musclecar Review Magazine.

The 1970 Monte Carlo SS 454 was not well promoted by Chevrolet; it was totally lacking in frontal identification. External identification was limited to a discrete "SS454" chrome emblem in the lower body chrome between the front wheelwell and door.

Decorative hood scoops were replaced by this functional cowl induction system for '70. It opened in response to engine demand. *Courtesy Musclecar Review Magazine.*

Chevelle SS interior was done in classic musclecar style: bucket seats, console, floor shifter and full gauges. This one also has power windows. *Courtesy Musclecar Review Magazine.*

El Camino SS 396/454

The El Camino underwent the same changes as the Chevelle. The front end was replaced by a more blunted "vee'd" version. A new grille, which was black-accented on the SS, was added. The El Camino was still offered in two versions, the standard and Custom models. But this year the SS was only available on the Custom. The Custom Pickup had bright trim, which ran from the front to rear bumper about a quarter of the way up the side. Bright trim also appeared on the wheelhouse molding. The popular cowl induction scoop was also optional on the El Camino SS. The 396/350 hp V-8 was available on the SS as well as both versions of the 454 cid engine.

Monte Carlo SS 454

Chevrolet celebrated the arrival of the '70s with a new spinoff. The Monte Carlo was introduced on September 18, 1969 and drew a cool reception from enthusiast magazines, who were caught up in muscle car mania. But the new Monte Carlo, which was available only as a coupe, was immediately accepted by the public, who quickly bought them. All Monte Carlos came with V-8s of at least 350 cubic inches. The Monte Carlo's body, which was derived from the Chevelle's, rode on an 116-inch wheelbase. The SS 454 was offered from the beginning. Though it did not appeal to many people, only 3,823 were built. Today, the 1970 SS 454 is one of the most sought after Monte Carlos. The SS option included special suspension components, "SS 454" emblems just behind the front wheelhouse, heavy-duty shocks and an automatic level-control feature built into the self-regulating rear air units. Though the sales literature does not mention it, it appears these Monte Carlos were also equipped with power front disc brakes. The SS

454 was not a very good accelerator; quarter-mile times as measured by *Car Life* were sluggish—it took the Monte Carlo 16.2 seconds to reach 90.1 mph. Its top speed, on the other hand, was an impressive 132 mph.

Nova SS

The Chevy Nova SS refined its basic package in 1970 and became one of the most popular street rods around. On the outside, the black-accented grille and rear panel with the "SS" emblem and the simulated front fender louvers just ahead of the door returned. The SS option included dual exhausts, power front disc brakes, simulated air louvers on the hood, white striping tires and hood insulation. Many options were available if you wanted a SS with a bit more pizazz. The 396 engine (which was really a 402) was still available on the Nova SS though this would be its last year. The large engine had caused some problems such as understeering and front end plowing in sharp turns. Like in the case of the Camaro, the 454 was supposedly slated for use on the Nova SS, but it too failed to materialize.

VIN NUMBERS

Vehicle Identification Number: 1( )( )( )( )0( )100001
Explanation:
First digit: GM line number: 1 = Chevrolet
Second digit: Series number: 2 = Camaro
Second digit: Series number: 3 = Chevelle*
Second digit: Series number: 6 = Impala
Second digit: Series number: 1 = Chevy Nova
Third digit: Model/engine number:
    Camaro V-8 = 4
    Chevelle Malibu V-8 = 6

(con't. next page)

Steel-backed Endura molding surrounded the mid-1970 RS grille. Wire wheel covers were optional.

Chevrolet promoted the 360-hp LS5 454, but not the brutal 450-hp LS6 454. It was up to the competition to gamble on which one was under the hood. Courtesy Musclecar Review Magazine.

VIN NUMBERS *(con't.)*

El Camino Custom = 6
   Impala V-8 = 4
   Monte Carlo = 8
   Chevy Nova V-8 = 4
Fourth & fifth digit: Body type number:
   Convertible = 67
   Coupe (Nova) = 27
   Coupe (Monte Carlo) = 57
   Hardtop (Camaro) = 87
   Hardtop (Sports Coupe-Impala, Chevelle) = 37
   Custom Coupe (Impala) = 47
   Sedan Pickup = 80
Sixth digit: Last digit of model year = 0
Seventh symbol: Letter indicating assembly plant
Eighth to thirteenth digit:
Sequential production number starting with 100001
*El Camino and Monte Carlo are listed under the Chevelle series

PRODUCTION TOTALS

Model	Total Units	Percent
Camaro	124,889	
Camaro RS opt.	27,136	21.7
Camaro SS opt.	12,476	10
Camaro Z-28 opt.	7,733	6.2
Chevelle Malibu V-8	354,700	
Chevelle SS 396 opt.	49,826	14.1
Chevelle SS 454 opt.	3,773	1.1
El Camino	47,707	
El Camino SS opt.	NA	
Monte Carlo	145,975	
Monte Carlo SS opt.	3,823	2.6
Nova V-8	139,242	
Nova SS opt.	19,558	14

DRIVETRAIN DATA

	Camaro Z-28 (Std.)	Nova SS Camaro SS 350 (Std.)	Chevelle SS El Camino SS (Std.) Camaro SS Nova SS 396 (Opt.)
Cyl:	V-8	V-8	V-8
Bore (in):	4.0	4.0	4.126
Stroke (in):	3.48	3.48	3.76
CID:	350	350	402
Carbs.:	1 4-bbl	1 4-bbl	1 4-bbl
Make:	Holley	Rochester	Rochester
Model:	800-cfm	4MV	4MV
Comp.:	11	10.25	10.25
Max. BHP:	360	300	350
@ RPM:	6000	4800	5200
Torque ft-lb:	380	380	415
@ RPM:	4000	3200	3400

	Camaro SS Chevelle SS Nova SS 396 (Opt.)	Impala Chevelle SS El Camino SS Monte Carlo SS 454 (Opt.)	Chevelle SS El Camino SS 454 (Opt.)
Cyl:	V-8	V-8	V-8
Bore (in):	4.126	4.251	4.251

(con't. next page)

Critics loved the '70-1/2 Z/28. Its 350 gave it the extra cubes needed for off-idle torque with better day-to-day manners. Courtesy Musclecar Review Magazine.

DRIVETRAIN DATA *(con't.)*

Stroke (in):	3.76	4.0	4.0
CID:	402	454	454
Carbs.:	1 4-bbl	1 4-bbl	1 4-bbl
Make:	Rochester	Rochester	Rochester
Model:	4MV	4MV	4MV
Comp.:	10.25	10.25	11.25
Max. BHP:	375	360(390*)	450
@ RPM:	5600	5400(4800*)	5600
Torque ft-lb:	415	500(800*)	500
@ RPM:	3600	3200(3400*)	3600

* Higher rating on full-size line though same engine.

TRANSMISSIONS

Camaro RS/SS 350, 396 (350 hp)
Std: 4-speed Fully Synchronized Floor-Mounted Manual
Opt: 3-speed Turbo Hydra-matic Column- or Floor-Mounted Automatic

Camaro RS/SS 396 (375 hp)
Std: 4-speed Fully Synchronized Floor-Mounted Manual
Opt: None

Camaro Z-28
Std: 4-speed Muncie Fully Synchronized Floor-Mounted Manual

Opt: 4-speed Close-Ratio Muncie Floor-Mounted Manual, 4-speed Wide-Ratio Muncie Floor-Mounted Manual, 3-speed Turbo Hydra-matic Column- or Floor-Mounted Automatic

Chevelle Malibu SS 396/454
Std: 4-speed Fully Synchronized Floor-Mounted Manual
Opt: 3-speed Turbo Hydra-matic Automatic

El Camino SS 396
Std: 4-speed Close-Ratio Fully Synchronized Floor-Mounted Manual
Opt: 4-speed Wide-Ratio Fully Synchronized Floor-Mounted Manual, 3-speed Turbo Hydra-matic Automatic

El Camino SS 454
Std: 3-speed Turbo Hydra-matic Automatic
Opt: 4-speed Special Close-Ratio Fully Synchronized Floor-Mounted Manual

Monte Carlo SS 454
Std: 3-speed Turbo Hydra-matic Automatic
Opt: 4-speed Fully Synchronized Floor-Mounted Manual*

*The four-speed was not listed in the sales literature, but specifications were filed with the Automobile Manufacturers' Association and reportedly some cars were delivered with a four-speed on special order

(con't. next page)

While Chevelle and Camaro grabbed the headlines, Nova was armed and dangerous with 396 power up to 375-hp. The '70 SS was also great looking. Courtesy Musclecar Review Magazine.

TRANSMISSIONS *(con't.)*

Nova SS
Std: 4-speed Close-Ratio Fully Synchronized
Floor-Mounted Manual
Opt: 2-speed Powerglide Column-Mounted Automatic,
3-speed Turbo Hydra-matic Automatic

REAR AXLE RATIOS
Camaro RS/SS 350
Std: 3.31 (man), 3.07 (auto)
Opt: 3.31 (man), 3.07 (auto)

Camaro RS/SS 396 (350 hp)
Std: 3.31
Opt: 3.31

Camaro RS/SS 396 (375 hp)
Std: 3.55
Opt: 4.10

Camaro Z-28
Std: 3.37
Opt: 4.10

Chevelle Malibu SS 396/454
Std: NA
Opt: NA

As was the custom for Chevrolet Super Sports, the SS Nova carried a pair of non-functional grilles in the hood. Courtesy Musclecar Review Magazine.

El Camino SS
Std: NA
Opt: NA
Monte Carlo SS 454
Std: 2.73
Opt: NA

Nova SS
Std: 3.31 (man), 3.08 (2-sp auto), 3.07 (3-sp auto)
Opt: 2.52 (auto)

EXTERIOR DATA
Camaro

	Hardtop
Length (in):	188
Width (in):	74.4
Height (in):	50.4
Wheelbase (in):	108
Weight (lb):	3172

(con't. next page)

EXTERIOR DATA (con't.)

Chevelle	Malibu Hardtop	Malibu Convertible	El Camino
Length (in):	197.2	197.2	NA
Width (in):	75.4	75.4	NA
Height (in):	52.8	52.8	NA
Wheelbase (in):	112	112	116
Weight (lb):	3307	3352	3321

Monte Carlo

	Coupe
Length (in):	205.8
Width (in):	75.6
Height (in):	52.6
Wheelbase (in):	116
Weight (lb):	3460

Nova SS

	Coupe
Length (in):	189.4
Width (in):	72.4
Height (in):	52.5
Wheelbase (in):	111
Weight (lb):	3048

FACTORY BASE PRICE DATA

Model	Coupe	Hardtop	Convertible
Camaro SS	$ —	$ 2905	$ —
Camaro Z-28	—	3412	—
Chevelle SS 396, 350 hp	—	3255	3454
Chevelle SS 454, 360 hp	—	3312	3512
Monte Carlo SS 454	3543	—	—
Nova SS 396	2794	—	—

Model	Custom Pickup
El Camino SS 396	$ 3305

NOTE: Rally Sport option available with Camaro for an additional cost of $188.

This is the Yenko Deuce, a non-SS Nova with a hot 360-hp 350. Chevrolet never offered the LT-1 as a regular production option, so Don Yenko, a Pennsylvania dealer, took matters into his own hands, swapped engines and dubbed his creation the Yenko Deuce. Courtesy Musclecar Review Magazine.

POPULAR FACTORY OPTIONS

Interior: Carpeted load floor, $53; Console, $54 (Monte Carlo, Nova, Chevelle), $59 (Camaro); Power door locks, $35; Special instrumentation including tachometer, ammeter and temperature gauges, $84 (Chevelle), $69 (Monte Carlo), $95 (Camaro, Nova); AM pushbutton radio, $61; AM/FM pushbutton radio, $134; AM/FM radio with FM stereo, $239; Stereo tape with AM radio, $195; Stereo tape with AM/FM radio with FM stereo, $373; Six-way power seat, $100; Power Strato Bucket seat, $121; Comfort-Tilt steering wheel, $46; Fingertip windshield wiper control, $19.

Exterior: Tinted glass, $25-$30; Vinyl top, $126 (Monte Carlo), $84 (Nova), $90 (Camaro), $95 (Chevelle); Rear fender skirts, $32 (Monte Carlo); Wheel covers, $21; Color-keyed wheel covers, $16 (Monte Carlo); Special wheel covers, $58-81; Six 15 x 7JK wheels, $11 (Monte Carlo); Rallye styled wheels, $36; Sport styled wheels, $79 (Nova); Rear deck lid spoiler, $33 (Camaro).

Miscellaneous: Comfortron air conditioning, $463; Four Season air conditioning, $363-$384; Air conditioning, $380 (Camaro); Power drum brakes, $41-$43; Power front disc brakes, $65; Electro-Clear rear defroster, $42; Standard rear defroster, $21-$29; Headlight delay system, $18; Vigilante light monitoring system, $26 (not available on Nova); Power steering, $90-$105; Powerglide automatic transmission, $159; Turbo Hydra-matic automatic transmission, $221-$290; Wide-ratio four-speed manual transmission, $185 (Chevelle, Nova, Monte Carlo), $205 (Camaro); Special Close-Ratio four-speed manual transmission, $221 (Chevelle), $232 (Camaro); Regular Close-Ratio four-speed manual transmission, $185 (Chevelle, Nova), $206 (Camaro); Cowl induction hood, $147; Posi-Traction differential, $42; Heavy-duty battery, $16; Dual exhausts, $24; Engine block heater, $11; Heavy-duty radiator, $15-$32.

LS6 convertibles are among the rarest Chevelles. Exact numbers are not known but less than 25 have been accounted for. Courtesy Musclecar Review Magazine.

One of the only ways you can tell that this is a 1971 Camaro SS as opposed to a 1970 model is by the high-back seats. These seats had tall, integral headrests, whereas 1970's had separate headrests. An optional two-position lever could adjust the tilt of the seat.

1971 Chevrolet

Chevrolet's 1971 model year production was up to 2,320,698 units manufactured. Its market share was also up by 2.46% from the year before to 22.35%. But Chevrolet's good fortune did not extend to its muscle cars. Production was down for most of the muscle cars. High insurance rates, federal emission laws and heightened concern over safety took their toll on the high-performance car market. The Chevy Nova SS was no longer available with the big 396. Furthermore, due to new federal emission laws, all new cars had to be able to run on unleaded gasoline. Compression ratios had to be lowered in order to accomplish this. Horsepower ratings were down for all the engines, with one exception — the less powerful 454 V-8's horsepower was actually increased by 5 so that it now was rated at 365 hp. In mid-1971, General Motors began giving its horsepower ratings in net terms rather than gross terms. Net ratings were always lower (and actually more accurate) than gross ratings because they were measured with all the equipment attached to the engine, whereas gross ratings were calcu-

lated without the equipment. (The drivetrain data listed here for 1971 is in gross terms, but after 1971 it is in net terms). In mid-year Chevrolet introduced a sort of mellowed out version of the Chevelle SS called the Heavy Chevy. It included a black grille, the Super Sport's domed hood, Rallye wheels and engine selections ranging from the 307 Turbo-Fire V-8 to the 400 Turbo-Jet.

Camaro RS/SS/Z-28

From the outside, one would be hard pressed to tell a mid-year 1970 Camaro from a 1971 Camaro. This was wholly understandable, though, since the new body had not even been around for a full year. The most noticeable external difference was the high back seats with integral headrests on the '71s. Under the hood was a different story altogether. The Z-28 was still powered by the 350 V-8. But the compression ratio had been reduced to 9:1 from 11:1. In fact, it was lucky to have a ratio this high since General Motors had mandated that all engines have a compression ratio of 8.5:1 or less, but they had let the Z-28 slip by. Its horsepower rating slid to 330. Heftier engine mounts and a bigger fuel filter were included in the Z-28 package. A new, three-piece spoiler, adapted from the one used on Pontiac's Firebird Trans Am, was made available on the Z-28. The SS was powered by the same 350 V-8, but it, too, was detuned. The 396 was available, but its horsepower was down to 300. A 400 cid engine seems to have been planned for mid-year introduction but it never materialized in the Camaro. The RS package was still available and, as in previous years, it could be teamed up with both the SS and the Z-28. It included round, driving-light style turn signals mounted in the catwalks between the grille and headlights, small bumperettes flanked by the blacked-out floating grille, which was circled by a body-color Endura bumper. "Rally Sport" chrome emblems adorned the front fenders. Both the SS and the RS package included hidden windshield wipers.

CHEVELLE SS

This year the Malibu Super Sport came in two versions, the Chevelle SS and the Chevelle SS 454. Externally, one could distinguish them by the "Chevelle SS" or "SS 454" emblem on the front grille, rear bumper and ahead of the doors. The major changes in 1971 were the new black-accented grille, the turn signal/parking lights which were now wrapped around the fender cap and the single head-lights, which replaced the traditional dual headlights of years past. The plain SS was offered with either a 245 or 270-hp Turbo-Fire 350 V-8 or the 300-hp Turbo-Jet 400 V-8. The SS 454 came with one of two powerplants, the 365-hp version and the detuned 425-hp version. The 454, 425-hp engine and the 350 engine for the Z-28 were the only Chevrolet engines allowed to have a compression ratio above 8.5:1. The lower-power version of the 454 was able to maintain its relatively high horsepower rating despite

lowered compression ratio by the use of a new head design and a revised camshaft.

EL CAMINO SS

Changes were minimal for the El Camino SS in 1971. It received the same modifications as did the Chevelle Malibu SS. But this was a significant year for the El Camino in that the Chevelle/El Camino body was introduced by Chevrolet to the GMC Division to be marketed under the name "Sprint." The SS package was again only available on the Custom pickup. It included a special instrumentation panel with a black steering wheel and column and an "SS" hub emblem. The engine availability was the same as that of the Chevelle SS.

MONTE CARLO SS 454

The Monte Carlo entered its second year of production with few changes. Rectangular front parking lamps replace the circular ones of the year before and a new finer textured grille and a spring-loaded hood-crest emblem were added. The SS option received more distinctive styling character-istics than it had the year before. Black-accented rear panels and "SS 454" inserts for the lower front fender decorated this car. Additionally, a small "SS" emblem was affixed to the right side of the panel. Still, the SS had no distinctive frontal identification. The two versions of the 454 were available on the SS. Special chassis parts were also part of the package, they included: special front and rear springs, heavy-duty shocks with the Automatic Level Control rear air units and a heavier front and rear stabilizer bar. Sales of the SS were down by almost 50% in 1971. This would be its last year of production before the Monte Carlo SS 454 was relegated to the muscle car history books.

The "Heavy Chevy" was part of Chevrolet's response to excruciating insurance premiums demanded for high-performance cars. Officially known as RPO YF3, 6,727 were built. Courtesy Musclecar Review Magazine.

The Rally Nova was also built as an insurance beating performance car for the budget minded. Standard engine was a 245-hp (gross) 350 and total production was 7,700. Courtesy Musclecar Review Magazine.

The 1971 Z-28 was available with two spoilers: one wrapped around the rear deck and the other up front. Other features included custom-styled chrome wheels, a vinyl roof covering, vinyl or cloth seats and the GS ornamentation in five places.

VIN NUMBERS

Vehicle Identification Number: 1( )( )( )( )1( )100001

Explanation:

First digit: GM line number: 1 = Chevrolet

Second digit: Series number: 2 = Camaro

Second digit: Series number: 3 = Chevelle*

Third digit: Model/engine number:

    Camaro V-8 = 4

    Chevelle Malibu V-8 = 6

    El Camino Custom = 6

    Monte Carlo = 8

Fourth & fifth digit: Body type number:

Convertible = 67

Coupe (Monte Carlo) = 57

Hardtop (Camaro) = 87

Hardtop (Chevelle) = 37

Sedan Pickup = 80

Sixth digit: Last digit of model year = 1

Seventh symbol: Letter indicating assembly plant

Eighth to thirteenth digit:

Sequential production number starting with 100001

*El Camino and Monte Carlo are listed under the Chevelle series

PRODUCTION TOTALS

Model	Total Units	Percent
Camaro	114,643	
Camaro RS opt.	18,404	16.1
Camaro SS opt.	8,377	7.3
Camaro Z-28 opt.	4,862	4.2
Chevelle Malibu V-8	240,200	
Chevelle SS 454 opt.	19,992	8.3
El Camino	41,606	
El Camino SS opt.	NA	
Monte Carlo	112,599	
Monte Carlo SS opt.	1,919	1.7

DRIVETRAIN DATA

	Camaro Z-28 (Std.)	Chevelle SS Nova SS Camaro SS 350 (Std.)	Chevelle SS Impala Camaro SS 396 (Opt.)
Cyl:	V-8	V-8	V-8
Bore (in):	4.0	4.0	4.126
Stroke (in):	3.48	3.48	3.76
CID:	350	350	402
Carbs.:	1 4-bbl	1 4-bbl	1 4-bbl
Make:	Holley	Rochester	Rochester
Model:	800-cfm	4MV	4MV
Comp.:	9.0:1	8.5:1	8.5:1
Max. BHP:	330	270	300
@ RPM:	5600	4800	4800
Torque ft-lb:	360	360	400
@ RPM:	4000	3200	3200

	Impala Chevelle SS 454 El Camino SS 454 Monte Carlo SS 454 (Std.)
Cyl:	V-8
Bore (in):	4.251
Stroke (in):	4.0
CID:	454
Carbs.:	1 4-bbl
Make:	Rochester
Model:	4MV
Comp.:	8.5:1
Max. BHP:	365
@ RPM:	4800
Torque ft-lb:	465
@ RPM:	3200

TRANSMISSIONS
Camaro RS/SS 350/396/Z-28
Std: 4-speed Fully Synchronized Floor-Mounted Manual
Opt: 3-speed Turbo Hydra-matic Column- or
Floor-Mounted Automatic

(con't. next page)

Chevelle SS performance carried on with fewer horses. A 365-hp 454 (LS5) was offered as the top engine with a 300-hp 400, 270 or 245-hp 350 V-8s. Courtesy Musclecar Review Magazine.

Z/28 was the same only different for '71. Its 350 felt cuts for emissions sake, but it still cranked out a healthy 330-hp (gross) thanks to big valve heads and a solid lifter camshaft. Courtesy Musclecar Review Magazine.

TRANSMISSIONS *(con't.)*

Chevelle SS 454
Std: 4-speed Special Fully Synchronized
Floor-Mounted Manual
Opt: 3-speed Turbo Hydra-matic Automatic

El Camino SS 454
Std: 4-speed Heavy-Duty Fully Synchronized
Floor-Mounted Manual
Opt: 3-speed Turbo Hydra-matic Automatic

Monte Carlo SS 454
Std: 3-speed Turbo Hydra-matic Automatic
Opt: 4-speed Fully Synchronized Floor-Mounted Manual*

*The four-speed was not listed in the sales literature, but specifications were filed with the Automobile Manufacturers' Association and reportedly some cars were delivered with a four-speed on special order.

REAR AXLE RATIOS
Camaro RS/SS 350
Std: 3.42 (man), 3.08 (auto)
Opt: None

Camaro RS/SS 396
Std: 3.42
Opt: None

Camaro Z-28
Std: 3.37
Opt: 4.10

Chevelle SS 454
Std: NA
Opt: NA

El Camino SS 454
Std: NA
Opt: NA

Monte Carlo SS 454
Std: NA
Opt: NA

EXTERIOR DATA
Camaro

	Hardtop
Length (in):	188
Width (in):	74.4
Height (in):	49.1
Wheelbase (in):	108
Weight (lb):	3218

Chevelle

	Malibu Hardtop	Malibu Convertible	El Camino
Length (in):	197.5	197.5	NA
Width (in):	75.4	75.4	NA
Height (in):	52.9	52.9	NA
Wheelbase (in):	112	112	116
Weight (lb):	3342	3390	3356

Monte Carlo

	Coupe
Length (in):	206.5
Width (in):	75.6
Height (in):	52.9
Wheelbase (in):	116
Weight (lb):	3488

FACTORY BASE PRICE DATA

Model	Coupe	Hardtop	Convert.	Custom Pickup
Camaro SS	$ —	$ 3330	$ —	
Camaro Z-28	—	3803	—	
Chevelle SS	—	3337	3617	
El Camino SS				$ 3439
Monte Carlo SS 454	3901	—	—	

NOTE: Rally Sport option available with Camaro for an additional cost of $179.

POPULAR FACTORY OPTIONS

Interior: Bucket seats, $137; Electric clock, $17; Special instrument panel, $85; Power bucket seats, $79; Power door locks, $47; Power windows, $116; AM pushbutton radio, $67; AM/FM pushbutton radio, $140; AM/FM stereo radio, $239; Adjustable steering wheel, $46; Sport or custom steering wheel, $16.

Exterior: Tinted glass, $44; Tinted windshield glass only, $31; Left remote control mirror, $13; Vinyl roof, $95 (Chevelle), $90 (Camaro); Wheel covers, $27; Custom wheel covers, $85; Rallye wheels, $46.

Miscellaneous: Air conditioning, $408; Cruise control, $64; Posi-Traction differential, $45; Power drum brakes, $48; Power disc brakes, $47; Power steering, $111; Rear window defroster, $32; Turbo Hydra-matic transmission, $238.

15 x 7 inch Rally wheels were part of the Z/28 package. Firestone Wide Oval 60s were OEM tires. Courtesy Musclecar Review Magazine.

Camaro interiors retained the enthusiast car image, helping to make Chevrolet's ponycar very successful throughout the 1970s. Courtesy Musclecar Review Magazine.

The Rally Sport front end remained essentially the same from 1970 to 1973. The 1972 RS option included concealed windshield wipers, a split front bumper, a special grille and an Endura rubber grille frame.

1972 Chevrolet

Due in part to President Nixon's price and wage controls enacted in August 1971, which included the elimination of a 7% excise tax on domestic automobile sales and a simultaneous introduction of a 10% surcharge on imported cars, production for the American car industry was up. Despite this economic windfall (which only lasted a few months), Chevrolet sales were slightly down; 2,151,076 cars were manufactured. This year came very close to being the last year for Camaros. Waning sales in the ponycar market and a 174 day strike at the Ohio plant where all Firebirds and Camaros were manufactured convinced many executives that the Camaro should be discontinued. To make matters worse, 1,100 unfinished Camaros had to be scrapped at the end of 1972 because they could not be modified to meet federal bumper safety standards. Fortunately for enthusiasts, those who were in favor of continuing the Camaro won the battle. It turned out to be a good decision on Chevrolet's part. When faced with poor sales, the Mustang and other cars were detuned, essentially eliminating them from the performance category. This left the door wide open for the Camaro and its sibling the Firebird, which hung in there with as much performance as they could get away with. The Chevelle SS would not be so fortunate; it had only one more year before being axed. Reported horsepower ratings for all muscle cars were down this year, but this was due, in large part, to the exclusive use of net horsepower ratings by GM rather than gross ratings.

Camaro RS/SS/Z-28

Considering that no Camaros were produced for almost half of a 1972, the seemingly dismal production figures for the Camaro were really not that bad. This year's Camaro differed most markedly from the previous year's in the grille texture of the straight across bumper. The grille mesh was coarser, with only seven vertical slats instead of the twelve used previously. The Rally Sport front ensemble was unchanged and still had twelve slats. Horsepower ratings for all Camaros were down, but as mentioned above, this was due in some part to the use of net rather than gross figures. The Z-28 continued to be the highest output Camaro. The standard Z-28 spoiler was somewhat revised and the optional spoiler package now came with a front air dam. Finally, variable-ratio power steering was replaced by a straight power-steering system. The SS again came with the 350 and the 396 and the RS package remained virtually the same as the year before.

CHEVELLE MALIBU SS

This year's Chevelle SS was almost identical to 1971's. New single-unit turn-signal/marker lamp units were the main distinguishing item on the front end—they were no longer stacked and were now one piece decorated with thin horizontal lines. The rear end was virtually the same as the year before. The SS equipment, which was unchanged from the previous year, was again offered on the convertible and coupe. But now it could be ordered with any Chevelle V-8. So it was possible to have a mean-looking machine powered by a tame 130-hp 307. Cowl induction was still a popular option to team up with the SS. The SS 454 was still available, but only in its 270-hp form. It was possible to construct the higher rated 454 from the parts bin and a few factory-built versions were allegedly delivered. California Chevelle enthusiasts were especially unhappy in 1972. Tough emissions laws kept the SS's with 307, 400 and 454 engines out of the state. The Heavy Chevy option was still available in much the same form as the year before.

EL CAMINO SS

Like the Chevelle Malibu, the El Camino was virtually unchanged for 1972. The turn signal/marker lamp units were changed in the same way as the Chevelle's and the Chevrolet bowtie was gone from the grille. The SS option continued as it had the previous year. The new grille was black, but the horizontal chrome divider piece was deleted from it. Cowl induction was still available on the SS. The 454 engine came in only one version, the 270-hp form, but it was possible, as with the Chevelle SS, to custom build the higher output 454. Both the weight and the price of the El Camino SS were down for 1972.

VIN NUMBERS

Vehicle Identification Number: 1( )( )( )( )2( )100001
Explanation:
First digit: GM line number: 1 = Chevrolet
Second letter: Series letter: Q = Camaro
Second letter: Series letter: D = Chevelle Malibu V-8
Second digit: Series number: 34 = El Camino
Third & fourth digit: Body type number:
  Convertible = 67
  Hardtop (Camaro) = 87
  Hardtop (Chevelle) = 37
  Sedan Pickup = 80
Fifth symbol: Engine symbol
Sixth digit: Last digit of model year = 2

California Chevelle SS fans were unhappy in '72. SSs equipped with the 307, 400, or 454 were not allowed in that state.

Seventh symbol: Letter indicating assembly plant
Eighth to thirteenth digit:
Sequential production number starting with 100001

PRODUCTION TOTALS

Model	Total Units	Percent
Camaro	68,656	
Camaro RS opt.	11,364	16.5
Camaro SS opt.	6,562	9.6
Camaro Z-28 opt.	2,575	3.6
Chevelle Malibu V-8	281,700	
Chevelle SS 454 opt.	5,333	1.9
El Camino	57,147	
El Camino SS opt.	NA	

DRIVETRAIN DATA

	Camaro Z-28 (Std.)	Chevelle SS Nova SS Camaro SS 350 (Std.)	Impala Chevelle SS Camaro SS 396 (Opt.)
Cyl:	V-8	V-8	V-8
Bore (in):	4.0	4.0	4.126
Stroke (in):	3.48	3.48	3.76
CID:	350	350	402
Carbs.:	1 4-bbl	1 4-bbl	1 4-bbl
Make:	Holley	Rochester	Rochester
Model:	800-cfm	4MV	4MV
Comp.:	9	8.5	8.5
Max. BHP:	255	200(175*)	240
@ RPM:	5600	4400(4000*)	4400
Torque ft-lb:	280	300(280*)	345
@ RPM:	4000	2800(2400*)	3200

* Reduced hp rating for Chevelle only

(con't. next page)

Hood and deck striping became a delete option on the 1972 Z-28 and the rear deck spoiler became optional.

DRIVETRAIN DATA *(con't.)*

	Impala Chevelle SS 454 El Camino SS 454 454 (Std.)
Cyl:	V-8
Bore (in):	4.251
Stroke (in):	4.0
CID:	454
Carbs.:	1 4-bbl
Make:	Rochester
Model:	4MV
Comp.:	8.5
Max. BHP:	270
@ RPM:	4000
Torque ft-lb:	390
@ RPM:	3200

TRANSMISSIONS

Camaro RS/SS 350, 396/Z-28
Std: 4-speed Fully Synchronized
Floor-Mounted Manual
Opt: 3-speed Turbo Hydra-matic Column- or
Floor-Mounted Automatic

Chevelle SS 454
Std: 4-speed Special Fully Synchronized
Floor-Mounted Manual
Opt: 3-speed Turbo Hydra-matic Automatic

El Camino SS 454
Std: 4-speed Heavy-Duty Fully Synchronized
Floor-Mounted Manual
Opt: 3-speed Turbo Hydra-matic Automatic

REAR AXLE RATIOS

Camaro RS/SS 350
Std: 3.42 (man), 3.08 (auto)
Opt: None

Camaro RS/SS 396
Std: 3.42
Opt: None

Camaro Z-28
Std: 3.37
Opt: 4.10

Chevelle SS 454
Std: NA
Opt: 3.31

El Camino SS 454
Std: NA
Opt: NA

EXTERIOR DATA

Camaro

	Hardtop
Length (in):	188
Width (in):	74.4
Height (in):	49.1
Wheelbase (in):	108
Weight (lb):	3248

Chevelle

	Malibu Hardtop	Malibu Convertible	El Camino
Length (in):	197.5	197.5	NA
Width (in):	75.4	75.4	NA
Height (in):	52.7	52.7	NA
Wheelbase (in):	112	112	116
Weight (lb):	3327	3379	3350

FACTORY BASE PRICE DATA

Model	Hardtop	Convertible	Custom Pickup
Camaro SS	$ 3126	$ —	
Camaro Z-28	3418	—	
Chevelle SS	3273	3573	
El Camino SS			$ 3310

NOTE: Rally Sport option available with Camaro for an additional cost of $118.

POPULAR FACTORY OPTIONS

Interior: Bucket seats; Electric clock, $18; Console, $58; Special instrument panel; Power door locks, $44; Power bucket seat; Power windows, $110; AM pushbutton radio, $63; AM/FM pushbutton radio, $132; AM/FM stereo radio, $227; Adjustable steering wheel, $43; Sport steering wheel, $50.

Exterior: Tinted glass, $41; Tinted windshield glass only, $29; Left remote control mirror, $12; Vinyl roof, $106; Wheel covers; Mag style wheel covers; Wire wheel covers, $80; Rallye wheels, $85.

Miscellaneous: Air conditioning, $405; Cruise control, $60; Posi-Traction differential; Power drum brakes, $47; Power disc brakes, $67; Power steering; Rear window defroster; Turbo Hydra-matic transmission, $230.

El Camino was available with the same engines as the Chevelle, including the top of the line 270-hp 454. Courtesy Musclecar Review Magazine.

The SS option was dropped for the Camaro in 1973, but the Rally Sport was still available. The RS still had its unique bumper which had been significantly altered to meet federal safety guidelines. Great pains were taken not to change its external design.

1973 Chevrolet

Production was up somewhat for 1973. Chevrolet manufactured 2,334,113 cars that year, though fewer of them were the muscle cars. Production of the performance cars continued to decline with the exception of the Camaro. The Camaro SS had been dropped from the line-up, so the Z-28 with its 350 engine was the only choice left for the serious high-performance car fan. The Z-28 would suffer the same fate as its brother, the SS, after 1974. This was to be the last year of the Chevelle SS, though the El Camino would retain this option for the rest of the 70's and into the 80's. The SS package dropped in price for 1973. This was done not only as a stimulation for sales, but also because the SS was rapidly becoming little more than a trim option. The Z-28 option's price was also lowered. Though the SS 454 and Z-28 were still available, their horsepower output had again been lowered. Federal emission and safety regulations as well as high insurance rates had helped to cripple the muscle car market; the Arab oil embargo of 1973 was the

final blow. After waiting in lines for hours on end for gasoline, it's no wonder that many American's became more concerned with miles-per-gallon than horsepower.

CAMARO Z-28

Though the SS option had been dropped for 1973, the Rally Sport trim option was still around. It still featured the turn signals mounted in the catwalks between the grille and the headlights. The grille was a floating style with bright vertical and horizontal accenting, circled by a body-color hard rubber frame which was flanked by bumperettes. A new option, Type LT, took the place of the SS option. It was basically a Camaro with a bit more luxury and not as much performance as its predecessor. It included a 2-barrel, 165-hp V-8, rallye wheels, hidden wipers, blackout rocker sills and moldings and sports mirrors. Inside was a full instrument panel trimmed with bright-beaded woodgrain. "LT" emblems were placed in the steering hub and on the exterior. This option could be combined with the RS and the Z-28. The Z-28 package continued, though its engine ratings had been lowered once again. Hydraulic lifters replaced the solid type that had been used in the Z-28 since its introduction. The aluminum manifold was also dropped and the Holley four-barrel carburetor was replaced by a Rochester Quadrajet. For the first time, air conditioning was available. Camaro recuperated well from the devastating strike of 1972; sales were up for all models, including the Z-28.

CHEVELLE MALIBU SS 454

The Chevelle Malibu received an all-new body in 1973. It was no longer a pillarless hardtop style, but now used doors with frameless windows. 1973 was also a memorable year since it was the first and only year that the SS was offered on a Malibu station wagon, in both the two- and three-seat style. Included in the SS package were "SS" emblems on the grille, fenders and over the rear bumper (or on the rear lift gate of the wagon), accent striping over the lower body, wheel cut-outs color keyed to the body and left and right sport mirrors. The special instrument panel continued and a special SS front and rear stabilizer bar was added. The 454 engine continued to lose power, rated at just 245 hp. Production was up for the Chevelle SS. But as Chevrolet was considering whether or not to retain this option, the oil embargo hit and ensured the demise of the SS.

EL CAMINO SS 454

The El Camino shared the new body of the Chevelle Malibu. The 116-inch wheelbase was retained, but body length was increased. A new grille and front end still featured the single-unit headlamps, but the wrap-around parking/turn signal lights were gone and the lights were now inserted into the front and rear bumpers. The boxy look of the rear tailgate was replaced by a more stylishly curved look, at the expense of some cargo space. The SS package continued as a trim option on the Custom pickup and featured a black-accented grille with the "SS" emblem as well as the other features included in the Chevelle SS package. The 454 was still the highest output engine offered for the SS. Production of the El Camino hit an all time high of 64,987.

VIN NUMBERS

Vehicle Identification Number: 1( )( )( )( )3( )100001
Explanation:
First digit: GM line number: 1 = Chevrolet
Second letter: Series letter: Q = Camaro
Second letter: Series letter: D = Chevelle Malibu V-8
Second digit: Series number: AC = El Camino
Third & fourth digit: Body type number:
  Hardtop (Camaro) = 87
  Coupe (Chevelle) = 37
  Sedan Pickup = 80
  Two-seat wagon = 36
  Three-seat wagon = 46

Fifth symbol: Engine symbol
Sixth digit: Last digit of model year = 3
Seventh symbol: Letter indicating assembly plant
Eighth to thirteenth digit:
Sequential production number starting with 100001

PRODUCTION TOTALS

Model	Total Units	Percent
Camaro	96,756	
Camaro Z-28 opt.	11,574	11.9
Chevelle Malibu SS	28,647	
Chevelle SS 454 opt.	2,500	8.7
El Camino	64,987	
El Camino SS opt.	NA	

DRIVETRAIN DATA

	Camaro Z-28 (Std.)	Impala Chevelle SS El Camino SS 454 (Std.)	Impala Chevelle Camaro Nova
Cyl:	V-8	V-8	V-8
Bore (in):	4.0	4.251	4.0
Stroke (in):	3.48	4.0	3.48
CID:	350	454	350
Carbs.:	1 4-bbl	1 4-bbl	1 4-bbl
Make:	Rochester	Rochester	Rochester
Model:	4MV	4MV	4MV
Comp.:	9.0:1	8.5:1	8.5:1
Max. BHP:	245	245	175
@ RPM:	5200	4000	4000
Torque ft-lb:	280	375	270
@ RPM:	4000	2800	2400

TRANSMISSIONS
Camaro Z-28
Std: 4-speed Special Fully Synchronized
Floor-Mounted Manual
Opt: 3-speed Turbo Hydra-matic Automatic

Chevelle SS 454
Std: 4-speed Close-Ratio Fully Synchronized
Floor-Mounted Manual
Opt: 3-speed Turbo Hydra-matic Automatic

El Camino SS 454
Std: 4-speed Close-Ratio Fully Synchronized
Floor-Mounted Manual
Opt: 3-speed Turbo Hydra-matic Automatic

REAR AXLE RATIOS
Camaro Z-28
Std: 3.73
Opt: 3.42

Chevelle SS 454
Std: NA
Opt: NA

El Camino SS 454
Std: NA
Opt: NA

EXTERIOR DATA
Camaro

	Hardtop
Length (in):	188.4
Width (in):	74.4
Height (in):	49.1
Wheelbase (in):	108
Weight (lb):	3283

Chevelle

	Malibu Coupe	Malibu Wagon	El Camino
Length (in):	202.9	213.6	213.2
Width (in):	76.6	76.6	76.6
Height (in):	53.3	55.2	53.8
Wheelbase (in):	112	116	116
Weight (lb):	3580	4027*	3350

*Three-seat wagon was 4075 lbs

FACTORY BASE PRICE DATA

Model	Coupe	Hardtop	Wagon	Custom Pickup
Camaro Z-28	$ —	$ 3374	$ —	
Chevelle SS	3253	—	3533, 3666†	
El Camino SS				$ 3318

†Three-seat wagon
NOTE: Rally Sport option available with Camaro for an additional cost of $118.

POPULAR FACTORY OPTIONS
Interior: Bucket seats; Electric clock, $18; Console, $59; Special instrument panel; Power door locks, $44; Power bucket seats, $103; Power windows, $75; AM pushbutton radio, $65; AM/FM pushbutton radio, $135; AM/FM stereo radio, $233; AM/FM stereo radio and tape, $363; Adjustable steering wheel, $44; Sport steering wheel, $44.

Exterior: Tinted glass, $42; Tinted windshield glass only, $30; Left remote control mirror, $12; Sky roof, $325; Vinyl roof, $92 (Chevelle), $87 (Camaro); Wheel covers, $26; Mag style wheel covers, $50; Wire wheel covers; Rallye wheels, $87.

Miscellaneous: Air conditioning, $397; Cruise control, $62; Posi-Traction differential, $45; Power drum brakes, $46; Power disc brakes, $92; Power steering, $113; Rear window defroster; Turbo Hydra-matic transmission, $210.

Chevrolet Engines And Specifications By Year And Car Line

LINE & RPO	CID/HP @ RPM	TORQUE @ RPM	COMPRESSION	NOTES

1964

FULL SIZE				
L30	327/250 @ 4400	350 @ 2800	10.5:1	
L74	327/300 @ 5000	360 @ 3200	10.5:1	
L33	409/340 @ 5000	420 @ 3200	10.0:1	
L31	409/400 @ 5800	425 @ 3600	11.0:1	Single 4 bbl
L80	409/425 @ 6000	425 @ 4200	11.0:1	Dual 4 bbl
CHEVELLE				
L30	327/250 @ 4400	350 @ 2800	10.5:1	
L74	327/300 @ 5000	360 @ 3200	10.5:1	

1965

CHEVY II				
L30	327/250 @ 4400	350 @ 2800	10.5:1	
L74	327/300 @ 5000	360 @ 3200	10.5:1	
FULL SIZE				
L30	327/250 @ 4400	350 @ 2800	10.5:1	
L74	327/300 @ 5000	360 @ 3200	10.5:1	
L33	409/340 @ 5000	420 @ 3200	10.0:1	
L31	409/400 @ 5800	425 @ 3600	11.0:1	
L35	396/325 @ 4800	410 @ 3200	10.25:1	
L78	396/425 @ 6400	415 @ 4000	11.0:1	
CHEVELLE				
L30	327/250 @ 4400	350 @ 2800	10.5:1	
L74	327/300 @ 5000	360 @ 3200	10.5:1	
L79	327/350 @ 5800	360 @ 3600	11.0:1	
Z16	396/375 @ 5600	420 @ 3600	11.0:1	

1966

CHEVY II				
L30	327/275 @ 4800	355 @ 4200	10.5:1	
L79	327/350 @ 5800	360 @ 3600	11.0:1	
FULL SIZE				
L30	327/275 @ 4800	355 @ 4200	10.5:1	
L35	396/325 @ 4800	410 @ 3200	10.25:1	
L36	427/390 @ 5200	470 @ 3600	10.25:1	
L72	427/425 @ 5600	460 @ 4000	11.0:1	
CHEVELLE				
L30	327/275 @ 4800	355 @ 4200	10.5:1	
L34	396/360 @ 5200	420 @ 3600	10.25:1	Opt. on SS 396
L35	396/325 @ 4800	410 @ 3200	10.25:1	Std. on SS 396
L78	396/375 @ 5600	415 @ 3600	11.0:1	Opt. on SS 396

1967

CHEVY II				
L30	327/275 @ 4800	355 @ 3200	10.0:1	
L79	327/350 @ 5800	360 @ 3600	11.0:1	

LINE & RPO	CID/HP @ RPM	TORQUE @ RPM	COMPRESSION	NOTES
FULL SIZE				
L30	327/275 @ 4800	355 @ 3200	10.0:1	
L35	396/325 @ 4800	410 @ 3200	10.25:1	
L36	427/385 @ 5200	460 @ 3400	10.25:1	
L36	427/390 @ 5400	460 @ 3600	10.25:1	Corvette Only
L72	427/425 @ 5600	460 @ 4000	11.0:1	
CAMARO				
L30	327/275 @ 4800	355 @ 3200	10.0:1	
L35	396/325 @ 4800	410 @ 3200	10.25:1	Opt. on Camaro SS
L48	350/295 @ 4800	380 @ 3200	10.25:1	Std. on Camaro SS
L78	396/375 @ 5600	415 @ 3600	11.0:1	Opt. on Camaro SS
Z28	302/290 @ 5800	290 @ 4200	11.0:1	Z/28 Only
CHEVELLE				
L30	327/275 @ 4800	355 @ 3200	10.0:1	
L34	396/350 @ 5200	415 @ 3400	10.25:1	Opt. on SS 396
L35	396/325 @ 4800	410 @ 3200	10.25:1	Std. on SS 396
L78	396/375 @ 5600	415 @ 3600	11.0:1	Opt. on SS 396
L89	396/375 @ 5600	415 @ 3600	11.0:1	Opt. on SS 396 aluminum heads
L79	327/350 @ 5800	360 @ 3600	11.0:1	

1968

LINE & RPO	CID/HP @ RPM	TORQUE @ RPM	COMPRESSION	NOTES
CHEVY II				
L30	327/275 @ 4800	355 @ 3200	10.0:1	
L34	396/350 @ 5200	415 @ 3400	10.25:1	
L48	350/295 @ 4800	380 @ 3200	10.25:1	
L78	396/375 @ 5600	415 @ 3600	11.0:1	
L79	327/325 @ 5600	355 @ 3600	11.0:1	
FULL SIZE				
L30	327/275 @ 4800	355 @ 3200	10.0:1	
L35	396/325 @ 4800	410 @ 3200	10.25:1	
L36	427/385 @ 5200	460 @ 3400	10.25:1	
L72	427/425 @ 5600	460 @ 4000	11.0:1	
CAMARO				
L30	327/275 @ 4800	355 @ 3200	10.0:1	
L34	396/350 @ 5200	415 @ 3400	10.25:1	Opt. on Camaro SS
L35	396/325 @ 4800	410 @ 3200	10.25:1	Opt. on Camaro SS
L48	350/295 @ 4800	380 @ 3200	10.25:1	Std. on Camaro SS
L78	396/375 @ 5600	415 @ 3600	11.0:1	Opt. on Camaro SS
L89	396/375 @ 5600	415 @ 3600	11.0:1	Opt. on Camaro SS aluminum head
Z28	302/290 @ 5800	290 @ 4200	11.0:1	Z/28 Only
CHEVELLE				
L30	327/275 @ 4800	355 @ 3200	10.0:1	
L73	327/325 @ 5600	355 @ 3600	11.0:1	
L34	396/350 @ 5200	415 @ 3400	10.25:1	Opt. on SS 396
L35	396/325 @ 4800	410 @ 3200	10.25:1	Std. on SS 396
L78	396/375 @ 5600	415 @ 3600	11.0:1	Opt. on SS 396
L89	396/375 @ 5600	415 @ 3600	11.0:1	Opt. on SS 396 aluminum head
L79	327/325 @ 5600	355 @ 3600	11.0:1	

1969

LINE & RPO	CID/HP @ RPM	TORQUE @ RPM	COMPRESSION	NOTES
NOVA				
LM1	350/255 @ 4800	365 @ 3200	9.0:1	
L34	396/350 @ 5200	415 @ 3400	10.25:1	
L48	350/300 @ 4800	380 @ 3200	10.25:1	
L78	396/375 @ 5600	415 @ 3600	11.0:1	
L89	396/375 @ 5600	415 @ 3600	11.0:1	

LINE & RPO	CID/HP @ RPM	TORQUE @ RPM	COMPRESSION	NOTES
FULL SIZE				
LS1	427/400 @ 5400	460 @ 3600	10.25:1	
L36	427/390 @ 5400	460 @ 3600	10.25:1	
L72	427/425 @ 5600	460 @ 4000	11.0:1	
CAMARO				
L34	396/350 @ 5200	415 @ 3400	10.25:1	
L35	396/325 @ 4800	410 @ 3200	10.25:1	
L78	396/375 @ 5600	415 @ 3600	11.0:1	
L89	396/375 @ 5600	415 @ 3600	11.0:1	Aluminum head
L72	427/425 @ 5600	460 @ 4000	11.0:1	COPO #9561 iron heads & block
ZL1	427/430 @ 5200	450 @ 4400	12.0:1	COPO #9560 aluminum heads & block
L65	350/250 @ 4800	345 @ 2800	9.0:1	
LM1	350/255 @ 4800	365 @ 3200	9.0:1	
L48	350/300 @ 4800	380 @ 3200	10.25:1	
Z28	302/290 @ 5800	290 @ 4200	11.0:1	Z/28 Only
CHEVELLE				
L34	396/350 @ 5200	415 @ 3400	10.25:1	
L35	396/325 @ 4800	410 @ 3200	10.25:1	
L78	396/375 @ 5600	415 @ 3600	11.0:1	
L89	396/375 @ 5600	415 @ 3600	11.0:1	Aluminum head
L72	427/425 @ 5600	460 @ 4000	11.0:1	COPO #9562
LM1	350/255 @ 4800	365 @ 3200	9.0:1	
L48	350/300 @ 4800	380 @ 3200	10.25:1	

1970

LINE & RPO	CID/HP @ RPM	TORQUE @ RPM	COMPRESSION	NOTES
NOVA				
L65	350/250 @ 4800	345 @ 2800	9.0:1	
L48	350/300 @ 4800	380 @ 3200	10.25:1	Std. on Nova SS
L34	396/350 @ 5200	415 @ 3400	10.25:1	
L78	396/375 @ 5600	415 @ 3600	11.0:1	
FULL SIZE				
L48	350/300 @ 4800	380 @ 3200	10.25:1	
LS4	454/345 @ 4400	500 @ 3000	10.25:1	
LS5	454/390 @ 4800	500 @ 3400	10.25:1	Same as Chevelle and Monte Carlo LS5 but higher hp rating in full size car
CAMARO				
L48	350/300 @ 4800	380 @ 3200	10.25:1	Std. on Camaro SS
L34	396/350 @ 5200	415 @ 3400	10.25:1	
L78	396/375 @ 5600	415 @ 3600	11.0:1	
Z28	350/360 @ 6000	380 @ 4000	11.0:1	Z28 only
CHEVELLE & MONTE CARLO				
L48	350/300 @ 4800	380 @ 3200	10.25:1	
* LS3	400/330 @ 4800	410 @ 3200	10.25:1	
* L34	396/350 @ 5200	415 @ 3400	10.25:1	
* L78	396/375 @ 5600	415 @ 3600	11.0:1	
* L89	396/375 @ 5600	415 @ 3600	11.0:1	Aluminum head
LS5	454/360 @ 4400	500 @ 3200	10.25:1	
LS6	454/450 @ 5600	500 @ 3600	11.25:1	

*402 CID

1971

LINE & RPO	CID/HP @ RPM	TORQUE @ RPM	COMPRESSION	NOTES
(Horsepower figures given in both Gross — Net)				
NOVA				
L48	350/270 — 175 @ 4800	360 @ 3200	8.5:1	
L65	350/245 — 165 @ 4800	250 @ 2800	8.5:1	

LINE & RPO	CID/HP @ RPM	TORQUE @ RPM	COMPRESSION	NOTES
FULL SIZE				
L48	350/270 — 175 @ 4800	360 @ 3200	8.5:1	
LS5	454/365 — 285 @ 4800	465 @ 3200	8.5:1	
* LS3	396/300 — 260 @ 4800	400 @ 3200	8.5:1	
CAMARO				
L48	350/270 — 175 @ 4800	360 @ 3200	8.5:1	
L65	350/245 — 165 @ 4800	250 @ 2800	8.5:1	
* LS3	396/300 — 260 @ 4800	400 @ 3200	8.5:1	SS only
Z28	350/330 — 275 @ 5600	360 @ 4000	9.0:1	Z28 only, solid lifters
CHEVELLE				
L48	350/270 — 175 @ 4800	360 @ 3200	8.5:1	
L65	350/245 — 165 @ 4800	250 @ 2800	8.5:1	
LS5	454/365 — 285 @ 4800	465 @ 3200	8.5:1	
* LS3	396/300 — 260 @ 4800	400 @ 3200	8.5:1	

*402 CID

1972

(Horsepower ratings are net only)

LINE & RPO	CID/HP @ RPM	TORQUE @ RPM	COMPRESSION	NOTES
NOVA				
L65	350/165 @ 4000	280 @ 2400	8.5:1	2 bbl
L48	350/200 @ 4400	300 @ 2800	8.5:1	Nova SS only
FULL SIZE				
LS5	454/270 @ 4000	390 @ 3200	8.5:1	
LS3	400/240 @ 4400	345 @ 3200	8.5:1	
CAMARO				
L65	350/165 @ 4000	280 @ 2400	8.5:1	2 bbl
L48	350/200 @ 4400	300 @ 2800	8.5:1	4 bbl, Camaro SS only
LS3	400/240 @ 4400	345 @ 3200	8.5:1	
Z28	350/255 @ 5600	280 @ 4000	9.0:1	Z28 only
CHEVELLE				
L65	350/165 @ 4000	280 @ 2400	8.5:1	2 bbl
L48	350/175 @ 4000	280 @ 2400	8.5:1	4 bbl, lower hp rating in Chevelle
LS5	454/270 @ 4000	390 @ 3200	8.5:1	SS only
LS3	400/240 @ 4400	345 @ 3200	8.5:1	

1973

LINE & RPO	CID/HP @ RPM	TORQUE @ RPM	COMPRESSION	NOTES
NOVA				
L48	350/175 @ 4000	270 @ 2400	8.5:1	4 bbl
L65	350/145 @ 4000	255 @ 2400	8.5:1	2 bbl
FULL SIZE				
L48	350/175 @ 400	270 @ 2400	8.5:1	4 bbl
LS4	454/245 @ 4000	375 @ 2800	8.5:1	
L65	350/145 @ 4000	255 @ 2400	8.5:1	2 bbl
CAMARO				
L65	350/145 @ 4000	255 @ 2400	8.5:1	2 bbl
L48	350/175 @ 4000	270 @ 2400	8.5:1	4 bbl
Z28	350/245 @ 5200	280 @ 4000	9.0:1	Z28 only
CHEVELLE				
L65	350/145 @ 4000	255 @ 2400	8.5:1	2 bbl
L48	350/175 @ 4000	270 @ 2400	8.5:1	4 bbl
LS4	454/245 @ 4000	375 @ 2800	8.5:1	

Pontiac
Muscle Cars
1964–1973

Pontiac in the Muscle Car Era

To enthusiasts under the age of 40, the name Pontiac has always been synonymous with sporting transportation in the American style. It was not always so. In fact, until the mid-1950s, the Pontiac Division had exactly the opposite reputation.

Pontiac had been conceived in the late 1920s as a six-cylinder upgrade to the low-priced four-cylinder Chevrolet. The idea was to provide a slightly fancier alternative to low-priced car buyers who wanted Chevrolet economy and affordability. From the mid-1930s, Pontiac was known for its "Silver Streak" styling (featuring chromed hood stripes — very Art Deco) and straight-eight engines, powerplants that were wonderfully smooth and dependable, but never noted for either startling performance or exceptional economy. As a consequence, Pontiac developed a reputation as a maker of solid, unexciting cars — built like the Rock of Gibraltar, and about as fast. So conservative was Pontiac management in this period that it delayed introduction of the new high compression V-8 engine for at least two years simply because it didn't feel the need. The 1953 models were designed to take the V-8, but it did not appear in production until 1955.

When the Pontiac 287 cubic-inch V-8 appeared, though, it was a superb engine with none of the early teething troubles associated with Chevy's new V-8. The Chevy engine had been a rush job and the initial examples showed it. The Pontiac engine had been in development far longer than necessary — at least since the end of World War II — and it

showed, too, in its refinement and potential. What was missing was someone to tap that potential, in both the figurative and literal sense of the term. That "someone" appeared on the scene in the summer of 1956 in the trio of Knudsen, Estes and DeLorean.

Semon "Bunkie" Knudsen was the son of a General Motors legend, William "Big Bill" Knudsen, a.k.a. the Great Dane, the man who had put Chevrolet on the map in the 1920s. When Big Bill Knudsen addressed his first meeting of Chevrolet dealers in 1923, he told them in his thick accent that he wanted them to match Ford sales "von for von." They all thought he was joking. By 1928, Chevrolet was actually out-selling Ford for the first time and, after that, no one ever laughed at Big Bill again.

Bunkie Knudsen's first significant act at Pontiac was to remove the Silver Streaks from the 1957 models, then nearly ready for series production. It was a symbolic decision, but an important one. Knudsen's famous dictum was: "You can sell a young man's car to an old man, but you can't sell an old man's car to a young man." In other words, Pontiac could only hope to grow in the marketplace by shedding its stuffy image and learning how to build youthful, exciting cars.

Knudsen's second significant act was to "hire" the engineering team of Elliott M. "Pete" Estes, as chief engineer, and John Z. DeLorean as director of advanced engineering. Estes had had a hand in designing the Oldsmobile Rocket engine of 1949, the first modern lightweight, high compression V-8 in the industry. DeLorean had worked for both Chrysler and Packard in advanced engineering. Estes was not only a great engineer, he was a solid manager, as well. The two do not always go hand-in-hand. DeLorean, for example, was to prove himself a mediocre executive but, as an engineer, even his detractors admit he was a near genius — and many of his former engineering colleagues at GM would readily delete the qualifier.

The first hard evidence that things were popping at Pontiac was the mid-year 1957 introduction of the first Bonneville, a limited-run convertible sporting Pontiac's first use of fuel injection. Only 630 were built, but the Bonneville reappeared as a standard series in 1958 and has led the Pontiac product roster ever since.

Pontiac's "fuelie" was a mixed success from an engineering standpoint, but the late fifties also saw a growing list of exciting engine developments — tri-power 389s, Super Duty options, etc. — concurrent with Pontiac's entry into stock car racing. From 1960 until 1962, Pontiac utterly dominated the stock car circuit, racking up an incredible record of 57 NASCAR victories. From two victories in 1958 and only one in 1959, Pontiac soared to six in 1960, 29 in 1961, 22 in 1962, and four in 1963. Pontiac's supremacy ended only when the old fogeys on the 14th floor of the General Motors building handed down their notorious edict of January, 1963, forbidding divisions to actively support racing competition. This decision hit Pontiac with special severity, since excitement had become Pontiac's chief claim to fame as it rose from sixth place in national sales in 1956 to third by 1961. The slogan "win on Sunday, sell on Monday" was more than a cliche for Pontiac, it was demonstrably true. So, how to

keep the fires burning without racing was a question of more than academic interest to Estes (who had succeeded Knudsen in 1962) and DeLorean (Pontiac's new chief engineer) as 1963 wore on.

Oddly enough, it may have been Oldsmobile that unwittingly supplied the answer. Olds had irritated Pontiac planners in early 1963 by their apparent intention to put their new 330 cubic-inch small-block V-8 in their 1964 standard size, B-body Jetstar 88. This move was seen as an unfair threat to the hot-selling Pontiac Catalina. The GM drill at that time went that small cars got small engines, big cars got big engines. Olds was cheating. Well, someone asked, why can't we do the same thing in reverse, i.e., put a big-block engine in an A-body Tempest or LeMans? There was, of course, that anti-performance edict to worry about. In addition to banning racing participation, it had mandated an upper limit of 330 cubic inches for any standard engine in an A-body GM car. That clearly ruled out Pontiac's big-block 389 V-8 — or did it? The ruling spoke of "standard" engines. What would happen if the 389 were made an *option* on the sporty LeMans? Thus, the legendary GTO was born as a mid-year option on the 1964 LeMans.

DeLorean and Jim Wangers, who handled Pontiac's advertising account at the time, were the primary co-conspirators in the GTO decision. Pontiac caught a tremendous amount of flak from GM upper management as soon as the option hit the nation's showrooms, and for a time it appeared that it would be killed. In the end, the 32,000 customers who lined up to buy GTOs probably settled the issue. GM has rarely been known to argue with success. The issue was certainly settled insofar as Buick and Olds were concerned. They had GTO clones of their own on the market before the end of the 1964 model year, the 4-4-2 and Skylark Gran Sport, respectively. The minions at Chevy dutifully waited for the final ruling from GM brass before launching their own answer to the Pontiac challenge: the Chevelle SS 396 in mid-year 1965. It was the Pontiac GTO, however, that started the muscle car era. Without the willful disobedience of a few brave souls at Pontiac, that era (and this book) might never have come to pass.

Also new in 1964, although hardly remembered today, was the Pontiac Catalina 2+2 option. This was a big car with an even bigger 421 cube engine intended to compete against the Chevy Impala Super Sport. It was a good idea as far as it went, but the concept was almost immediately eclipsed by the runaway success of the GTO. Although the 2+2 lingered through the 1968 model run, it never recorded much enthusiasm at the cash register. A clean, original 2+2 is, however, a rare and highly desirable collectible today.

John DeLorean moved into the general manager's office in July, 1965, when Estes was promoted to Chevrolet. Steve Malone was named chief engineer and continued the enthusiastic devotion to high performance detail for which Pontiac had by that point become famous. (Bunkie Knudsen, for his part, was promoted to an administrative job, then passed over for the GM presidency in 1969 and bolted to Ford Motor Company. After serving for a few months as president in Dearborn, he and Hank the Deuce had a terminal falling out, but the move completed the circle in a sense. Big Bill Knudsen had left Ford in 1922 after a dispute with Henry I to join Chevrolet.)

DeLorean's first big effort as general manager was to secure a slice of the Camaro program. Pontiac planners had been trying for years without success to "sell" GM man-agement on an affordable Pontiac sporty car and wasn't about to let the ponycar program leave without them. Chevy resisted, but Pontiac won — sort of. At DeLorean's insistence Pontiac was given last minute approval to build a Camaro derivative and a pitifully small budget with which to do it. Pontiac designers Jack Humbert (exteriors) and Fedele Bianco (interiors) managed to instill genuine Pontiac flavor into the styling despite having to use mostly Camaro parts. Malone and his engineering team managed to tweak the Camaro/Firebird chassis just enough to give the Pontiac-powered F-car its own distinct driving personality.

Although introduced as a mid-year 1967 model, the most exciting Firebird was the mid-year 1969 Trans Am, a car destined for great fame but one that was literally an afterthought at the time. The real push that year was the GTO Judge, essentially a gee-whiz cosmetic package for the Goat. The Trans Am was the same idea for the Firebird crowd.

When the second generation Firebird went into development, Pontiac made sure it had more say in the process. In fact, it can be said that the 1970 1/2 F-cars were joint efforts all the way. The Firebird design work was guided by Bill Porter (exteriors) and John Shettler (interiors). The engineering was accomplished by a team directed by Malone.

It was about this time that the high performance market began to evaporate under the combined pressure of the insurance industry and the safety crusaders. The GTO was functionally gone by 1972, although it lingered on in diluted form for another three years. The Firebird line was very nearly killed, along with the Camaro, at the end of the 1972 model run. Fortunately, wiser heads prevailed. It was, however, the end of an era in which Pontiac had played a key role.

This special 1964 GTO show car exhibits the basic elements that would be developed over the next five years: a split grille, twin hood scoops, and a peaked center. Originally Pontiac called the GTO a "sports car" to differentiate it from race cars.

1964 Pontiac

The 1964 model year was one of Pontiac's most important of the modern era. Production rose 20% to 715,261 enabling Pontiac to easily maintain its third place in the auto sales competition. Its closest rival was 175,000 units behind. The Tempest was Pontiac's greatest success that year, with the all-new intermediate-size Tempest's production up by an incredible 80%. Though virtually all the special features that had made the Tempest so remarkable in the 1961-1963 model years had been dropped (such as the slant-four engine and the flexible transaxle), the Tempest's popularity rose at an unprecedented rate. Pontiac was sensitive to those who wanted more than the conventional car and in 1964 introduced the ground-breaking GTO (short for Gran Turismo Omologato or Homologated Grand Touring in English) option on the Tempest LeMans. For the first time, a powerful V-8 was officially placed in a (relatively) small car, creating a super-powerful, relatively inexpensive car that even threatened the

fabled Corvette, but cost a whole lot less. The GTO could truly be considered the trailblazer of muscle cars.

Catalina 2+2

The Catalina underwent a few mild styling changes. The crisp angles of the previous year had been softened so that the contours were now more rounded. The 2+2 option was introduced for the Catalina in 1964 and became the first officially designated regular performance model in the big Pontiacs. It was basically a trim option, designed to give the Catalina a sporty look. The 389 cid 283 hp V-8 was the standard power for this model; but for those who wanted a high performance engine as well as a sporty appearance, three 421 cid engines were available including the 421 cid, 370 hp V-8.

LeMans GTO

In the previous year, General Motors' top executives decided to end Pontiac's involvement in stock car racing. This left Pontiac with the problem of maintaining its attraction to the youthful performance market it had traditionally appealed to, without the visual hype of a perform-

For the second year in a row, Pontiac achieved record production totals. The Catalina 2+2, which was the first officially designated regular performance model among the big Pontiacs, would help keep Pontiac sales strong.

ance car. The GTO option introduced in 1964 was Pontiac's answer to this problem. They dropped a large 389 cid engine into the relatively lightweight LeMans and came up with the powerhouse known as the GTO. This option was not included in the original 1964 catalog; in fact it is possible the GM top executives were unaware of the GTO until it hit the showroom floor. Forecasters had predicted that a market for about 10,000 GTO's existed; they were not even close. By the end of the 1964 model year, over 34,000 GTO's had been sold. If GM top brass had any qualms about the GTO, sales figures soothed their fears. The GTO's performance was truly exceptional, and its price made it affordable for most performance car enthusiasts. *Road & Track* measured the standard GTO's top speed at 122 mph and the tri-power 348 hp's 0 to 60 time at 5.7 seconds. *Car & Driver* clocked the Tri-Power GTO, with an optional 3.90 rear axle ratio at 115 mph in 13.1 seconds in the standing quarter-mile. The GTO not only had great performance but it was also styled like a supercar. Two nonfunctional air scoops on the hood, horizontal headlights and a blacked-out grille gave the GTO a face that oozed muscle. Chrome GTO nameplates were mounted

on the grille and rear deck and a different GTO monogram was positioned on each front fender.

VIN NUMBERS
Vehicle Identification Number: 8( )4( )1001 and up
Explanation:
First digit: Number of cylinders = 8
Second digit: Series number:
  Catalina = 3
  Custom = 1
  LeMans = 2
  Tempest = 0
Third digit: Last digit of model year = 4
Fourth digit: Letter indicating assembly plant
Last four digits: Sequential production number

PRODUCTION TOTALS

Model	Total Units	Percent
Catalina	257,768	
2+2 opt.	7,998	3

The GTO had a comfortable and stylish interior. A sports wheel, Morrokide seats and carpeting were all standard.

Some car enthusiasts criticized the GTO's hood scoops because they only imitated functional ones on "true sports cars."

LeMans	235,855	
GTO opt.	32,450	14

DRIVETRAIN DATA

	Catalina 2+2 (Std.)	Catalina 2+2 (Opt.)	Catalina 2+2 (Opt.)
Cyl:	V-8	V-8	V-8
Bore (in):	4.06	4.09	4.062
Stroke (in):	3.75	4.00	3.75
CID:	389	421	421
Carbs.:	1 2-bbl	1 4-bbl	3 2-bbl
Make:	Rochester	Rochester	Rochester
Model:	2GC	4GC	2GC
Comp.:	10.5	10.5	10.75
Max. BHP:	283	320	350
@ RPM:	4400	4400	4600
Torque ft-lb:	418	455	454
@ RPM:	2800	2800	3200

	Catalina 2+2 (Opt.)	LeMans GTO (Std.)	LeMans GTO (Opt.)
Cyl:	V-8	V-8	V-8
Bore (in):	4.09	4.062	4.062
Stroke (in):	4.00	3.75	3.75
CID:	421	389	389
Carbs.:	3 2-bbl	1 4-bbl	3 2-bbl
Make:	Rochester	Rochester	Rochester
Model:	2GC	4GC	2GC
Comp.:	10.75	10.75	10.75
Max. BHP:	370	325	348
@ RPM:	5200	4800	4900
Torque ft-lb:	460	428	428
@ RPM:	3800	3200	3200

TRANSMISSIONS

Catalina 2+2
Std: 4-speed Console-Mounted Manual or Hydra-matic Console-Mounted Automatic
Opt: NA

LeMans GTO
Std: 3-speed Column-Mounted Manual
Opt: 4-speed Floor-Mounted Manual Wide-Ratio, 4-speed Floor-Mounted Manual Close-Ratio, 2-speed Lever-Mounted Torque Convertor Automatic

REAR AXLE RATIOS

Catalina 2+2 (std. 389 cid, 283 hp)
Std: 3.42
Opt: NA

Catalina 2+2 (421 cid, 320 hp)
Std: 3.08 (auto), 3.23 (3-sp man), 3.42 (4-sp man)
Opt: Ratios up to 4.10 available

Catalina 2+2 (421 cid, 350 hp)
Std: 3.08 (auto), 3.23 (man)
Opt: Ratios up to 4.10 available

Catalina 2+2 (421 cid, 370 hp)
Std: 3.42
Opt: Ratios up to 4.10 available

LeMans GTO
Std: 3.23
Opt: 3.08, 3.36, 3.55, 3.90

The "GTO 6.5 Liter" emblem could be found on both sides of the GTO. Pontiac observed that "If you don't think this is enough warning, you could always fly the skull and crossbones." The "GTO" letters were sometimes translated as "Get The Others."

EXTERIOR DATA

Catalina 2+2

	Sports Coupe	Convertible
Length (in):	213.8	213.8
Width (in):	79.2	79.2
Height (in):	NA	NA
Wheelbase (in):	120	120
Weight (lb):	3750	3825

LeMans GTO

	Hardtop	Sports Coupe	Convertible
Length (in):	203	203	203
Width (in):	73.3	73.3	73.3
Height (in):	53.5	53.5	53.5
Wheelbase (in):	115	115	115
Weight (lb):	3443	3423	3623

FACTORY BASE PRICE DATA

Model	Coupe	Hardtop	Convertible
Catalina 2+2	$ 3160	$ —	$ 3472
LeMans GTO	2787	2852	3092

POPULAR FACTORY OPTIONS

Interior: Rally clock, $19; Console, $48; Rear window defogger, $21; Saf-T-Track differential, $37; Tri-power engine, $116; Padded instrument panel, $16; Power windows, $102; AM radio, $64; AM/FM radio, $151; Verba-Phonic rear speaker system, $54; Retractable seat belts, $18; Custom sports steering wheel, $39; Tilt steering wheel, $43; Tachometer & rally gauge cluster, $86; Tonneau cover, $50.

Exterior: Backup lights, $13; Tinted glass, $31; Tinted windshield glass only, $20; Outside mirror, $4; Outside remote controlled mirror, $12; Vinyl roof covering, $75; Custom wheel discs, $36; Rally wheels, $53; Windshield washer, $13.

Miscellaneous: Air conditioning, $345; Aluminum brake drums, $50; Metallic brake linings, $38; Handling package, $4; Transistorized ignition, $65; Power brakes, $43; Power steering, $97; Quick-ratio steering, $11; Four-speed manual transmission; Two-speed automatic transmission; Remote trunk lid release, $11.

The 1965 GTO was considered by many to be the best GTO. It was stylish and virtually every car magazine that tested it found its performance to be exceptional. The 1965 GTO was so popular that there were two top-ten hits about it that year.

1965 Pontiac

Pontiac's remarkable production record of 1964 was surpassed in 1965; 802,000 cars were built that year including the 10 millionth Pontiac built since 1926. The performance cars were hotter than ever. A total of 75,352 GTO's were built that year, up by a whopping 132%. The standard-size Pontiacs received a new body that made them look much larger than the previous year's models. This was done with a few styling tricks and, in actuality, the new bodies of many of the standard-sized cars were lighter than they had been previously. All models featured bold new grilles and heavily sculptured side contours; seat belts were standard and an automatic temperature control option was available. General Motors also introduced the new Turbo Hydra-matic transmission on the full-size Pontiac, replacing the old Hydra-matic as its automatic transmission. This was an important improvement in automatics — it was more responsive and smoother than the old transmission in almost every way. On the corporate level, John Z. DeLorean was

named general manager of Pontiac, replacing Elliott M. Estes, who moved on to Chevrolet. While most GM general managers retained a low-profile, it was clear that John Z. DeLorean was cast from a different mold. A brilliant engineer, he also had an astute understanding for the importance of promotion and the excitement it could generate within the division.

Catalina 2+2

Catalina 2+2 sales were up by 44% from the year before, with over 11,000 cars sold. The Catalina's new body rode on a new, slightly longer chassis, with a wheelbase of 121 inches. The 2+2's standard engine was the 421-cid motor with an output of 338 hp. Two other more powerful 421 cid engines were available, one with an output of 356 hp, the other with 376 hp. Standard features of the 2+2 included heavy-duty springs and shock absorbers, a three-speed transmission with a Hurst shifter, dual exhausts and a performance axle ratio. Special treatment was also accorded to the interior and exterior, with bucket seats, seat belts, full carpeting, custom pinstriping and vertical louvers on the front fenders all standard. *Car and Driver's* Walt Hansgen compared the Catalina 2+2 with the Ferrari

Changes on the 1965 GTO included stacked headlights, a recessed grille and a single hood scoop.

The Catalina 2+2 became a true performance option in 1965 when the 421 cid, 338-hp engine was offered.

2+2 and said "If one totalled their relative strengths and weaknesses and took an average for each car, the net result would be nearly equal.... They provide their drivers with a brand of automotive excitement seldom experienced off the race course." But the Catalina had one important advantage over the Ferrari—it was about $10,000 less. Hansgen measured the 2+2's top speed at over 130 mph and its 0 to 60 time at a fast 3.9 seconds.

TEMPEST LEMANS GTO

The GTO was altered very little from the previous year's highly successful model. Front and rear styling were modified slightly — headlights were set vertically, one on top of the other and the grille was slightly recessed. Overall body length was increased by three inches. Horsepower on the standard engine was boosted by 10 hp and on the Tri-Power engine, it was raised by 12 hp. A new engine featuring Ram Air was available in mid-year. Its horsepower ratings were the same as the Tri-Power, but it made use of the air-scoops on the hood. The GTO came with heavy-duty springs, shocks and stabilizer bar, as well as custom pinstriping and performance red-circle tires (nicknamed tiger paws). Pontiac came out with a rather unusual (and rare) promotional folder for the GTO, that included a 45 rpm record with such moving lyrics as: "Listen to her growl! She's always on the prowl! Gee-TO Tiger, GO!"

VIN NUMBERS

Vehicle Identification Number: 2(   )5( )( )00001 and up
Explanation:
First digit: GM line number: 2 = Pontiac
Second to fifth digit: Body number:
   Catalina Sports Coupe = 5237
   Catalina Convertible = 5267

   LeMans GTO Sports Coupe = 3727
   LeMans GTO Hardtop = 3737
   LeMans GTO Convertible = 3767
Sixth digit: Last digit of model year = 5
Seventh digit: Letter indicating assembly plant
Eight digit: Number of cylinders 8 = 1
Last five digits: Sequential production number

PRODUCTION TOTALS

Model	Total Units	Percent
Catalina	271,058	
2+2 opt.	11,519	4
LeMans	182,905	
GTO opt.	75,352	41

DRIVETRAIN DATA

	Catalina 2+2 (Std.)	Catalina 2+2 (Opt.)	Catalina 2+2 (Opt.)
Cyl:	V-8	V-8	V-8
Bore (in):	4.09	4.09	4.09
Stroke (in):	4.00	4.00	4.00
CID:	421	421	421
Carbs.:	1 4-bbl	3 2-bbl	3 2-bbl
Make:	Rochester	Rochester	Rochester
Model:	4GC	2GC	2GC
Comp.:	10.5	10.75	10.75
Max. BHP:	338	356	376
@ RPM:	4600	4800	5000
Torque ft-lb:	459	459	461
@ RPM:	2800	3200	3600

(con't. next page)

The Catalina 2+2 came with a fully synchronized 3-speed transmission with a Hurst shifter, dual exhausts, and heavy duty springs and shocks. The more responsive Turbo Hydra-matic automatic transmission replaced the old Hydra-matic.

DRIVETRAIN DATA *(con't.)*

	LeMans GTO	LeMans GTO Ram Air	LeMans GTO Tri-Power
	(Std.)	*(Opt.)*	*(Opt.)*
Cyl:	V-8	V-8	V-8
Bore (in):	4.062	4.062	4.062
Stroke (in):	3.75	3.75	3.75
CID:	389	389	389
Carbs.:	1 4 bbl	1 2-bbl	3 2-bbl
Make:	Rochester	Rochester	Rochester
Model:	4GC	2GC	2GC
Comp.:	10.75	10.75	10.75
Max. BHP:	335	360	360
@ RPM:	5000	5200	5200
Torque ft-lb:	431	424	424
@ RPM:	3200	3600	3600

TRANSMISSIONS

Catalina 2+2
Std: 3-speed All-Synchro Floor-Mounted Manual with Hurst Shifter
Opt: 4-speed All-Synchro Floor-Mounted Manual with Hurst Shifter, Turbo Hydra-matic Console-Mounted Automatic

LeMans GTO
Std: 3-speed Floor-Mounted Manual with Hurst Shifter
Opt: 3-speed Fully Synchro Floor-Mounted Manual with Hurst Shifter, 4-speed Floor-Mounted Manual Close-Ratio with Hurst Shifter, 4-speed Floor-Mounted Manual Wide-Ratio with Hurst Shifter, 2-speed Lever-Mounted Torque Convertor Automatic

REAR AXLE RATIOS

Catalina 2+2
Std: 3.42 (man), 3.23 (auto)
Opt: 3.23 (man), 3.42 (auto), 3.55, 3.73, 4.11 (man)

LeMans GTO (389 355 hp)
Std: 3.23
Opt: 3.08, 3.36, 3.55, 3.90

LeMans GTO (389 cid 360 hp)
Std: 3.55
Opt: 3.08, 3.23, 3.36, 3.90

The Firebird 400 came equipped with non-functional air scoops. For $263 the Ram Air option, which made use of the scoops, could be ordered. Stiffer valve springs and cold, dense air from the scoops in the carburetor allowed 6000 rpm without float or pump-up.

1967 Pontiac

Sales for the automobile industry were down by about 7% in 1967. Likewise, Pontiac's sales were down, but not nearly as much as the entire industry. In fact, Pontiac's market penetration reached its highest level in its history at 9.98%. In other words, almost one out of ten cars purchased in the United States was a Pontiac. All full-sized Pontiacs received styling changes that made them look longer and more sleek than they had in previous years. One of the most distinctive styling additions was new front bumpers with grilles built into them. The 2+2 reverted to being an option on the Catalina, rather than a separate series. The GTO maintained its status as well as its popularity. The most notable event for Pontiac in 1967 was the mid-year introduction of the Firebird, Pontiac's entry into the ponycar market. By the time GM's management had given the green light to produce the Firebird, had barely six months to get their ponycar out. Five different models were available, the most powerful of which was the Firebird 400.

CATALINA 2+2

After its brief moment of glory as a separate series, the 2+2 reverted to being an option package on the Catalina. For the 2+2 package, the large 428 cid, 360 hp was stuffed into a specially trimmed Catalina. The Quadra-Power 428 was optional for those who wanted more performance. Other goodies included in this option were a three-speed all-synchro floor-mounted heavy-duty transmission, bucket seats, carpeting and a special suspension. The 2+2 logo could be seen on the front deck hood and various other strategic locations. Although overall Pontiac sales were down by only 2%, sales of big Pontiacs were down by 8%. Only 1,768 Catalina 2+2's were sold, down by 4,615, and total Catalina sales also declined.

FIREBIRD 400

Ever since the 1964 introduction of the Ford Mustang and the creation of the ponycar market, it had been a foregone conclusion that Chevrolet would introduce a competing model. In September of 1966, Chevy introduced the Camaro as an early '67 model. But Pontiac fought hard to get a piece of the action, and in mid 1967, it released the Firebird into

The 2+2 reverted to optional status on the Catalina in 1967. It was now powered by a 428-cid engine that produced either 360 or 376 hp. One of the most distinctive styling changes on the 2+2 was the introduction of the disappearing windshield wipers.

the hot ponycar market. The Firebird shared most of the Camaro's exterior sheet metal and its interior trim. But its grille and taillights were specifically designed for the Firebird and such touches as pleating of the seats gave it some distinction. Mechanically, though, the Firebird and Camaro were miles apart. Five different Firebirds were available. The base Firebird came with a 165 hp, 230 cid overhead cam six. The Firebird Sprint was powered by a four-barrel, 215-hp version of this engine. The Firebird 326 featured the two-barrel version of the 326 cid, 250-hp V-8. The Firebird HO used a four-barrel version of this engine that produced 285 hp. Finally, for those who craved performance, the Firebird 400 featured the 400-cid, 325-hp four-barrel powerhouse V-8. A Ram Air version of this engine that turned the hood scoops into functional entities was also available. Officially, the ratings of the Ram Air version were the same as the standard engine (a ploy supposed to fool insurance companies and thereby keep rates down), but in reality it increased performance considerably. Included in the Firebird 400 package were chrome engine parts, a three-speed heavy-duty floor shift and a sports type suspension. The number '400' was clearly

displayed on the righthand side of the deck lid. The Firebird was a tremendous success in its inaugural year—production hit 82,560, despite the fact that the Firebird was a mid-year introduction.

GTO

Though the GTO was still very popular among muscle car enthusiasts, the competition in 1967 had heated up tremendously. Production of the GTO was down by 15%, but considering the quantity and quality of the competition, this could be seen as an achievement. Externally, the GTO was little changed. The grille work was altered so that it looked something like two pieces of chain-link fencing. New safety features, such as an energy-absorbing steering column, a dual braking system, a four-way flasher, a lane changing signal and an inside rear-view glareless tilting mirror became standard on the GTO. The most notable change, though, was in the engine. The engine block was bored out just 1/16th of an inch so that displacement increased to 400 cubic inches. Quoted horsepower was unchanged, but the Ram Air option was still available. The Tri-Power engine, with its three two-barrel carburetors was

A number of safety features were standard on the GTO in 1967 including an energy-absorbing steering column, dual brakes, a four-way warning flasher and lane changer signal. Shoulder straps and power-assisted front-wheel disc brakes were optional.

dropped from the option list and a new high output (HO) engine, equipped with a four-barrel carburetor called the Quadrajet, was offered instead. Though many were afraid that performance would suffer because of this, others felt that the Quadrajet could be reworked so that it would be as effective as the Tri-Power. For those who liked muscular appearances, but were timid at heart, an economy 400 cid engine with 255 hp was available.

VIN NUMBERS

Vehicle Identification Number: 2(   )7( )( )00001 and up
Explanation:
First digit: GM line number: 2 = Pontiac
Second to fifth digit: Body number:
  Catalina Hardtop = 5287
  Catalina Convertible = 5267
  Firebird Hardtop = 2337
  Firebird Convertible = 2367
  GTO Sports Coupe = 4207
  GTO Hardtop = 4217
  GTO Convertible = 4267

Sixth digit: Last digit of model year = 7
Seventh digit: Letter indicating assembly plant
Eight digit: Number of cylinders 8 = 1
Last five digits: Sequential production number

PRODUCTION TOTALS

Model	Total Units	Percent
Catalina	211,405	
2+2 opt.	1,768	1
GTO	81,722	
Firebird	82,256	
400 opt.	NA	

DRIVETRAIN DATA

	Catalina 2+2 (Std.)	Catalina 2+2 (Opt.)	Firebird 400 (Std.)
Cyl:	V-8	V-8	V-8
Bore (in):	4.12	4.12	4.12
Stroke (in):	4.00	4.00	3.75

(con't. next page)

An 8-track tape was optional on the Firebird, but it couldn't be ordered with air conditioning, console gauges or a floor stick.

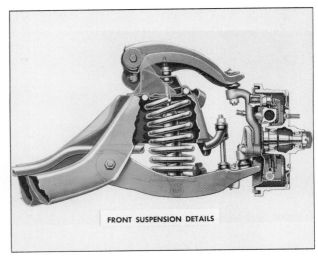

FRONT SUSPENSION DETAILS

The Firebird's suspension system was developed largely through the use of computer models.

DRIVETRAIN DATA *(con't.)*

CID:	428	428	400
Carbs.:	1 4-bbl	1 4-bbl	1 4-bbl
Make:	Rochester	Rochester	Rochester
Model:	4MV	4MV	4MV
Comp.:	10.5	10.75	10.75
Max. BHP:	360	376	325
@ RPM:	4600	5100	4800
Torque ft-lb:	472	462	410
@ RPM:	3200	3400	3400

	GTO (Std.)	GTO HO (Opt.)	GTO Ram Air (Opt.)
Cyl:	V-8	V-8	V-8
Bore (in):	4.12	4.12	4.12
Stroke (in):	3.75	3.75	3.75
CID:	400	400	400
Carbs.:	1 4 bbl	1 4-bbl	1 4-bbl
Make:	Rochester	Rochester	Rochester
Model:	4MV	4MV	4MV
Comp.:	10.75	10.75	10.75
Max. BHP:	335	360	360
@ RPM:	5000	5100	5400
Torque ft-lb:	441	438	438
@ RPM:	3400	3600	3800

	GTO Economy (Opt.)
Cyl:	V-8
Bore (in):	4.12
Stroke (in):	3.75
CID:	400
Carbs.:	1 2 bbl

Make:	Carter
Model:	AFB
Comp.:	8.6
Max. BHP:	255
@ RPM:	4400
Torque ft-lb:	397
@ RPM:	4400

TRANSMISSIONS

Catalina 2+2
Std: 3-speed All-Synchro Floor-Mounted Manual
Opt: 4-speed All-Synchro Floor-Mounted Manual with Hurst Shifter, 4-speed All-Synchro Floor-Mounted Manual Close-Ratio with Hurst Shifter, Turbo Hydra-matic Console-Mounted Automatic

Firebird 400
Std: 3-speed Heavy-Duty Floor-Mounted Manual
Opt: 4-speed Floor-Mounted Manual, 3-speed Turbo Hydra-matic Console-Mounted Automatic

GTO
Std: 3-speed Column-Mounted Manual
Opt: 3-speed Fully Synchro Floor-Mounted Manual with Hurst Shifter, 4-speed Floor-Mounted Manual Close-Ratio with Hurst Shifter, 4-speed Floor-Mounted Manual Wide-Ratio with Hurst Shifter, 3-Speed Lever-Mounted Turbo Hydra-matic Automatic

REAR AXLE RATIOS

Catalina 2+2
Std: 3.42 (3-sp man), 3.23 (auto), 4.11 (4-sp man)
Opt: NA

(con't. next page)

A Quadra-Power 428 V-8 was optional on the 2+2. Its compression ratio was 10.75:1 and premium fuel was required.

For the second year in a row, production of all big Pontiacs declined. The 2+2's fell by over 4,000 units from 1966.

REAR AXLE RATIOS *(con't.)*

Firebird 400
Std: 3.36 (man), 3.08 (auto)
Opt: 3.23, 3.55, 3.90, 4.33

GTO (255 hp)
Std: 3.36 (auto), 2.93 (man)
Opt: 2.56

GTO (335 hp)
Std: 3.23 (auto), 3.55 (man)
Opt: 3.90, 4.11, 4.33

GTO (360 hp)
Std: 3.55 (man), 3.36 (auto)
Opt: 3.90, 4.11, 4.33

EXTERIOR DATA

Catalina 2+2

	Hardtop	Convertible
Length (in):	215.6	215.6
Width (in):	79.7	79.7
Height (in):	55.3	55.3
Wheelbase (in):	121	121
Weight (lb):	3860	3910

Firebird

	Hardtop	Convertible
Length (in):	188.8	188.8
Width (in):	72.8	72.8
Height (in):	51.5	51.4
Wheelbase (in):	108.1	108.1
Weight (lb):	3123	3415

GTO

	Hardtop	Sports Coupe	Convertible
Length (in):	206.6	206.6	206.6
Width (in):	74.7	74.7	74.7
Height (in):	53.7	53.7	53.6
Wheelbase (in):	115	115	115
Weight (lb):	3430	3425	3515

FACTORY BASE PRICE DATA

Model	Coupe	Hardtop	Convertible
Catalina 2+2	$ —	$ 3549	$ 3664
Firebird 400	—	2777	3177
GTO	2891	2935	3165

POPULAR FACTORY OPTIONS

Interior: Electric clock, $16; Console, $47 (Firebird), $68 (GTO); Head rests, $53; Rally & hood tach instruments, $32 (Firebird); Remote control mirror, $9; Power windows, $100; Pushbutton radio, $61; AM/FM radio, $134; Fold-down rear seat, $37 (Firebird); Rear speaker, $16; Custom front & rear seat belts, $6; Front shoulder straps, $23; Safeguard speedometer, $11 (Firebird); Deluxe steering wheel, $12 (GTO); Custom steering wheel, $30; Tilt steering wheel, $42; Stereo tape deck, $128; Four-way power seat, $70 (GTO); Right reclining bucket seat, $84 (GTO).

Exterior: Exhaust tailpipe extensions, $20 (Firebird & GTO); Hood-mounted tachometer, $63 (Firebird); Tinted glass, $30; Tinted windshield glass only, $21; Tonneau cover, $48 (GTO); Remote trunk lid release, $13; Vinyl roof, $84; Deluxe wheel discs, $17; Custom wheel discs, $19 (Firebird), $36 (GTO); Wire wheel

(con't. next page)

This GTO hardtop with optional wire wheel covers and a vinyl top shows the distinctive 1967 waffle-mesh grille. This year it was polished aluminum instead of painted-black as it had been previously. The GTO emblem was lowered and bolted to the rocker panels

POPULAR FACTORY OPTIONS *(con't.)*

discs, $53 (Firebird), $73 (GTO); Rally I wheels, $50 (Firebird), $57 (GTO); Rally II wheels, $53 (Firebird), $73 (GTO); Cordova top, $84 (GTO); Outside mirror, $7; Power antenna, $29 (GTO).

Miscellaneous: Air conditioning, $356; Disc brakes, $63 (Firebird); Front disc brakes, $110 (GTO); Cruise control, $53; Saf-T-Track differential, $42 (Firebird); Heavy-duty differential, $63 (GTO); Dual exhaust, $30 (Firebird); Handling package, $9 (Firebird), $4 (GTO); Drum power brakes, $42 (Firebird); Front disc power brakes, $105 (GTO); Power steering, $95; Power top, $53 (convertibles only); Rear window defogger, $21; Four-speed manual transmission, $184; Two-speed Turbo Hydra-matic transmission, $184 (Firebird); Three-speed Turbo Hydra-matic transmission, $226 (Catalina and GTO); Quadra-Power engine, $77 (GTO); Ram Air engine, $263 (GTO and Firebird); Economy engine (GTO); Superlift shock absorbers, $40 (GTO); Capacitor discharge ignition, $104 (GTO); Transistorized ignition, $75 (GTO).

Pontiac called the GTO "An idea on wheels — the idea that there's more to driving than moving in isolated indifference."

The 1968 Firebird was little changed; wraparound front parking lamps and the removal of the front vent windows were the most noticeable changes. A Ram Air and a High Output V-8, which were both rated at 335 hp, were available on the Formula 400.

1968 Pontiac

Industry-wide sales were up to a new record for 1968 and, likewise, Pontiac's sales were up to a new record high of 910,977. Due to the dismal sales of 2+2s in the previous year, this option was dropped. But a 428 cid engine could be ordered, so in effect, you could build your own 2+2, without calling it such. All intermediate Pontiacs received new bodies in 1968. Two-door models came on a chassis with a 112-inch wheelbase, while four-door models rode on a larger 116-inch wheelbase. Overall styling was more rounded than before and included disappearing windshield wipers. The Firebird, on the other hand, remained much as it had been before. The major change was renaming the Firebird Sprint the Firebird 350.

FIREBIRD 400

Few changes were made to the Firebird in 1968. Side vent windows were eliminated and side marker lights were added to this car. Additionally, the rear suspension was refined and the interior was slightly altered. The Firebird 400 had three possible engines. The standard engine produced 330 hp; its maximum speed was recorded by *World Car* at 122 mph. The HO (or high output) option increased horsepower by five to 335 hp. The most performance-oriented engine was again the Ram Air, which put the decorative Firebird's air scoops to good use. The Firebird 400 package consisted of a chrome air cleaner, chrome rocker covers, a chrome oil cap, sports type springs and shock aborbers, a heavy-duty battery, dual exhausts, special decals, red stripe or whitewall tires, and the "Power Flex" variable pitch cooling fan. Production went up considerably from the previous year (but 1967 was only a partial model year) — 107,122 units were produced. The Firebird continued to gain prominence in the increasingly competitive ponycar market.

GTO

The GTO, like all intermediate-size Pontiacs, received a new body. Despite the fact that it rode on a smaller 112-inch wheelbase, it was slightly heavier than the year before. One of the most innovative and unusual new styling fea-

The rear suspension of the Firebird was revised in 1968 — multi-leaf rear springs replaced the old mono-plates.

Motor Trend *named the '68 GTO Car of the Year for "confirming the correlation between safety, styling and performance."*

tures on the GTO was the dramatic Endura rubber front bumper. Because it could be molded into any shape and painted the same color as the car, it opened up new dimensions in design. The bumper no longer had to appear as if it were a functional afterthought to the design of the car. It was now an integral part of the overall design. Of course, the Endura rubber bumper had more than styling potential; it was extremely resilient and flexible. Many will remember the Pontiac commercial in 1968 in which John DeLorean was shown battering the GTO bumper with a sledgehammer, with no effect on the bumper. Many people had mixed feelings about this new bumper that made the car look "bumperless." Thus Pontiac made it a delete option, that is, one could choose not to have it installed and not pay for it. The same engines were available this year. Awards and praise for the GTO abounded in 1968. It was named by *Motor Trend* as Car of the Year. It came in second in the *Car and Driver* Fifth Annual Readers' Choice Winners in the Best Super Car category. In September of 1968 it was chosen by *Car Life* as one of the Ten Best Test Cars. In presenting the award *Car Life* said that the GTO "has become a classic in its own time. It's an unmistakable car, slightly erotic, highly romantic, full of verve, optimism, grace and beauty."

VIN NUMBERS
Vehicle Identification Number: 2( )8( )( )00001 and up
Explanation:
First digit: GM line number: 2 = Pontiac
Second to fifth digit: Body number:
   Firebird Hardtop = 2337
   Firebird Convertible = 2367
   GTO Hardtop = 4237
   GTO Convertible = 4267

Sixth digit: Last digit of model year = 8
Seventh digit: Letter indicating assembly plant
Eight digit: Number of cylinders 8 = 1
Last five digits: Sequential production number

PRODUCTION TOTALS
Model	Total Units	Percent
GTO	87,684	
Firebird	107,112	
Firebird 400 opt.	NA	

DRIVETRAIN DATA
	Firebird 400 (Std.)	Firebird 400 HO (Opt.)	Firebird 400 Ram Air (Opt.)
Cyl:	V-8	V-8	V-8
Bore (in):	4.12	4.12	4.12
Stroke (in):	3.75	3.75	3.75
CID:	400	400	400
Carbs.:	1 4-bbl	1 4-bbl	1 4-bbl
Make:	Rochester	Rochester	Rochester
Model:	4MV	4MV	4MV
Comp.:	10.75	10.75	10.75
Max. BHP:	330	335	335
@ RPM:	4800	5000	5300
Torque ft-lb:	430	430	430
@ RPM:	3300	3400	3600

	GTO (Std.)	GTO HO (Opt.)	GTO Ram Air (Opt.)
Cyl:	V-8	V-8	V-8
Bore (in):	4.12	4.12	4.12

(con't. next page)

The 1968 GTO began the year with an all-new body. The trademark two-piece horizontal grille was kept, but the new revolutionary Endura front bumper, horizontal headlights (in this case, hidden) and a hood-mounted tach gave this GTO its distinctive appearance.

DRIVETRAIN DATA *(con't.)*

Stroke (in):	3.75	3.75	3.75
CID:	400	400	400
Carbs.:	1 4 bbl	1 4-bbl	1 4-bbl
Make:	Rochester	Rochester	Rochester
Model:	4MV	4MV	4MV
Comp.:	10.75	10.75	10.75
Max. BHP:	350	360	360
@ RPM:	5000	5100	5400
Torque ft-lb:	445	445	438
@ RPM:	3000	3500	3800

	GTO Economy (Opt.)
Cyl:	V-8
Bore (in):	4.12
Stroke (in):	3.75
CID:	400
Carbs.:	1 2 bbl
Make:	Rochester
Model:	2GC

Comp.:	8.6
Max. BHP:	265
@ RPM:	4600
Torque ft-lb:	397
@ RPM:	2400

TRANSMISSIONS
Firebird 400
Std: 3-speed Heavy-Duty Floor-Mounted Manual
Opt: 4-speed Floor-Mounted Manual, 3-speed Turbo Hydra-matic Console-Mounted Automatic

Firebird 400 Ram Air
Std: 4-speed Heavy-Duty Floor-Mounted Manual
Opt: 4-speed Floor-Mounted Manual, 3-speed Turbo Hydra-matic Console-Mounted Automatic

GTO
Std: 3-speed Floor-Mounted Manual
Opt: 4-speed Floor-Mounted Manual Close-Ratio with Hurst Shifter, 4-speed Floor-Mounted Manual Wide-

Ratio with Hurst Shifter, 3-Speed Turbo Hydra-matic Lever-Mounted Automatic

REAR AXLE RATIOS

Firebird 400 (330 hp)
Std: 3.36 (man), 3.08 (auto)
Opt: 3.23, 3.55, 2.56, 3.90, 4.33

Firebird 400 (335 hp)
Std: 3.36 (man), 3.08 (auto)
Opt: 2.56, 3.55, 3.90, 4.33

Firebird 400 Ram Air (335 hp)
Std: 3.90
Opt: 4.33

GTO (265 hp)
Std: 2.93
Opt: 2.56, 2.78, 3.23

GTO (350 hp)
Std: 3.55 (man), 3.36 (auto)
Opt: 2.93, 3.08, 3.23, 3.36, 3.55, 3.90, 4.33

GTO (360 hp)
Std: 3.55
Opt: 3.08, 3.23, 3.36, 3.90, 4.33

GTO Ram Air (360 hp)
Std: 4.33
Opt: NA

EXTERIOR DATA
Firebird

	Hardtop	Convertible
Length (in):	188.8	188.8
Width (in):	72.8	72.8
Height (in):	50	49.9
Wheelbase (in):	108.1	108.1
Weight (lb):	3061	3346

GTO

	Hardtop	Convertible
Length (in):	200.7	200.7
Width (in):	74.8	74.8
Height (in):	52.2	52.5
Wheelbase (in):	112	112
Weight (lb):	3123	3415

FACTORY BASE PRICE DATA

Model	Hardtop	Convertible
Firebird 400	$ 3054	$ 3269
Firebird Ram Air	3397	3612
GTO	3101	3327

POPULAR FACTORY OPTIONS

Interior: Electric clock, $16 (Firebird), $19 (GTO); Console, $51 (Firebird), $53 (GTO); Head rests, $42 (Firebird), $53 (GTO); Rally & hood tack instruments, $82; Clock with rally cluster, $51 (GTO); Clock with rally cluster & inside tachometer, $84 (GTO); Power windows, $100; Pushbutton radio, $61; AM/FM radio, $134; AM/FM stereo radio, $239; Stereo tape player, $134; Fold-down rear seat, $42; Rear speaker, $16; Custom front & rear seat belts, $13; Front shoulder straps, $26; Safeguard speedometer, $16 (Firebird); Deluxe steering wheel, $15; Custom sports steering wheel, $45 (Firebird), $31 (GTO); Tilt steering wheel, $42; Power bucket seat, $70.

Exterior: Exhaust tailpipe extensions, $21; Tinted glass, $31 (Firebird), $35 (GTO); Tinted windshield glass only, $21 (Firebird), $25 (GTO); Remote control outside mirror, $7 (Firebird), $9 (GTO); Rally stripes, $15 (Firebird), $11 (GTO); Hood-mounted tachometer, $63; Vinyl roof, $84; Deluxe wheel discs, $21; Custom wheel discs, $41; Wire wheel discs, $74; Rally I wheels, $61; Rally II wheels, $84; Cordova Top, $95 (GTO); Power antenna.

Miscellaneous: Air conditioning, $360; Front disc brakes, $63; Cruise control, $53; Trunk lid release, $14; Saf-T-Track differential, $42; Heavy-duty differential, $63 (GTO); Dual exhaust, $31; Handling package, $9 (Firebird), $4 (GTO); Power brakes, $42; Power disc brakes, $62; Power steering, $95; Power top, $53; Rear window defogger, $21; Three-speed manual transmission, $42; Four-speed manual transmission, $184; Three-speed Turbo Hydra-matic transmission, $237; Superlift shock absorbers, $53 (GTO).

An all-new frame was designed for the 1968 GTO.

The Ram Air engine was standard on the new 1969 Trans Am. The cold air induction system was improved with the addition of another cold air source from two openings in the front grille, which took in more fresh air at high speeds than the hood scoops alone.

1969 Pontiac

Pontiac production was down in 1969 to 870,528 units manufactured; market penetration, which had reached almost 10% only two years ago, declined ominously. GTO sales, which had been phenomenal over the last few years, were down 17% and would never significantly recover. In fact, over 85% of all GTO's were sold during the first five years of production. There were a number of factors that led to the decline of the GTO. Increasing competition from worthy opponents and even from the Firebird cut into GTO sales. The muscle car market itself was shrinking. Many buyers of super cars were unable to obtain insurance. Those that did often paid exorbitant premiums. In an attempt to drum up more enthusiasm, Pontiac offered two mid-year introductions: *The Judge,* an option on the GTO and the *Trans Am,* an option on the Firebird. These options would have vastly different outcomes. The Judge would be a short-lived package for the GTO, but the Trans Am would become one of Pontiac's most enduring ponycars.

FIREBIRD *400*

In 1969, the Firebird underwent its first major styling revision, just like its twin, the Camaro. It still used the same body, but the front end was revamped. The grille was now in two parts and the headlights were outside the grille assembly. Firebird's rear chevrons were eliminated and new extractor vents appeared in the trailing edges of the front-fender cutouts. Internally, the instrument panel received a new setting. This new styling was not particularly popular; most people felt that the new Firebird just didn't look as good as the old one. Sales were far below the year before. Despite the fact that the 1969 model year ran for seventeen months, well into the 1970 calender year, production was down 19% from the normal 1968 model year. The Firebird 400's standard engine remained virtually unchanged. But the Ram Air option, now officially called Ram Air IV, had an increased output of 5 hp. The HO engine, which was given Ram Air, was called by engineers Ram Air III, but it was still referred to by Pontiac as HO and by others as just Ram Air. Its horsepower output was also slightly up. The Firebird 400 package consisted of chrome

Simulated air exhausts behind the front wheel openings gave the side of the 1969 Firebird a more sporty look.

In designing the new 1969 Firebird, Pontiac designers had to adapt to the general lines laid down by the Camaro stylists.

engine parts, dual exhausts, a heavy-duty battery, red stripe or whitewall tires and a variable pitch cooling fan. The Ram Air II package included all these goodies as well as an additional de-clutching fan and twin functional hood scoops. The Ram Air IV option included all the above plus special decals for the hood scoops.

FIREBIRD TRANS AM

It was difficult to foresee that the mid-year introduction of the Trans Am would make such an impact on Pontiac sales in the next few years. Less than 700 Trans Ams were built in 1969, only eight of these were convertibles (hence, these eight are some of the most valuable cars of the era). There was no special fanfare to introduce it; there wasn't even any customer sales literature available in the first year. It was introduced as basically a companion car to the GTO Judge and not much more than a cosmetic option. The Ram Air III was the standard engine for the Trans Am, but the Ram Air IV was available. A three-speed with a heavy-duty shifter was its standard transmission and heavy-duty springs, shocks and a one-inch stabilizer bar were included in the package. Other performance items included power front disc brakes, variable ratio power steering and engine air exhaust louvers.

GTO

The 1969 GTO's were very close in styling to the revamped 1968's. Grilles were now of a honeycomb texture and the taillights were no longer in the rear bumpers but now sat on top of them. Finally, the vent windows were removed and a new "upper level ventilation system" was installed to bring air in from the outside. New safety features were also introduced on the 1969 GTO. Padded headrests and padding on the dash helped to cushion passengers during a

crash. The biggest change for the GTO was under the hood. The HO option, which had an output of 360 hp, was dropped and replaced with a 366 hp Ram Air version. The old Ram Air engine was supplanted by the new Ram Air IV. With an officially rated output of 370 hp, it was the most powerful engine ever put in a GTO. The Ram Air IV made use of four cold-air intakes. Two of these were the functional air scoops on the hood which could be opened or closed by the driver through a cable-operated valve. The other two were ducts to the carburetor located behind the grille. The Ram Air version of the GTO could be identified by Ram Air stickers placed on the hood scoops.

GTO JUDGE

Rumors abounded that Pontiac would introduce a new version of the GTO. Some thought it would be a "new thin-pillar coupe" and it would be a budget GTO, an economy supercar that would compete with the new Plymouth Road Runner. It was rumored that Pontiac would have a contest to name this new GTO and prizes and television fanfare would accompany its introduction. The rumor mongers were right about Pontiac introducing a new version of the GTO, but everything else was wrong. The Judge was a mid-year release. It cost about $400 dollars more than the standard GTO and featured the Ram Air engine, dual exhausts, a floor-mounted Hurst T-handled shifter, Morrokide bucket seats, low-restriction mufflers, a blacked-out grille, black wall tires, Rally II wheels and a distinctive rear deck spoiler. The Ram Air IV engine was optional, as well as various rear axle ratios, a Rally gauge package and a hood-mounted tachometer. The Judge's name came from a popular line uttered in the very successful television program, Rowan and Martin's *Laugh In.* "Heah come da Judge." The Judge was a very noticeable car. Though it was available in many colors, the vast majority of them were

The Trans Am chief designer added blue stripes to the hood reluctantly. He felt that the car should be purely functional.

A one-inch stabilizer bar helped the Trans Am's cornering. Stiffer valving gave the power steering more road feel.

painted Carousel Red (later called Orbit Orange by Pontiac). This very bright, more-orange-than-red car was made even more striking by a three-color slash stripe that ran from the upper edge of the front fender to the door. Finally "The Judge" stickers, which matched the slash stripe in color, were liberally placed on the car. A 60-inch floating deck airfoil (or spoiler) enabled the color-blind to identify the GTO. The Judge's performance was as striking as its colors. *Mechanix Illustrated* measured the standard Judge's 0 to 60 time at a speedy 5.9 seconds and *High-Performance Pontiac* measured the optional Judge's time at an impressive 5.1 seconds. Steve Kelly of *Hot Rod* wrote that the Judge is "...bound to discourage the performance-minded competition for many months to come."

VIN NUMBERS

Vehicle Identification Number: 2( )9( )( )00001 and up
Explanation:
First digit: GM line number: 2 = Pontiac
Second to fifth digit: Body number:
  Firebird Hardtop = 2337
  Firebird Convertible = 2367
  GTO Hardtop = 4237
  GTO Convertible = 4267
Sixth digit: Last digit of model year = 9
Eight digit: Number of cylinders 8 = 1
Seventh digit: Letter indicating assembly plant
Last five digits: Sequential production number

PRODUCTION TOTALS

Model	Total Units	Percent
GTO	72,287	
The Judge opt.	6,833	9.5
Firebird	107,112	
Firebird 400 opt.	NA	
Trans Am opt.	697	1

DRIVETRAIN DATA

	Firebird 400 (Std.)	Firebird 400 (Opt.) Trans AM (Std.) Ram Air	Firebird 400 Trans Am Ram Air IV (Opt.)
Cyl:	V-8	V-8	V-8
Bore (in):	4.12	4.12	4.12
Stroke (in):	3.75	3.75	3.75
CID:	400	400	400
Carbs.:	1 4-bbl	1 4-bbl	1 4-bbl
Make:	Rochester	Rochester	Rochester
Model:	4MV	4MV	4MV
Comp.:	10.75	10.75	10.75
Max. BHP:	330	335	345
@ RPM:	4800	5000	5400
Torque ft-lb:	430	430	430
@ RPM:	3300	3400	3700

	GTO (Std.)	GTO (Opt.) Judge (Std.) Ram Air	GTO Judge (Opt.) Ram Air IV (Opt.)
Cyl:	V-8	V-8	V-8
Bore (in):	4.12	4.12	4.12
Stroke (in):	3.75	3.75	3.75
CID:	400	400	400
Carbs.:	1 4 bbl	1 4-bbl	1 4-bbl

(con't. next page)

Vent windows were removed in the 1969 GTO. A new "upper level ventilation system" replaced the lost ventilation.

The GTO Judge with the super-powerful Ram Air IV engine was easily identifiable by the decal on its hood scoops.

DRIVETRAIN DATA *(con't.)*

Make:	Rochester	Rochester	Rochester
Model:	4MV	4MV	4M
Comp.:	10.75	10.75	10.75
Max. BHP:	350	366	370
@ RPM:	5000	5100	5500
Torque ft-lb:	445	445	445
@ RPM:	3000	3600	3900

	GTO
	(Opt.)
Cyl:	V-8
Bore (in):	4.12
Stroke (in):	3.75
CID:	400
Carbs.:	1 2 bbl
Make:	Rochester
Model:	2GC
Comp.:	8.6
Max. BHP:	265
@ RPM:	4600
Torque ft-lb:	397
@ RPM:	2400

TRANSMISSIONS

Firebird 400, Trans Am
Std: 3-speed Heavy-Duty Floor-Mounted Manual
Opt: 4-speed Floor-Mounted Manual, 3-speed Turbo Hydra-matic Console-Mounted Automatic

Firebird 400 Ram Air IV
Std: 4-speed Heavy-Duty Floor-Mounted Manual
Opt: 4-speed Floor-Mounted Manual, 3-speed Turbo Hydra-matic Console-Mounted Automatic

GTO
Std: 3-speed Floor-Mounted Manual
Opt: 4-speed Floor-Mounted Manual Close-Ratio with Hurst Shifter, 4-speed Floor-Mounted Manual Wide-Ratio with Hurst Shifter, 3-Speed Turbo Hydra-matic Lever-Mounted Automatic

Judge
Std: 3-speed Floor-Mounted Manual
Opt: 4-speed Floor-Mounted Manual Close-Ratio with Hurst Shifter, 3-Speed Turbo Hydra-matic Column or Console-Mounted Automatic

REAR AXLE RATIOS
Firebird 400 (330 hp)
Std: 3.36 (man), 3.08 (auto)
Opt: 3.23 (auto), 3.55, 3.90, 4.33

Firebird 400, Trans Am (335 hp)
Std: 3.36 (man), 3.08 (auto)
Opt: 3.55, 3.90, 4.33

Firebird 400, Trans Am Ram Air IV (345 hp)
Std: 3.90
Opt: NA

GTO (265 hp)
Std: 2.93
Opt: 2.56, 2.78, 3.23

GTO (350 hp)
Std: 3.55 (man), 3.36 (auto)
Opt: 3.08, 3.23, 3.36, 3.55, 3.90, 4.33

(con't. next page)

The Judge featured a 60-inch fiberglass spoiler supported by a pair of stands. At low speeds the effect of the spoiler was negligible, but at high speeds a one-hundred-pound downward pressure was created on the rear end, assuring better traction and stability.

REAR AXLE RATIOS *(con't.)*
GTO, Judge Ram Air (366 hp)
Std: 3.55
Opt: 3.08, 3.23, 3.36, 3.90, 4.33

GTO, Judge Ram Air IV (370 hp)
Std: 3.90
Opt: 4.33

EXTERIOR DATA
Firebird
	Hardtop	Convertible
Length (in):	189.1	189.1
Width (in):	73.9	73.9
Height (in):	49.6	49.6
Wheelbase (in):	108.1	108.1
Weight (lb):	3080	3498

GTO
	Hardtop	Convertible
Length (in):	201.2	201.2
Width (in):	75.8	74.8
Height (in):	52.3	52.3
Wheelbase (in):	112	112
Weight (lb):	3503	3553

FACTORY BASE PRICE DATA
Model	Hardtop	Convertible
Firebird 400	$ 3106	$ 3320
Firebird Ram Air	3182	3396
Firebird Ram Air IV	3663	3877
Trans Am	3556	3770

GTO	3156	3382
Judge	3488	3714

POPULAR FACTORY OPTIONS
Interior: Electric clock, $16; Console, $54 (Firebird), $72 (GTO); Head rests, $17; Rally & clock instruments, $47; Rally & tach instruments, $84; Remote control mirror, $11; Left bucket power seat, $74; Reclining right bucket seat, $42 (GTO); Power windows, $105; Push-button radio, $61; AM/FM radio, $134; AM/FM stereo radio, $239; Stereo tape, $134; Rear speaker, $16; Verba-Phonic rear radio speaker, $53; Custom front & rear seat belts, $13; Safeguard speedometer, $16 (GTO); Sports steering wheel, $51 (Firebird), $35 (GTO); Tilt steering wheel, $45; Hood-mounted tachometer, $63.

Exterior: Tinted glass, $33; Tinted windshield glass only, $22; Hidden head lights, $53 (GTO); Ram Air hood inlet, $84 (Firebird); Tailpipe extensions, $21 (GTO); Vinyl roof, $90 (Firebird); Cordova top, $100 (GTO); Deluxe wheel discs, $21; Custom wheel discs, $41; Wire wheel discs, $74; Rally II wheels, $84.

Miscellaneous: Air conditioning, $376; Cruise control, $58; Saf-T-Track Differential, $63; Ram Air III engine, $351; Ram Air IV engine, $558; Handling package, $4 (GTO); Power brakes, $42; Disc power brakes, $64; Power steering, $105; Power top, $53 (convertible only); Rear window defogger, $22; Superlift shock absorbers, $42 (GTO); Three-speed automatic transmission, $227; Four-speed manual transmission, $195; Remote control trunk lid release, $15.

The new Firebird, introduced in mid-1970, was dramatically restyled inside and out. Handling and cornering had been improved by shortening the width of the Firebird and widening the front and rear tread as well as completely revising the suspension.

1970 Pontiac

For the first time since 1960, Pontiac lost its third place standing in the auto sales competition. Sales were down by over 20%, while industry sales were down by only 11%. Market penetration was at its lowest point since 1961. The late introduction of the 1970 Firebird only served to exacerbate waning sales. The new, redesigned Firebird finally made its appearance at the end of February, coinciding almost perfectly with the collapse of the ponycar market. In the meanwhile Pontiac tried to sell the 1969 Firebirds by not mentioning that they were 1969's. In March of 1969 all Firebird literature was revised to delete references to the year "1969," in the hopes that customers would think that the 1969 models were something like early 1970 models or not-quite 1970 models. One can imagine that Pontiac dealers became very adept at avoiding the issue of model years. On the GTO front, production almost half of 1968's. In an effort to spike sales, Pontiac advertising gave the GTO a new nickname, "The Humbler."

FIREBIRD FORMULA 400

The all new Firebird was finally introduced in February of 1970. Though 1970 was not a good year in terms of sales for Firebirds, it was a watershed year in terms of engineering and styling. Many thought the new body of the Firebird was gorgeous. It seemed to be a piece of rolling sculpture. The front bumper/grille was molded out of Endura rubber and painted the same color as the car. The sides sported full wheel cut-outs and were unencumbered by superfluous trim. The suspension was completely revised for the Firebird. Springs rates were softened for a less bumpy ride without sacrificing cornering ability. The front stabilizer bar was thickened, and for the first time a rear stabilizer bar was added. The convertible was no longer available. The model designations were also changed for 1970. Instead of six Firebirds, there were now only four. The base Firebird came as either a six or V-8. The Firebird Esprit came with either the 350 cid V-8 or the 265 hp, two-barrel version of the Pontiac 400 cid V-8. The Firebird Formula 400 came with either the 330 cid V-8 or the 345 hp Ram Air version of the 400 V-8. Finally the Trans Am was equipped with the 345 hp Ram Air V-8 and special exterior trim. The Ram Air

The Formula 400 was easily recognized by its specially-molded fiberglass hood with air scoops.

For the first time, the big-engined Firebirds, like this Firebird 400, were equipped with a rear stabilizer bar.

IV engine was available for both the Trans Am and The Formula 400, but since it was intended primarily for drag racing, only 88 Firebirds were equipped with this engine. The Formula 400 also included an air cleaner with twin snorkels, front and rear stabilizer bars, special high-rate springs and a special wind-up control for the rear axle. The Formula's external styling was clean and plain; this was a designed to be a pure driving machine. The instrument panel was designed with functionality in mind. *Car and Driver* tested the standard Formula 400's 0 to 60 time at 6.4 seconds and its standing quarter-mile speed and time at 98.9 mph in 14.7 seconds

Firebird Trans Am

The 1970 Trans Am was the highest performance Firebird of the year. With functional air scoops and a standard engine rated at 345 hp, it was a car to be reckoned with. *Car and Driver* clocked its 0 to 60 time at 5.7 seconds and its standing quarter-mile at 103.2 miles in 14.1 seconds. In addition to the new body all Firebirds received, the Trans Am was fitted with air dams across the bottom of the front and in front of the wheels, a shaker hood, air extractors on the front fenders and an airfoil on the rear deck. All these features were designed to make the Trans Am aerodynamically sound. The front air dam and side air extractors created 50 pounds of downward pressure on the front end at expressway speeds. The spoilers at the wheels kept air pressure from building up in the wheel wells. The rear spoiler was supposed to create a downward pressure of 50 pounds at expressway speeds, to maintain stability. The shaker hood had a rear-facing air scoop at the base of the windshield where airflow over the hood created a maximum amount of pressure to feed the Ram Air engine. In contrast to the Firebird 400 the Trans Am had distinctive ornamentation. Full-length racing stripes contrasted with the Trans Am's blue or white color. The aerodynamically styled outside mirrors further distinguished the Trans Am. A four-speed manual transmission with a Hurst shifter was standard on the Trans Am as well as heavy-duty springs and shock absorbers.

GTO

All intermediate sized Pontiacs received a new face lift in 1970. The sheet metal was new, though the body chassis was not. The two-part grille was split by a protruding fin that melted into the hood center and then passed through the hood scoops, giving the front-end a sort of snub-nose look. The concealed headlights were gone, mainly due to mechanical problems. The front end of the GTO now had a more massive appearance than it had in previous years. The economy engine was dropped from the option list this year, but a new 455 cid, 360 hp engine was available. All the other engines, including the Ram Air (which made use of the hood scoops) were available, but with a reduced compression ratio. GTO sales were even worse than they had been in the previous year. Production fell by almost 45%. Clearly the muscle car market was shrinking. The GTO had grown larger and heavier. The interior had been redesigned so that it was more spacious and luxurious. More convenience and appearance options were available in an attempt to broaden the GTO's appeal to a larger market than pure performance-car enthusiasts.

GTO Judge

The Judge also received a facelift in 1970. In addition to the changes that were made on all GTO's, the Judge received a blacked-out grille and a slightly modified rear deck air foil. The overall effect of these changes was to make the Judge a bit more conspicuous. The standard engine was

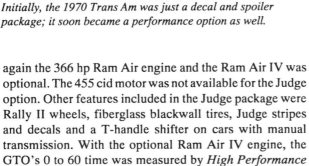

Initially, the 1970 Trans Am was just a decal and spoiler package; it soon became a performance option as well.

The Trans Am came with Rally II wheels. Its performance tires and wheels made for an exceptionally good handling car.

again the 366 hp Ram Air engine and the Ram Air IV was optional. The 455 cid motor was not available for the Judge option. Other features included in the Judge package were Rally II wheels, fiberglass blackwall tires, Judge stripes and decals and a T-handle shifter on cars with manual transmission. With the optional Ram Air IV engine, the GTO's 0 to 60 time was measured by *High Performance Pontiac* at an impressive 5.1 seconds. In a quarter-mile standing run it was clocked at 107 mph in 13.99 seconds.

VIN NUMBERS

Vehicle Identification Number: 2( )0( )( )00001 and up
Explanation:
First digit: GM line number: 2 = Pontiac
Second to fifth digit: Body number:
   Firebird Formula 400 Hardtop = 2687
   Trans AM Hardtop = 2887
   GTO Hardtop = 4237
   GTO Convertible = 4267
Sixth digit: Last digit of model year = 0
Seventh digit: Letter indicating assembly plant
Eight digit: Number of cylinders 8 = 1
Last five digits: Sequential production number

PRODUCTION TOTALS

Model	Total Units	Percent
GTO	40,149	
The Judge opt.	3,797	9.46
Firebird	48,739	
Formula 400 opt.	7,708	15.8
Trans Am opt.	3,196	6.6

DRIVETRAIN DATA

	Firebird Formula 400 (Std.)	Firebird Formula 400 (Opt.) Trans AM (Std.) Ram Air	Firebird Formula 400 (Opt.) Trans AM (Opt.) Ram Air IV
Cyl:	V-8	V-8	V-8
Bore (in):	4.12	4.12	4.12
Stroke (in):	3.75	3.75	3.75
CID:	400	400	400
Carbs.:	1 4-bbl	1 4-bbl	1 4-bbl
Make:	Rochester	Rochester	Rochester
Model:	4MV	4MV	4MV
Comp.:	10.25	10.5	10.75
Max. BHP:	330	345	345
@ RPM:	4800	5000	5400
Torque ft-lb:	430	430	430
@ RPM:	3000	3400	3700

	GTO (Std.)	GTO (Opt.) Judge (Std.) Ram Air	GTO (Opt.) Judge (Opt.) Ram Air IV
Cyl:	V-8	V-8	V-8
Bore (in):	4.12	4.12	4.12
Stroke (in):	3.75	3.75	4.21
CID:	400	400	400
Carbs.:	1 4 bbl	1 4 bbl	1 4-bbl
Make:	Rochester	Rochester	Rochester
Model:	4MV	4MV	4MV
Comp.:	10.25	10.5	10.5
Max. BHP:	350	366	370
@ RPM:	5000	5100	5500

(con't. next page)

To cut costs the GTO medallions were replaced by decals in 1970. This actually contributed to the smooth look of the GTO.

The GTO's grille was split by a protruding fin which tapered into the hood center and passed between the hood scoops.

DRIVETRAIN DATA *(con't.)*

Torque ft-lb:	445	445	445
@ RPM:	3000	3600	3900

	GTO
	(Opt.)
Cyl:	V-8
Bore (in):	4.15
Stroke (in):	4.21
CID:	455.4
Carbs.:	1 4-bbl
Make:	Rochester
Model:	4MV
Comp.:	10.25
Max. BHP:	360
@ RPM:	4300
Torque ft-lb:	500
@ RPM:	2700

TRANSMISSIONS

Firebird Formula 400 (std.)
Std: 3-speed Heavy-Duty Floor-Mounted Manual with Hurst Shifter
Opt: 4-speed Floor-Mounted Manual with Hurst Shifter, 3-speed Turbo Hydra-matic Console-Mounted Automatic

Firebird Formula 400 (Ram Air opt.), **Trans Am**
Std: 4-speed Heavy-Duty Floor-Mounted Manual with Hurst Shifter
Opt: 3-speed Turbo Hydra-matic Console-Mounted Automatic

GTO, Judge (350 hp, 366 hp)
Std: 3-speed Floor-Mounted Manual
Opt: 4-speed Floor-Mounted Manual Close-Ratio with Hurst Shifter, 4-speed Floor-Mounted Manual Wide-Ratio with Hurst Shifter, 3-Speed Turbo Hydra-matic Lever-Mounted Automatic

GTO, Judge (360 hp)
Std: 3-speed Floor-Mounted Manual
Opt: 4-speed Floor-Mounted Manual Close- Ratio with Hurst Shifter, 3-Speed Turbo Hydra-matic Column or Console-Mounted Automatic

GTO, Judge (370 hp)
Std: 4-speed Floor-Mounted Manual Close-Ratio with Hurst Shifter
Opt: 3-Speed Turbo Hydra-matic Lever-Mounted Automatic

REAR AXLE RATIOS

Firebird Formula 400 (330 hp)
Std: 3.55 (man), 3.07 (auto)
Opt: 3.31 (auto), 3.73

Firebird Formula 400 (345 hp)
Std: 3.55
Opt: 3.73

Firebird Formula 400, Trans Am Ram Air (350 hp)
Std: 3.55
Opt: NA

GTO (350 hp)
Std: 3.55, 3.23 (with air conditioning)
Opt: 3.23, 3.08, 3.90 (4-sp close-ratio), 4.33 (same)

If a free-floating spoiler and bright paint weren't enough decoration for your Judge, body striping was optional.

Height (in):	52	52
Wheelbase (in):	112	112
Weight (lb):	3641	3691

FACTORY BASE PRICE DATA

Model	Hardtop	Convertible
Firebird Formula 400	$ 3370	$ —
Firebird Ram Air	3539	—
Trans Am	4305	—
GTO	3267	3492
The Judge	3604	3829

POPULAR FACTORY OPTIONS

Interior: Electric clock, $16; Console, $59 (Firebird), $72 (GTO); Power bucket seat, $73 (GTO); Power door locks, $68 (GTO); Reclining bucket seat; Custom sports steering wheel, $35 (GTO); Rally & clock instruments, $47 (Firebird), $51 (GTO); Rally & hood tach instruments, $95; Power windows, $105; Pushbutton radio, $61; AM/FM radio, $134; AM/FM stereo radio, $239; Rear speaker, $16; Custom front & rear seat belts, $39; Deluxe steering wheel, $16 (Firebird); Formula steering wheel, $42 (Firebird); Tilt steering wheel, $45; Stereo tape player, $134.

Exterior: Cordova top, $90 (Firebird), $100 (GTO); Tinted glass, $33; Tinted windshield glass only, $26; Two mirrors, left remote control, $36 (Firebird); Hood-mounted tachometer, $63; Wire wheel covers, $74; Rally II wheels, $84; Wheel discs, $21 (GTO); Custom wheel discs, $41 (GTO).

Miscellaneous: Air conditioning, $376; Cruise Control, $58 (GTO); Deck lid release, $15; Rear window defroster, $53 (GTO); Saf-T-Track differential, $42 (Firebird), $64 (GTO); Driver controlled exhaust (tiger button), $63 (GTO); Handling package, $4 (GTO); Head light delay, $13 (GTO); Heavy-duty suspension (GTO); Superlift shock absorbers (GTO); Power brakes, $42 (Firebird); Front disc power brakes, $65 (GTO); Power steering, $105; Rear window defogger, $26; Three-speed automatic transmission, $227; Four-speed manual transmission, $195.

REAR AXLE RATIOS *(con't.)*

GTO (360 hp)
Std: 3.31 (man), 3.07 (auto)
Opt: 3.31 (auto), 3.55 (man)

GTO, Judge (366 hp)
Std: 3.55, 3.23 (with air conditioning)
Opt: 3.90 (4-sp close ratio), 4.33 (4-sp close ratio)

GTO, Judge (370 hp)
Std: 3.90
Opt: 4.33 (man)

EXTERIOR DATA

Firebird

	Formula Hardtop	Trans Am Hardtop
Length (in):	191.6	191.6
Width (in):	73.4	73.4
Height (in):	50.4	50.4
Wheelbase (in):	108	108
Weight (lb):	3470	3550

GTO

	Hardtop	Convertible
Length (in):	202.9	202.9
Width (in):	76.7	76.7

The Firebird Formula 400's standard engine produced 300 hp. In order to enable GM cars to run on low- or no-lead fuel, compression ratios for all GM engines were lowered to 8.5 or below.

1971 Pontiac

Pontiac sales continued their downward slide in 1971. Production fell to 261,088 for the model year, the lowest since 1961. Aside from a continuing slump in the market, a long GM strike also contributed to the decline in production. But since industry-wide sales were down even more, Pontiac was able to regain its traditional third place in the automobile sales race. GTO sales were miserable in 1971; production fell by 74% from the previous dismal year. The Judge's sales were even worse. Only 374 Judges were sold, 17 of which were convertibles. Consequently, this was to be the last year of the Judge and of the GTO as a separate model. Federal emission standards caused the horsepower output of all engines to be lowered. The compression ratio had to be lowered so that the engine could run on low- or no-lead fuel. Thus, overall performance suffered. Federal pollution and safety regulations forced car companies to adopt new marketing strategies. Automobile literature now tended to emphasize safety rather than performance.

FIREBIRD FORMULA 400/455

The Firebirds were barely revised for 1971; in fact they were almost indistinguishable from their predecessors. The most significant changes were seen in engine availability. For the Formula 400, a 400 cid 300 hp engine was standard. Both Ram Air engines were dropped from the lineup. Instead two 455 cid engines were available, rating 325 hp or 335 hp. The higher output one was standard on the Trans Am. The Formulas with 455 cid engines were referred to as Formula 455 instead of Formula 400 because of the higher displacement. The highest output 455 cid could be ordered with functional air scoops and Ram Air; but this did not officially increase horsepower output. Compression ratios were lower on all engines because General Motors had decreed that no 1971 engine should have a compression ratio higher than 8.5:1.

FIREBIRD TRANS AM

Trans Am sales dropped by about a third in 1971 due to a slump in the ponycar market. Nevertheless, Trans Am was building a solid reputation and it would only be a few years before sales took off once again. The '71 Trans Am was equipped with striking new honeycomb wheels, front and rear stabilizer bars, a Formula steering wheel, functional front fender air extractors, a black textured grille insert and Trans Am identification decals. The 455 cid HO Ram Air engine, rated at 335 hp, was the one and only engine available for the Trans Am.

GTO

Only a third as many GTO's were produced in 1971 as had been produced in the first year of the GTO, when most people had never heard of the car. Styling changes were made to the front end of the GTO. The Endura bumper was no longer cleanly integrated into the front end, but now protruded out from it. The grille featured a chain-like mesh, much like the 1967 GTO's, but this time it took up more surface area. Though styling changes helped give the GTO a more aggressive look, government emissions regulations took the verve out of the engine. The compression ratio for the standard engine and the 455 cid optional engine was down to 8.2:1. For the high output Ram Air engine, which was optional with the GTO and standard with the Judge, the compression ratio was 8.4:1. Pontiac attempted to compensate for the lost performance by keeping what Pontiac called "tractive force" up to par. "Tractive force" was defined by Pontiac as "...the net result of all its drivetrain components....The force exerted by the turning of the drive wheels." Axle ratios were lowered to prevent the engines from being noticeably lower in power and the carburetor was modified for improved starting and acceleration. Nevertheless, performance did suffer somewhat. Maximum speed for the GTO equipped with the standard engine, the optional engine, and the optional high output engine, as measured by the *World Car Catalog*, was 108, 109 and 111 mph, respectively.

GTO JUDGE

This was to be the third and final year for the flamboyant Judge. Like the GTO, it was essentially unchanged from the previous year. It included the high output 455 cid engine with functional air-intake hood scoops, a heavy-duty three-speed transmission with a floor-mounted Hurst T-handled shifter, a black textured grille and a rear deck spoiler, which could be ordered in black when the Judge was ordered in white. Judge stripes, decals and emblems in "some of the keenest colors this side of a light show" gave the Judge its distinctive gaudy identity. A special handling package included wide Rally II wheels, heavy-duty shocks and a sway-bar making it exceptionally good in handling. *Hot Rod* compared the Judge with the Trans Am and found its performance and handling to be similar.

VIN NUMBERS
Vehicle Identification Number: 2( )1( )( )00001 and up

Explanation:
First digit: GM line number: 2 = Pontiac
Second to fifth digit: Body number:
  Firebird Formula Hardtop = 2687
  Trans AM Hardtop = 2887
  GTO Hardtop = 4237
  GTO Convertible = 4267
Sixth digit: Last digit of model year = 1
Seventh digit: Letter indicating assembly plant
Eight digit: Number of cylinders 8 = 1
Last five digits: Sequential production number

PRODUCTION TOTALS

Model	Total Units	Percent
GTO	10,532	
The Judge opt.	374	3.6
Firebird	53,125	
Formula opt.	7,802	14.7
Trans Am opt.	2,116	4

DRIVETRAIN DATA

	Firebird Formula 400 (Std.) GTO (Std.)	Firebird Formula 455 (Opt.) GTO (Opt.)	Firebird Formula 455 (Opt.) Trans Am GTO (Opt.) Judge (Std.) HO
Cyl:	V-8	V-8	V-8
Bore (in):	4.12	4.15	4.15
Stroke (in):	3.75	4.21	4.21
CID:	400	455	455
Carbs.:	1 4-bbl	1 4-bbl	1 4-bbl
Make:	Rochester	Rochester	Rochester
Model:	4MV	4MV	4MV
Comp.:	8.2	8.2	8.4
Max. BHP:	300	325	335
@ RPM:	4800	4400	4800
Torque ft-lb:	400	455	480
@ RPM:	3600	3200	3600

TRANSMISSIONS
Firebird Formula 400
Std: 3-speed Heavy-Duty Floor-Mounted Manual with Hurst Shifter
Opt: 4-speed Floor-Mounted Manual with Hurst Shifter, 3-speed Turbo Hydra-matic Console-Mounted Automatic

(con't. next page)

The only engine available on the 1971 Trans Am was the new 455 H-O V-8, which developed 335 hp at 4800 rpm (gross ratings). It used the Ram Air IV's aluminum intake manifold and its heads; its camshaft came from the 1969 Ram Air engine.

TRANSMISSIONS *(cont.)*
Firebird Formula 455 (325 hp)
Std: 3-speed Turbo Hydra-matic Console-Mounted Automatic
Opt: NA

Firebird Formula 455 (335 hp), **Trans Am**
Std: 3-speed Heavy-Duty Floor-Mounted Manual with Hurst Shifter
Opt: 4-speed Heavy-Duty Floor-Mounted Manual with Hurst Shifter, 3-speed Turbo Hydra-matic Console-Mounted Automatic

GTO, Judge
Std: 3-speed Floor-Mounted Manual
Opt: 4-speed Floor-Mounted Manual Close-Ratio with Hurst Shifter, 4-speed Floor-Mounted Manual Wide-Ratio with Hurst Shifter, 3-Speed Turbo Hydra-matic Lever-Mounted Automatic

REAR AXLE RATIOS
Firebird Formula 400 (300 hp)
Std: 3.42 (man), 3.08 (auto)
Opt: 3.73

Firebird Formula 455 (325 hp)
Std: 3.42
Opt: 3.08

Firebird Formula 455 (335 hp), **Trans Am**
Std: 3.42
Opt: 3.08, 3.42

GTO (400 cid 300 hp)
Std: 3.55 (3-sp man, 4-sp wide-ratio, auto), 3.23 (with air conditioning), 3.90 (4-sp close-ratio)
Opt: 3.08 (auto), 3.23 (3-sp man, 4-sp wide-ratio), 3.55, 3.90 (3-sp man, 4-sp wide-ratio), 4.33 (man)

GTO (455 cid 325 hp)
Std: 3.31, 3.07 (with air conditioning)
Opt: NA

GTO, Judge (455 cid 335 hp)
Std: 3.55 (3-sp man, 4-sp wide-ratio, auto), 3.07 (auto with air conditioning), 3.90 (4-sp close-ratio)
Opt: NA

EXTERIOR DATA

Firebird	Formula Hardtop	Trans Am Hardtop
Length (in):	191.6	191.6
Width (in):	73.4	73.4
Height (in):	50.4	50.4
Wheelbase (in):	108	108
Weight (lb):	3473	3578

GTO	Hardtop	Convertible
Length (in):	203.3	203.3
Width (in):	76.7	76.7
Height (in):	52	52
Wheelbase (in):	112	112
Weight (lb):	3619	3664

FACTORY BASE PRICE DATA

Model	Hardtop	Convertible
Firebird Formula 400	$ 3446	$ —
Trans Am	4595	—
GTO	3446	3676
The Judge	3841	4071

POPULAR FACTORY OPTIONS

Interior: Electric clock, $16; Clock with rally gauges, $51 (GTO); Console, $61; Rear console, $26 (Firebird); Rally & clock instruments, $47 (Firebird); Rally & hood tach, $95 (Firebird); Power bucket seat, $79 (GTO); Power door locks, $45; Power windows, $115; Pushbutton radio, $66; AM/FM radio, $139; AM/FM stereo radio, $239; Rear speaker, $19; Custom front & rear seat belts, $16; Custom steering wheel, $16 (GTO); Formula steering wheel, $42; Tilt steering wheel, $45; Stereo eight-track tape, $134; Stereo cassette tape, $134.

Exterior: Bumper guards, $16 (Firebird); Outside remote control mirror, $13 (GTO); Outside body color mirror, $27 (GTO); Two left remote control mirrors, $26 (Firebird); Tinted glass, $41; Tinted windshield glass only, $38; Hood air inlet, $84 (Firebird); Rear air spoiler, $33 (Firebird); Hood mounted tachometer, $64 (GTO); Custom wheel discs, $32 (Firebird); Wire wheel discs, $84; Honeycomb wheels, $37 (Firebird), $63 (GTO); Rally II wheels, $90 (Firebird).

Miscellaneous: Air conditioning, $402; Cruise control, $64 (GTO); Saf-T-Track differential, $44; Saf-T-Track HD differential, $67 (Firebird); 325 hp engine, $158 (Firebird); 335 hp engine, $237 (Firebird); 455 cid engine, $58 (GTO); 455 H-O engine, $358 (GTO), $137 (Judge); Heavy-duty suspension (GTO); Power brakes, $47; Power front disc brakes, $70 (GTO); Power steering, $111; Rear window defogger, $32; Rear window defroster, $63; Space-Saver spare tire, $16 (Firebird); Three-speed automatic transmission, $222 (Firebird), $243 (GTO); Four-speed manual transmission, $206 (Firebird), $196 (GTO); Remote control trunk lid release, $15.

Pontiac warned the "demure and meek" against the flamboyant Judge. They called it "an extrovert's car. Something for the movers.... Subtle it's not. It comes in some of the keenest colors this side of a light show. And with some equally keen features."

The GTO front end was optional on any LeMans or LeMans Sport, such as this LeMans Sport convertible. If you coupled this with a big V-8, a 3-speed manual transmission with Hurst shifter and dual exhausts you ended up with a pretty good substitute for the GTO.

1972 Pontiac

For the first time in four years, production was up at Pontiac, though the division failed to maintain their third place in the automobile sales competition. Nothing much was new at Pontiac, but they managed to produce 706,978 units. The Firebird and the GTO were little changed except for lowered engine output. In looking at the engine specifications, horsepower ratings were significantly lower than the previous year's. This was due in large part to the change of rating output from gross horsepower to net horsepower. The lower net horsepower ratings were thought to be more accurate of the actual power delivered to the rear wheels.

FIREBIRD FORMULA 400/455

Prices actually dropped for the Formula in 1972, but this did not spur sales as was hoped. Only 5,250 were produced that year, down by more than 2,000 units from the year before. General Motors considered dropping Firebirds altogether in 1972. Lackluster sales, safety considerations,

the waning appeal of muscle cars and skyrocketing insurance rates had already conspired to put an end to many a muscle car and there were those who predicted the demise of the Firebird. On top of all this, a 174 day strike by the United Auto Workers at the only plant that produced Firebirds prevented an estimated 39,000 Firebirds from being built. Fortunately, a few dedicated Pontiac executives managed to convince the GM front office not to pull the plug on the Firebird just yet. Therefore the Firebird was little changed; slight modifications were made to the grille. Engines were altered to meet federal emissions standards, but the same basic ones from 1971 were used.

FIREBIRD TRANS AM

Trans Am sales plummeted to their lowest depths, just 1,286 cars were produced. On the bright side, Trans Am sales had no place to go but up, which they soon would. The 1972 Trans Am was little changed from the previous year. It still used the 455 cid HO engine, but this year horsepower was at a low 250 hp net. A four-speed manual transmission was standard, but the Turbo Hydra-matic transmission could be ordered at no extra cost.

A bird decal had been available on the Trans Am since 1970. In earlier models this decal tended to wrinkle and crack.

The GTO reverted to option status in 1972. It was available on any LeMans or LeMans Sport with a big V-8.

LeMans Sports/GTO

Federal pollution regulations and safety standards, as well as changing attitudes about fast cars and high insurance rates, spelled the imminent demise of the muscle-bound GTO. Pontiac attempted to rescue the GTO by toning down its image as a supercar. First they got rid of the flamboyant Judge, then they relegated the GTO to the option list for the LeMans and the LeMans Sport. Finally, they even discontinued the convertible GTO. To add insult to injury, the unique Endura bumper that the GTO alone had sported for so long became an option on any LeMans or LeMans Sport equipped with a V-8 engine. After all this, it was not surprising that GTO production fell to a new record low of 5,807 cars . GTO styling was virtually unchanged from the year before. The grille mesh was slightly different and functional air extractors were installed in the front fender. A rear spoiler, which was like a lip on the rear deck, was listed as an option and shown in early ads, but, according to Pontiac, not one spoiler-equipped GTO was ever built. Engine options were limited to the same basic engines as the year before: the standard 400 cid 250 hp V-8 and the 455 cid, 250 hp or HO 300 hp engine.

VIN NUMBERS

Vehicle Identification Number: 2( )2( )( )00001 and up
Explanation:
First digit: GM line number: 2 = Pontiac
Second digit: Series number:
  Firebird Formula = U
  Firebird Trans Am = V
  LeMans = D
Third to fourth digit: Body number:
  Firebird Coupe = 87
  LeMans Coupe = 27

  LeMans Hardtop = 37
Fifth digit: Letter indicating engine:
  T = 400 cid, 250 hp
  Y = 455 cid, 250 hp
  X = 455 cid, 300 hp
Sixth digit: Last digit of model year = 2
Seventh digit: Letter indicating assembly plant
Eight digit: Number of cylinders 8 = 1
Last five digits: Sequential production number

PRODUCTION TOTALS

Model	Total Units	Percent
LeMans	120,299	
GTO opt.	5,807	4.8
Firebird	29,951	
Formula opt.	5,249	17.5
Trans Am opt.	1,286	4.3

DRIVETRAIN DATA

	Firebird Formula 400 (Std.) LeMans GTO (Std.)	Firebird Formula 455 (Std.) Trans Am (Std.) LeMans GTO (Opt.)	LeMans GTO (Opt.)
Cyl:	V-8	V-8	V-8
Bore (in):	4.12	4.15	4.15
Stroke (in):	3.75	4.21	4.21
CID:	400	455	455
Carbs.:	1 4-bbl	1 4-bbl	1 4-bbl
Make:	Rochester	Rochester	Rochester

(con't. next page)

DRIVETRAIN DATA *(con't.)*

Model:	4MV	4MV	4MV
Comp.:	8.2	8.4	8.2
Max. BHP:	250	300	250
@ RPM:	4400	4000	3700
Torque ft-lb:	325	415	325
@ RPM:	3200	3200	2400

TRANSMISSIONS

Firebird Formula 400
Std: 4-speed Heavy-Duty Floor-Mounted Manual with Hurst Shifter
Opt: 4-speed Floor-Mounted Close-Ratio Manual with Hurst Shifter, 3-speed Turbo Hydra-matic Console-Mounted Automatic

Firebird Formula 455, Trans Am
Std: 4-speed Heavy-Duty Floor-Mounted Manual with Hurst Shifter,
Opt: 3-speed Turbo Hydra-matic Console-Mounted Automatic

LeMans GTO
Std: 3-speed Floor-Mounted Manual
Opt: 4-speed Floor-Mounted Manual Close-Ratio with Hurst Shifter, 4-speed Floor-Mounted Manual Wide-Ratio with Hurst Shifter, 3-Speed Turbo Hydra-matic Lever-Mounted Automatic

REAR AXLE RATIOS

Firebird Formula 400
Std: 3.42 (man), 3.08 (auto)
Opt: 3.42

Firebird Formula 455, Trans Am
Std: 3.42 (man), 3.08 (auto)
Opt: NA

LeMans GTO (400 cid 250 hp)
Std: 3.55, 3.23 (with air conditioning)
Opt: 3.08 (auto), 3.23 (3-sp man)

LeMans GTO (455 cid 250 hp)
Std: 3.31, 3.07 (with air conditioning)
Opt: NA

LeMans GTO (455 cid 300 hp)
Std: 3.55. 3.31 (man with air conditioning), 3.07 (auto with air conditioning)
Opt: NA

EXTERIOR DATA

Firebird	Formula Hardtop	Trans Am Hardtop
Length (in):	191.6	191.6
Width (in):	73.4	73.4
Height (in):	50.4	50.4
Wheelbase (in):	108	108
Weight (lb):	3424	3564

LeMans	GTO Coupe	GTO Hardtop
Length (in):	203.3	203.3
Width (in):	76.7	76.7
Height (in):	52	52
Wheelbase (in):	112	112
Weight (lb):	3510	3450

Firebird sales were very poor in 1972; Trans Am sales fell to just over 1,200. Pontiac reduced prices for all Firebirds, including the Trans Am in an effort to increase sales, but a devastating strike at GM's Norwood, Ohio plant shattered that hope.

FACTORY BASE PRICE DATA

Model	Coupe	Hardtop
Firebird Formula 400	$ —	$ 3318
Firebird Formula 455	—	3452
Trans Am	—	4256
LeMans GTO	3108	3237

POPULAR FACTORY OPTIONS

Interior: Electric clock, $16; Console, $59; Rear console, $26 (Firebird); Rally & clock instruments, $47; Rally, clock & tach instruments, $95; Four-way power seat, $75 (GTO); Power door locks, $45; Power windows, $116; Pushbutton radio, $66; AM/FM radio, $139; AM/FM stereo radio, $239; Rear speaker, $19; Custom front & rear seat belts, $16; Custom steering wheel, $15 (GTO); Custom sport steering wheel, $55 (GTO); Formula steering wheel, $55 (GTO); Tilt steering wheel, $44; Eight-track tape player, $134; Stereo tape cassette player, $127.

Exterior: Bumper guards, $16 (Firebird); Cordova top, $95 (GTO); Tinted glass, $38; Tinted windshield glass only, $31; Left remote control mirror, $26 (Firebird); Outside remote control mirror, $12 (GTO); Rear deck spoiler, $45 (GTO); Wire wheel discs, $80 (GTO); Deluxe wheel discs, $32; Honeycomb wheels, $126; Rally II wheels, $90.

Miscellaneous: Air conditioning, $408 (Firebird), $387 (GTO); Cruise Control, $60 (GTO); Saf-T-Track differential, $46; 455 cid engine, $55 (GTO); 455 cid GTO engine, $130 (GTO); Power brakes, $47; Front disc power brakes, $67 (GTO); Power steering, $116; Rear window defogger, $32; Rear window defroster, $63; Space-Saver spare tire, $16 (Firebird); Remote trunk lid release, $14; Three-speed automatic, $243 (Firebird, no cost on Trans Am), $230 (GTO); Four-speed manual transmission, $206 (Firebird), $238 (with HO engine), $185 (GTO).

Buick
Muscle Cars
1965–1972

Buick in the Muscle Car Era

Without Buick, there wouldn't be a General Motors.

By the turn of the century, William C. "Billy" Durant had parlayed a minor investment into the largest horse-drawn carriage works in America — the Durant Dort Carriage Company of Flint, Michigan. Billy Durant did not, however, gain any special pleasure from being a successful businessman. What attracted him was the thrill of the hunt, the sheer excitement of putting companies together and building them up.

During the first few years of this century, the automobile went from a curiosity to a necessity. Automobile companies were springing up all over, and one of the first was in Flint, Michigan.

David Dunbar Buick was trying doggedly to make a go of his car company in Flint when he met Billy Durant. Durant felt that the future lay with the automobile and it wasn't long before he had gained control of Buick. By 1908, his burgeoning empire included Buick, Oldsmobile and Oakland (later to become Pontiac). Soon after that, he bought Cadillac — and General Motors was born.

Durant's wheeling and dealing brought General Motors to the brink of ruin in 1911. The bankers came to the rescue but Durant was out. Out, that is, but not down. He bankrolled a little car company headed by Louis Chevrolet and, by 1917, had used Chevrolet to regain control of General Motors! Now bigger than ever, he began wheeling and dealing on an unprecedented scale until the stock market plunge of 1921 wiped him out and nearly took General Motors down with

him. Again, the bankers intervened, but Durant was gone from GM for good.

In truth, it was probably only the solid profits of Buick that saved GM in 1921. Chevrolet was not yet a serious competitor in the low-priced field and few of the other GM divisions were making money. Buick was the cash cow that provided the investment money to build Chevrolet into the number one nameplate in America, and the Chevy and Buick divisions have been the primary profit centers in GM ever since.

Buicks have always been good performing cars, rather than high performance cars. Still, Buick had the essential formula for the muscle car as early as 1936. At that time, Buick offered both small- and large-bodied cars, as did many upscale manufacturers, and it was customary to increase engine size as the size and weight of the car increased. In 1936, Buick introduced the Century series on its smallest body, but equipped it with the big Roadmaster engine. Voila! Big engine, little car — a muscle car, right? Well...it was the right idea, and a good performer for its day, but you can't get neck-snapping performance out of a straight eight. If Buick had had a decent V-8, the muscle car era might have dawned thirty years sooner!

By the time Buick developed its modern, high compression V-8 in 1953, Buicks were saddled with two-speed Dynaflow automatic transmissions that, while smooth, were not especially rugged and definitely not capable of truly hot performance. Buick was into big, comfortable cars; not little, exciting cars.

The first suggestion that Buick might be onto a different track was the compact Buick Special of 1961. Available as an option, was a brand new aluminum V-8, the first such engine in any volume production American car. This powerplant was not only technically interesting, it put forth a respectable 155 horsepower. This was enough to give the Special unusually good performance for a compact — especially considering it weighed 1,600 pounds less than a standard 1961 Buick. Not spine-tingling performance, mind you, but getting there. As a demonstration of the potential inherent in this engine, Mickey Thompson modified one to deliver 330 horsepower on dynamometer tests.

By 1963, however, GM brass had decided the engine was more expensive than it was worth and the tooling was sold to Rover in England, where it resides to this day. As such it has powered a succession of Rover cars, as well as the contemporary Range Rover. It appeared briefly in the MG-TC, although it was never very satisfactory in that application. According to Jaguar engineers, British Leyland even tried to use it in the car that was to become the current Jaguar XJ-6.

In 1962, Buick introduced its cast-iron V-6, again the first such powerplant ever put in a production American car. It worked well, but after a few years was sold to Kaiser Jeep, which was later bought by American Motors. In 1974, in the wake of the fuel crunch, Buick bought the engine back from AMC and it formed the basis for all the high performance T-Type and Grand National Buicks of the 1980s.

In the mid-1960s, Buick's high performance instincts went into hibernation again. True, the Wildcat series was launched in 1962, but it was a pale shadow of the Chevrolet Impala SS *genre*. The Riviera Gran Sport was introduced for 1965, but it, too, was

more "gran" than "sport." One buff magazine referred to it as "Daddy Warbucks' high-powered runabout."

By that year, Buick general manager Ed Rollert had come to the conclusion that Buick needed some help to capture the growing "youth" market. The Riviera Gran Sport was one attempt to instill some youthful excitement into the Buick line-up, but a more meaningful effort was the Skylark Gran Sport.

The Skylark GS boasted a 400 cubic inch V-8 rated at 325 horsepower. On paper it was a real tiger. On the road, however, it was not quite as exciting as its counterparts offered by Chevy, Pontiac and Olds. Still, the Skylark GS was good for 0-60 mph in around seven seconds and was a very refined piece of machinery — sort of Daddy Warbucks' playboy son's runabout.

David Holls was Buick's chief designer into the mid-1960s. It was under his direction that the early Gran Sports were styled. Later, Wayne Kady assumed his role. Other designers who influenced Gran Sport styling included Jerry Hirschberg and Ron Hill. All of these designers were to have influential careers at GM Design.

Buick big-block engines were entirely new for 1967, an expenditure that took some explaining when the GM bean-counters came calling. Buick engineers, headed by chief engineer Lowell Kintigh and chief engine specialist Cliff Studaker, were convinced Buick needed to start with a fresh sheet of paper. The 1953 V-8 had reached the limits of its development, so the old 401/425 cubic-inch powerplants were supplanted by new units displacing 400 and 430 cubic inches, respectively.

The Skylark Gran Sports were faster than ever before with the new engines. While still not the fastest cars on the market, they were capable of holding their own against the competition and they still retained the reputation for refinement and luxury for which they had always been known.

In 1968, Kintigh was named GM's director of advanced planning and Phillip Bowser became chief engineer at Buick. It was left to him to shepherd the Gran Sports through what remained of the muscle car era.

The biggest news to come from Buick in the Bowser era was the 455 cube V-8 in 1970. This awesome powerplant found its way into the Gran Sport as the Skylark GS 455. Moreover, there was a Stage I package that offered a special high-lift cam, a low-restriction exhaust system, heavy duty valve springs and a set of functional hood scoops to gain even more snap than usual when the fast pedal was depressed. The Stage I was capable of 0-60 times in the mid-six second range, the best Buick muscle car of the era. It was also one of the last.

A "Stage II" version was developed by Buick in conjunction with the famed Buick drag racing team of Kenne-Bell. Buick cast 50 sets of Stage II heads, which featured larger intake and oval exhaust ports and larger valve seats. Kenne-Bell installed their own pistons, camshaft and Edelbrock manifold.

During testing, the Buick Gran Sport Stage II turned a 10.90 elapsed time with a top speed of 121 mph in the quarter-mile! The Stage II, however, never made it to the showroom floor, as Buick cancelled the program in late 1971.

The Stage I option was listed as late as 1974, but the last editions were pale copies of the 1970 version. By 1975, it was all over for Buick. If Buick Gran Sports in their various guises were never the fastest muscle cars, they were, nonetheless, refined and impressive machines.

The Skylark Gran Sport was equipped with a modified heavy-duty perimeter frame featuring a torque box construction plus rigid cross-members. A recirculating ball-bearing steering system and a specially calibrated suspension ensured superior handling.

1965 Buick

Numerous trim and model variations were offered by Buick in 1965 so that the buyer could custom build his Buick. Standard, Deluxe and Skylark versions of the Special were offered. The Gran Sport option, equipped with $250 worth of roadability improvements, made its debut on the mid-size Skylark and full-size Riviera. The Skylark Gran Sport, introduced in mid-1965, served as Buick's entry into the supercar market, following the example of the Pontiac GTO, which had successfully broken through the barrier of General Motors' anti-performance policy.

RIVIERA GRAN SPORT

Few styling charges were made in 1965 Rivieras. Headlights were hidden behind the grille, and the taillights were integrated into the rear bumper. The Gran Sport option included a 360 horsepower Super Wildcat V-8 engine with a dual four-barrel carburetor, large diameter dual exhausts, Posi-Traction differential and bright metal engine accents

including a large chromed air cleaner and polished ribbed valve covers. The styling of the Gran Sport body was subtly distinguished from other Rivieras with its special full wheel covers and Gran Sport lettering on the rear deck below the Riviera script and on the front fenders. *Car and Driver*, in June 1965, estimated the Riviera Gran Sport's maximum speed at 130 mph. In December 1964 *Motor Trend*, estimating its speed at a more conservative 125 mph, pronounced the Gran Sport superb in every category: "It goes and handles better than before, and that's quite an improvement." Buick called the Gran Sport "a Riviera with muscles on its muscles...for those whose love of performance is insatiable."

SKYLARK GRAN SPORT

In mid-1965, Buick put a 401 cubic-inch, 325 hp V-8 engine into the mid-size Skylark and branded it the Skylark Gran Sport. Since GM policy prohibited the use of any engine larger than 400 cubic inches in its intermediate models, the engine was called a 400 cubic-inch V-8, but this engine was the same as the standard power in the big Electra and Wildcat and wasn't detuned for the smaller

Buick called the new Riviera Gran Sport an "iron fist in a velvet glove...otherwise known as the Executive's Express." Power assisted brakes and steering were standard and an optional extra-quick 15:1 gear ratio was available.

sized and lighter Skylark. It was fitted with a single four-barreled carburetor, a heavy-duty cross-flow radiator and a dual exhaust manifold, with oversized pipes. With a weight of 642 pounds, the engine was 134 pounds heavier than the 300 cid V-8 used in other Skylarks. Externally, the Gran Sport models were the same as other Skylark V-8s, but with the addition of the Gran Sport name in red letters on the roof quarters (rear fenders on the convertibles), deck and the driver's side grille. Interior identification was limited to the Gran Sport logo placed on the instrument panel. The Gran Sport option also included oversized 7.75 x 14-inch tires mounted on 6JK rims. Buick advertised this high performance Gran Sport Skylark as "a howitzer with windshield wipers."

VIN NUMBERS
Vehicle Identification Number: 4( )( )( )( )5( )100001
Explanation:
First five digits: Same as model number
First digit: GM line number: 4 = Buick
Second digit: Series number: 9 = Riviera
Second digit: Series number: 4 = Skylark
Third digit: Model/engine number:
  Riviera = 4
  Skylark V-8 = 4
Fourth & fifth digit: Body type number:
  2-dr Sports Coupe = 47
  Convertible = 67
Sixth digit: Last digit of model year = 5

Seventh symbol: Letter indicating assembly plant
Eighth to thirteenth digit:
Sequential production number

PRODUCTION TOTALS

Model	Total Units	Percent
Buick Riviera	34,586	
Gran Sport opt.	NA	
Buick Skylark	98,787	
Gran Sport opt.	NA	

DRIVETRAIN DATA

	Riviera Gran Sport (Std.)	Skylark Gran Sport (Std.)
Cyl:	V-8	V-8
Bore (in):	4.31	4.19
Stroke (in):	3.64	3.64
CID:	425	401
Carbs.:	2 4-bbl	1 4-bbl
Make:	Carter	Carter
Model:	AFB	AFB
Comp.:	10.25	10.25
Max. BHP:	360	325
@ RPM:	4400	4400
Torque ft-lb:	465	445
@ RPM:	2800	2800

TRANSMISSIONS
Riviera Gran Sport
Std: 3-speed Torque Convertor Console-Mounted Automatic
Opt: None

Skylark Gran Sport
Std: 3-speed Floor-Mounted Manual
Opt: 4-speed Fully Synchronized Manual, 2-speed Super Turbine Automatic (both available with console), 2-speed Torque Convertor Automatic

REAR AXLE RATIOS
Riviera Gran Sport:
Std: 3.42
Opt: 3.23, 3.58

Skylark Gran Sport:
Std: 3.36 (man), 3.08 (auto)
Opt: 3.08 (man), 3.55, 3.73, 2.78, 3.23 (auto), 3.36 (auto)

EXTERIOR DATA
Riviera Gran Sport:

	sports coupe
Length (in):	209
Width (in):	76.6
Height (in):	53
Wheelbase (in):	117
Weight (lb):	4036

Skylark Gran Sport:

	sports coupe	convertible
Length (in):	203.4	203.4
Width (in):	73.9	73.9
Height (in):	53.5	53.5
Wheelbase (in):	115	115
Weight (lb):	3198	3294

FACTORY BASE PRICE DATA

Model	Sports Coupe	Convertible
Riviera Gran Sport	$ 4508	$ —
Skylark Gran Sport	3149	3299

POPULAR FACTORY OPTIONS
Interior: Four-way or Six-way power seat controls; AM radio; AM-FM radio (full size-only); Seven position tilt steering wheel; Tachometer; Consoles for Skylark bucket seats; Front seat belt deletion; Electric clock (Skylark).

Exterior: Tinted glass; Electric antenna (Riviera); Backup lights (Skylark); Trunk light (Skylark); Whitewall tires.

Miscellaneous: Power steering; Power brakes; Power windows; Power vent windows (Riviera); Air conditioning; Remote control outside rearview mirror; Four-note horn; Heater/defroster deletion; Automatic trunk release; Rear window defroster.

Many convenience options were available on the GS including back-up lights, a trunk light and a rear window defroster.

Buick marketed its 1966 Skylark GS as the "Tuned Car." Its styling, performance, ride and handling were designed to work together in harmony. This "tuning" included a special chassis for the GS, designed to hold the extra power of the 325 hp Wildcat V-8.

1966 Buick

1966 was a banner year for the Gran Sport label at Buick. Not only was it offered again on both the Skylark and the Riviera, but for the first and only time it was an option on the full-sized Wildcat. It is not known how many Wildcats were produced with the Gran Sport option, but the top selling Wildcat models were not available with the GS option. Most of Buick's line were carry-overs from the previous year, with the exception of the Riviera, which received a new body many regard as one of the best looking among American cars of the modern era.

RIVIERA GRAN SPORT

The 1966 Riviera Gran Sport was a rare blend of outstanding styling and high performance. The Riviera had a new body, which it shared with the new Oldsmobile Toronado, but retained its own rear-wheel-drive chassis and distinctive styling. Its wheelbase was increased by 2 inches, its

length was stretched by 3 inches. Only one engine, a 340 hp single carburetor was available on the Riviera; but a two-carburetor dealer-installed version could be ordered, with an increased output of 360 hp at 4000 rpm. The Gran Sport option included high-performance springs and shocks, as well as Posi-Traction rear axle. It sported 8.45 x 15 white-wall or redline tires and the GS logo on the front fenders and the instrument panel. In a quarter-mile acceleration test by *Motor Trend*, its speed was clocked at 87 mph in 16.4 seconds. With the two-barrel carburetor, *Mechanix Illustrated* measured its top speed at 125 mph.

SKYLARK GRAN SPORT

The Skylark went through few styling changes in 1966. The Gran Sport was set apart from the other Skylarks with the introduction of a blacked-out grille, Gran Sport labels in the grille and on the rear deck, simulated twin hood scoops, and a black matte finish for the rear cove panel. The engine and transmission were unchanged from the previous year. *Motor Trend* recorded the GS's 0 to 60 time at 7.6 seconds. Though it came in last in a quarter-mile comparison test of six supercars conducted by *Car and Driver*, in its March 1966 issue, it was by far the participant most likely to be bought for street use. The Skylark Gran Sport's speed and acceleration time were measured at 95.13 mph in 14.13 seconds.

WILDCAT GRAN SPORT

The Super Sport option, available for the first and only time on the Wildcat, included a chrome plated air-cleaner, cast aluminum rocker arm covers, dual exhausts, heavy-duty front and rear suspension, positive traction differential, and GS identification plates front and rear. The GS package could only be ordered on the two-door Sport Coupe or convertible in either the base or Custom versions. *Mechanix Illustrated* tested the 0 to 60 acceleration of the Wildcat Gran Sport at just 7.5 seconds. Even more impressive was this high performance demon's top speed which was measured at 125 mph. Clearly, Buick engineers had packed a lot of muscle into this Wildcat.

VIN NUMBERS

Vehicle Identification Number: 4( )( )( )( )6( )100001
Explanation:
First five digits: Same as model number
First digit: GM line number: 4 = Buick
Second digit: Series number: 9 = Riviera
Second digit: Series number: 4 = Skylark
Second digit: Series number: 6 = Wildcat
Third digit: Model/engine number:
   Riviera = 4
   Skylark Gran Sport = 6
   Wildcat = 4
   Wildcat Custom = 6
Fourth & fifth digit: Body type number:
   Convertible = 67

2-dr Sports Coupe (Riviera) = 87
2-dr Coupe (Skylark) = 07
2-dr Sports Coupe (Skylark) = 17
2-dr Coupe (Wildcat) = 37
Sixth digit: Last digit of model year = 6
Seventh symbol: Letter indicating assembly plant
Eighth to thirteenth digit:
Sequential production number

PRODUCTION TOTALS

Model	Total Units	Percent
Buick Riviera	45,348	
Gran Sport opt.	NA	
Buick Skylark	106,217	
Gran Sport opt.	13,816	12
Buick Wildcat	68,584	
Gran Sport opt.	NA	

DRIVETRAIN DATA

	Riviera Gran Sport (Std.)	Skylark Gran Sport (Std.)	Wildcat Gran Sport (Std.)
Cyl:	V-8	V-8	V-8
Bore (in):	4.31	4.19	4.31
Stroke (in):	3.64	3.64	3.64
CID:	425	401	425
Carbs.:	1 4-bbl	1 4-bbl	1 4-bbl
Make:	Carter	Carter	Carter
Model:	AFB	AFB	AFB
Comp.:	10.25	10.25	10.25
Max. BHP:	340	325	340
@ RPM:	4400	4400	4400
Torque ft-lb:	465	445	465
@ RPM:	2800	2800	2800

Front end of the '66 Skylark Gran Sport had a corporate GM look. Twin hood scoops (non-functional), blacked out grille and a Gran Sport emblem distinguished it from base Skylarks. Courtesy Musclecar Review Magazine.

Simple "GS" emblems on the rear quarter-panel identify the Gran Sport, a far cry from the outrageous GSX exterior, still a few years down the road. Courtesy Musclecar Review Magazine.

TRANSMISSIONS

Riviera Gran Sport
Std: 3-speed Torque Convertor Column-Mounted Automatic
Opt: NA

Skylark Gran Sport
Std: 3-speed Floor-Mounted Manual
Opt: 4-speed Floor-Mounted Manual, 2-speed Super Turbine Console-Mounted Automatic

Wildcat Gran Sport
Std: Super Turbine
Opt: None

REAR AXLE RATIOS

Riviera Gran Sport:
Std: 3.23
Opt: 3.42

Skylark Gran Sport:
Std: 3.36 (man), 2.93 (auto)
Opt: 3.08 (man), 3.55, 3.73, 2.78 (auto), 3.23 (auto), 3.36

Wildcat Gran Sport:
Std: 3.23
Opt: NA

EXTERIOR DATA

Riviera Gran Sport:

	Sports Coupe
Length (in):	211.2
Width (in):	79.3
Height (in):	56.1
Wheelbase (in):	119
Weight (lb):	4180

Skylark Gran Sport:

	Coupe	Sports Coupe	Convertible
Length (in):	204	204	204
Width (in):	75	75	75
Height (in):	53.2	53.2	54
Wheelbase (in):	115	115	115
Weight (lb):	3479	3428	3532

Wildcat Gran Sport:

	Sports Coupe	Convertible
Length (in):	219.9	220.1
Width (in):	80	80
Height (in):	54.5	54.3
Wheelbase (in):	126	126
Weight (lb):	4003	4065

FACTORY BASE PRICE DATA

Model	Coupe	Sports Coupe	Convertible
Riviera G S	$ —	$ 4601	$ —
Skylark G S	2956	3019	3167
Wildcat G S	—	3581	3735
Wildcat Custom GS	—	3802	3956

POPULAR FACTORY OPTIONS

Interior: Four-way power seat controls, $69; Six-way power seat controls, $95 ; AM radio, $88; AM-FM radio, $175; Seven position tilt steering wheel, $42.

Exterior: Remote control outside rearview mirror, $7; Tinted glass, $42; Tinted windshield glass only, $28; Cornering lights, $34; Simulated wire wheel covers, $58; Five-spoke chromed wheels, $89.

Miscellaneous: Power steering, $121; Power brakes, $42; Power windows, $105; Air conditioning, $421; Four-note horn, $16; Automatic trunk release, $13; Electro cruise, $63, $56; Heater/Defroster deletion, $96 credit.

Interior of the '66 Skylark Gran Sport was straightforward. This convertible carried the bench seat and optional two-speed automatic transmission. Courtesy Musclecar Review Magazine.

1966 was the only year for a GS Wildcat. Though now rare, it obviously did not lack horsepower. Courtesy Musclecar Review Magazine.

In styling, the GS 340 was almost identical to the GS 400, but it was offered only as a 2-door hardtop. Yet it was easily distinguishable from the GS 400 because it came only in white or platinum and its broad rally stripes and hood scoops were painted red.

1967 Buick

For 1967 Buick introduced one of its largest engines ever, the 430 cid V-8 on the Electra, Wildcat and Riviera. The engine's horsepower was no greater than previous engines, but it offered a slight increase in torque and ran more smoothly. The Skylark Gran Sport became the GS 400 and was joined by a new, lower priced and less powerful version, the GS 340. The GS 340 was Buick's entry into the popular low-priced supercar market, which would soon be overcrowded with competitors.

GS 340

The GS 340 was introduced as "the GS 400's running mate...for people who look for a large measure of sporting flavor at a low price." Its engine was smaller than the 400's, only displacing 340 cubic inches. A four-speed gearbox was the standard transmission and the only alternative was the two-speed Super Turbine automatic. The suspension of the GS included special front and rear springs and a large

diameter front stabilizer bar. An optional "Sport Pac" suspension that included heavy-duty springs and shocks, a heavy-duty rear stabilizer bar and a 15:1 steering ratio was also offered. Few options were offered externally. Body colors were limited to white or platinum contrasting with broad rally stripes and hood scoops, both finished in red. The interior was limited to black all-vinyl bench seats. Furthermore, the GS 340 was only offered on the two-door hardtop coupe.

GS 400

Powering the GS 400 was a completely new 401 cid engine. Horsepower had been boosted to 340 at 5000 rpm — up 15 from the year before. As in earlier years, many optional rear axle ratios for the GS were available. And, for the first time, Buick offered the three-speed Super Turbine automatic on the Gran Sport. Externally, the GS 400 was set apart from other Skylarks with the GS monogram in red letters incorporated into the front grille and placed on the rear deck. The Gran Sport lacked the rear fender skirts that were standard on other Skylarks but was equipped with twin hood scoops, thin side body stripes and 14-inch wheels, either whitewall or redline style. *World Car Catalog* clocked the GS 400's top speed at 122 mph, two mph higher than the 1966 Gran Sport. The 0 to 60 time was measured by *Motor Trend* at 6.9 seconds with the automatic and 6.6 seconds with the four-speed manual transmission.

RIVIERA GRAN SPORT

The Riviera saw few styling changes in 1967, but there was a difference under the hood. A new, 430 cid engine replaced the smaller 1966 engine. The Gran Sport option consisted of heavy duty front and rear shocks, Posi-Traction differential, wide oval red or white stripe tires and the GS monogram on the front fender and instrument panel. It used the same engine as the standard Riviera, but there was little need for a different one, since it was one of the largest motors offered that year and it had the highest horsepower rating of any standard 1967 muscle car engine. *Motor Trend* timed the Riviera's 0-to-60 acceleration at 7.8 seconds and its speed at the end of a standing quarter-mile at 86 mph, the same as the Thunderbird's, and 1 mph under the best time set by the Pontiac Grand Prix.

VIN NUMBERS

Vehicle Identification Number: 4( )( )( )( )7( )100001
Explanation:
First five digits: Same as model number
First digit: GM line number: 4 = Buick
Second digit: Series number: 9 = Riviera
Second digit: Series number: 4 = Skylark
Second digit: Series number: 3= Special*
Third digit: Model/engine number:
  GS 400 = 6
  Riviera = 4
Fourth & fifth digit: Body type number:
  Convertible = 67
  2-dr Sports Coupe (Riviera) = 87
  2-dr Coupe (GS) = 07
  2-dr Sports Coupe (GS) = 17
Sixth digit: Last digit of model year = 7
Seventh symbol: Letter indicating assembly plant
Eighth to thirteenth digit:
Sequential production number
* GS 340 was numbered in the Special V-8 series

PRODUCTION TOTALS

Model	Total Units	Percent
GS 340	3,692	
GS 400	13,813	
Riviera	42,799	
Gran Sport opt.	NA	

DRIVETRAIN DATA

	GS 340 (Std.)	GS 400 (Std.)	Riviera Gran Sport (Std.)
Cyl:	V-8	V-8	V-8
Bore (in):	3.75	4.19	4.18
Stroke (in):	3.85	3.64	3.9
CID:	340	401	430
Carbs.:	1 4-bbl	1 4-bbl	1 4-bbl
Make:	Rochester	Rochester	Rochester
Model:	4MV	4MV	4MV
Comp.:	9.0	10.25	10.25
Max. BHP:	260	340	360
@ RPM:	4200	5000	5000
Torque ft-lb:	365	440	475
@ RPM:	2800	3200	3200

TRANSMISSIONS

GS 340
Std: 3-speed Floor-Mounted Manual
Opt: 2-speed Super Turbine Automatic

GS 400
Std: 3-speed Floor-Mounted Manual
Opt: 4-speed Floor-Mounted Manual, 3-speed Super Turbine Automatic

Riviera Gran Sport
Std: Super Turbine Column-Mounted Automatic
Opt: Super Turbine Console-Mounted Automatic

REAR AXLE RATIOS

GS 340:
Std: 3.23
Opt: 3.63, 3.90

GS 400:
Std: 3.63 (man), 2.93 (auto)
Opt: 3.55, 3.90, 4.30, 3.36 (auto)

Riviera Gran Sport:
Std: 3.42
Opt: NA

EXTERIOR DATA

GS 340:

	Coupe
Length (in):	205
Width (in):	75.4
Height (in):	53.2
Wheelbase (in):	115
Weight (lb):	3283

(con't. next page)

Top of the Skylark line was this GS 400 convertible. With its chrome wheels, simulated hood scoops, side vents and assorted GS badges, the GS 400 was quite a handsome automobile. Courtesy Musclecar Review Magazine.

The GS 340 was a '67-only option aimed at those wanting Buick quality and performance for a few less bucks. The GS 340 was powerd by a 340 cid V-8 rated at 260 hp at 4200 rpm. Courtesy Musclecar Review Magazine.

EXTERIOR DATA *(con't.)*
GS 400:

	Coupe	Sports Coupe	Convertible
Length (in):	205	205	205
Width (in):	75.4	75.4	75.4
Height (in):	53.2	53.2	53.2
Wheelbase (in):	115	115	115
Weight (lb):	3439	3500	3505

Riviera Gran Sport:

	Sports Coupe
Length (in):	216
Width (in):	79
Height (in):	53.2
Wheelbase (in):	119
Weight (lb):	4222

FACTORY BASE PRICE DATA

Model	Coupe	Sports Coupe	Convertible
GS 340	$ 2845	$ —	$ —
GS 400	2956	3019	3167
Riviera GS	—	4607	—

POPULAR FACTORY OPTIONS

Interior: Front seat headrests; Tilt steering wheel (standard on Riviera); Full-length console with bucket seats; AM radio; AM/FM radio; Stereo radio; Reclining bucket seat; Reclining Strato bench seat (Riviera only); Power seat adjustment.

Exterior: Five-spoke plated sport wheels; Wire wheel covers; DeLuxe wheel covers; Vinyl roof cover; Cornering lights.

Miscellaneous: Power steering (standard on Riviera); Power brakes (standard on Riviera); Front power disc brakes; Automatic air conditioning; Air conditioning; Power door locks; Electro-cruise (automatic transmission only, not available on GS 400); Power windows; Four-note horn; Remote control mirror; Automatic trunk release; Rear window defroster; Speed alert.

The 1967 Gran Sport name was changed to "GS 400." The GS emblems could be found on the grille and rear fenders.

Buick stylists did a great job on the A-body. The GS 400 was a fine looking car with a 340-hp punch. Courtesy Musclecar Review Magazine.

The 1968 California GS, a mid-year introduction, was basically a GS 350 with a little more panache. Standard features included custom-styled chrome wheels, a vinyl roof covering, vinyl or cloth seats and the GS ornamentation in five places.

1968 Buick

In 1968 all of Buick's intermediate models received new styling. The two door models were placed on a 112-inch wheelbase chassis, shortened three inches from the year before. This made for a highly maneuverable car with a sportier appearance. Additionally a number of styling changes, pertaining to safety, were made. These included larger outside rear-view mirrors, side marker lights on front fenders and rear quarter panels, safety armrests and improved door latches. The GS models' production was up by 55% from the year before. Buick's full-sized models, including the Riviera, received new grilles, altered rear bumpers and concealed windshield wipers.

CALIFORNIA GS

In mid-1968, Buick introduced the California GS, which was exclusively designed and engineered for Golden State motorists. This Gran Sport was essentially the same as the GS 350 but with a special trim and a standard two-speed

automatic transmission. The California GS was equipped with a vinyl top, chrome exterior trim, chrome plated "Super Sport" wheels and the DeLuxe steering wheel. The GS California emblems decorated the grille, roof sail panels and rear fenders. Buick advertised this model as "The Distinctive Personal Car for Americana on the GO!"

GS 350

A new, more potent 350 cid engine replaced the GS 340 in 1968, hence the name change. Horsepower was increased to 280 at 4600 rpm. A three-speed manual transmission was standard and an optional four-speed manual was available. Both transmissions were regarded as heavy-duty models and could be linked to a Hurst linkage for an additional cost. A new upper level instrument panel ventilation system was introduced, justifying the elimination of front ventipanes. On the inside, the GS 350 was trimmed like the Skylark Custom, but on the outside, finned simulated air intakes, lower body paint accent stripes and bright wheelhouse mouldings gave it a more muscular look. For easy identification, a GS 350 plaque was placed on the center of the deck lid. The GS monogram could be found on the grille, the door panels and rear fenders.

The powerful, new 350 cid engine and superior styling made the California GS the choice for "Americana on the GO!"

The GS received a new body for 1968. Placed on a smaller wheelbase, the GS gained a sportier, more muscular look.

GS 400

This year the GS 400 was only offered in the Sport Coupe and the convertible. Though the body had been changed, the engine remained virtually the same. The only major revision was the addition of a "controlled emission system." This was the biggest overall production year for the GS — over 13,000 GS 400's were manufactured, of which 2,514 were convertibles. The GS 400 was identifiable by wide oval white-stripe tires, fake fender vents, functional hood scoops and GS ornamentation on the front fenders, radiator grille, rear end panel and instrument panel. Buick advertised the GS 400 as the car for "the person who truly gets a thrill out of driving.... If it takes something extra to get you excited, be excited." And the GS 400's performance was exciting. Its top speed was measured by *World Car Catalog* at an impressive 120 mph, down slightly from 1967, probably due to the extra weight of the new body.

Riviera Gran Sport

In addition to the styling changes given to all the full-size Buicks, the Riviera got a new, much heavier divided grille, giving this car a more distinctive look. In 1968 there was little mechanical change in the Riviera; it was still powered by the muscular 430 cid engine. The Gran Sport equipment consisted of heavy-duty front and rear suspension, Posi-Traction differential, H70 x 15 red or white stripe tires and the GS monogram on the front fenders and the instrument panel. Though the Riviera's weight was up by over 30 pounds, its performance was as good as ever. *Mechanix Illustrated* timed the 0 to 60 run at 8.1 seconds and rated the Riviera's top speed at 125 mph, while *World Car Catalog* listed it as 132 mph. *Mechanix Illustrated* declared that the Riviera Gran Sport was "just about the best of any of the 1968 cars we have tested."

VIN NUMBERS

Vehicle Identification Number: 4( )( )( )( )8( )100001
Explanation:
First five digits: Same as model number
First digit: GM line number: 4 = Buick
Second digit: Series number: 9 = Riviera
Second digit: Series number: 4 = Skylark Custom
Second digit: Series number: 3= Special*
Third digit: Model/engine number:
  GS 350 = 4
  GS 400 = 6
  Riviera = 4
Fourth & fifth digit: Body type number:
  Convertible = 67
  2-dr Sports Coupe (Riviera) = 87
  2-dr Sports Coupe (GS) = 37
  2-dr Coupe (California GS) = 27
Sixth digit: Last digit of model year = 8
Seventh symbol: Letter indicating assembly plant
Eighth to thirteenth digit:
Sequential production number
*California GS was actually numbered in the Special Deluxe series

PRODUCTION TOTALS

Model	Total Units	Percent
California GS	NA	
GS 350	8.317	
GS 400	13,197	
Riviera	49,284	
Gran Sport opt.	NA	

GS 350's standard features included a long-lasting dual exhaust system composed of aluminized and stainless steel.

The GS 400's sporty styling features included chrome molding, accent stripes, and the GS 400 plaque on the deck lid lip.

DRIVETRAIN DATA

| | California GS | | Riviera |
| | GS 350 | GS 400 | Gran Sport |
	(Std.)	(Std.)	(Std.)
Cyl:	V-8	V-8	V-8
Bore (in):	3.80	4.19	4.18
Stroke (in):	3.85	3.64	3.9
CID:	340	401	430
Carbs.:	1 4-bbl	1 4-bbl	1 4-bbl
Make:	Rochester	Rochester	Rochester
Model:	4MV	4MV	4MV
Comp.:	10.25	10.25	10.25
Max. BHP:	280	340	360
@ RPM:	4600	5000	5000
Torque ft-lb:	375	440	475
@ RPM:	3200	3200	3200

TRANSMISSIONS

California GS
Std: 2-speed Super Turbine Automatic Column or Console-Mounted
Opt: NA

GS 350
Std: 3-speed Column-Mounted Manual
Opt: 2-speed Super Turbine Automatic Column or Console-Mounted, 3-speed Consolette or Floor-Mounted Manual, 4-speed Consolette or Floor-Mounted Manual

GS 400
Std: 3-speed Floor-Mounted Manual
Opt: 4-speed Consolette or Floor-Mounted Manual, Super Turbine Automatic

Riviera Gran Sport
Std: Super Turbine Column-Mounted Automatic
Opt: Super Turbine Console-Mounted Automatic

REAR AXLE RATIOS

California GS:
Std: 3.42 (man), 2.93 (auto)
Opt: NA

GS 350:
Std: 3.23
Opt: NA

GS 400:
Std: 3.42 (man), 2.93 (auto)
Opt: NA

Riviera Gran Sport:
Std: 3.42
Opt: NA

EXTERIOR DATA

California GS, GS 350:

	coupe
Length (in):	200.6
Width (in):	75.6
Height (in):	52.8
Wheelbase (in):	112
Weight (lb):	3375

GS 400:

	sports coupe	convertible
Length (in):	200.6	200.6

(con't. next page)

Heavy duty springs and direct-acting shock absorbers made for spectacular handling on the GS 400.

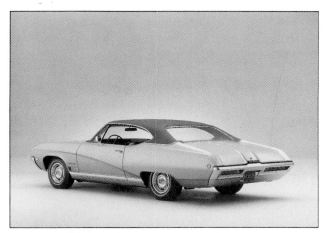

The GS 400, redesigned to fit on a 112-inch wheelbase, rode on wide oval white-striped tires (red-striped was optional).

EXTERIOR DATA *(con't.)*

Width (in):	75.6	75.6
Height (in):	52.8	52.7
Wheelbase (in):	112	112
Weight (lb):	3514	3547

Riviera Gran Sport:

	sports coupe
Length (in):	215.2
Width (in):	78.8
Height (in):	53.4
Wheelbase (in):	119
Weight (lb):	4222

FACTORY BASE PRICE DATA

Model	Sports Coupe	Convertible
California GS	$ NA	$ —
GS 350	2926	—
GS 400	3127	3271
Riviera Gran Sport	4747	—

POPULAR FACTORY OPTIONS

Interior: Four-way power seat; Six-way power seat; Seven-position tilt steering column; AM radio; AM/FM radio; AM/FM stereo radio; Tape deck; Strato seats (Riviera only); GS 350/GS 400 consolette, tachometer, for manual transmission; Full-length console (bucket seats and Super Turbine transmission required).

Exterior: Vinyl top; Chrome road wheels; Whitewall tires; DeLuxe wheelcovers; Cornering lights (Riviera); Remote control outside rear view mirror; Super DeLuxe wheelcovers; Radial ply tires.

Miscellaneous: Power steering; Power brakes; Power windows; Air conditioning; Soft-Ray glass; Cruise Master; Automatic Climate Control; Power front disc brakes; Automatic door locks; Trailer hitch; Rear window defroster; Speed alert.

Superior styling and high performance led to a banner sales year. Production of GS's was up by more than 55%.

The 1969 GS's styling was little changed from the previous year. A new grille with a thick center bar and a prominent hood scoop arrangement were the most notable changes. The latter was more than cosmetic — it was part of Buick's "Cool Air" induction system.

1969 Buick

The year 1969, was a record breaking year, in which 713,832 cars were produced—more than any year that decade and second only to the record of 781,296 in 1955. 1969 also saw few styling changes. Most of the changes that were made emphasized safety and increased performance. The Turbo Hydra-matic transmission was offered as an option for the first time. A new suspension named Accu-Drive was also introduced. It was designed to keep the car on a straight path; Buick engineers claimed that this suspension provided "the best directional stability ever experienced in an automobile." Among the new safety features available that year, were an anti-theft ignition lock on a redesigned collapsible steering column, headrests, larger rear-view mirrors and impact bars within the doors and quarter panels of some models.

More minor styling changes in the GS's included a new grille with a thick vertical center bar and the removal of the front vent windows.

CALIFORNIA GS

The California GS model was again essentially the same as the GS 350, but only available in California. Though it looked a bit more like a GS 400, it was powered by the GS 350 engine. A vinyl covered roof was standard, as was the Turbo Hydra-matic automatic transmission. The GS logo was placed on the roof quarters and on the deck lid. "California" was spelled out in script on the rear fenders. *Mechanix Illustrated* tested the California GS's 0 to 60 time at 9.5 seconds and its top speed at over 110 mph.

GS 350

The GS 350 underwent few mechanical or styling changes in 1969. The hood scoop became considerably more prominent to accommodate Buick's new "Cool Air" induction system. The new hood scoops were linked to a special air cleaner with twin snorkels. Although Buick claimed that this system increased maximum horsepower by eight percent and provided a six-and-one-half percent boost in peak torque, the company left the GS engine ratings unchanged. A GS 350 plaque was placed on the center of the deck lid and the GS monogram decorated the grille and door panels.

GS 400

In 1969 the GS 400 received a few styling changes designed to set it apart from other Skylarks and the GS 350. A unique grille was fitted to the GS 400 and several vertical elements were changed. It also received the "Cool Air" induction system. The engine was virtually unchanged. But an important dealer-installed option could be purchased. This option, called the "Stage I Special Package," included a cam with greater lift and duration, a 11:1 compression ratio, forged pistons with solid skirts, stronger valve springs and revised spark advance curve and carburetor calibration. This engine was officially rated at 345 hp at 4800 rpm and 440 ft-lb of torque at 3200 rpm, but most engine authorities considered the Stage I V-8 to have a horsepower output closer to 400. Buick offered a Stage II package as over-the-counter parts. Ports and valves were enormous and made tremendous horsepower on the high cube 455 block.

RIVIERA GRAN SPORT

The 1969 Riviera underwent few styling changes and virtually no changes in its engine. Despite this, the changes were enough to lower overall weight by 23 pounds. Production was up from the year before; 52,872 cars were produced, setting a record for the second consecutive year. The Gran Sport option consisted of front and rear heavy-duty suspension, a chrome covered air cleaner, performance axle with Posi-Traction differential and white sidewall tires. The GS was identifiable by special narrow rocker panel covers, the absence of gravel deflectors and a thin side trim molding. The GS monogram remained in the same locations as in the previous year. *Motor Trend* timed the Riviera's 0 to 60 time at 9.2 seconds and *World Car Catalog* measured its top speed at 132 mph for the second year in a row.

VIN NUMBERS

Vehicle Identification Number: 4( )( )( )( )9( )100001
Explanation:
First five digits: Same as model number
First digit: GM line number: 4 = Buick
Second digit: Series number: 9 = Riviera
Second digit: Series number: 4 = Skylark Custom
Second digit: Series number: 3 = Special*
Third digit: Model/engine number:
  GS 350 = 4
  GS 400 = 6
  Riviera = 4
Fourth & fifth digit: Body type number:
  Convertible = 67
  2-dr Sports Coupe (Riviera) = 87
  2-dr Sports Coupe (GS) = 37
  2-dr Coupe (California GS) = 27
Sixth digit: Last digit of model year
Seventh symbol: Letter indicating assembly plant
Eighth to thirteenth digit:
Sequential production number
*California GS was numbered in the Special Deluxe series

PRODUCTION TOTALS

Model	Total Units	Percent
California GS	4,831	
GS 350	4,933	
GS 400	7,532	
Riviera	52,872	
Gran Sport opt.	NA	

Cool air induction was part of the performance upgrade made to the '69 GS. Foam gaskets fit over the air intakes of the breather and mated to the bulging scoop in the hood which was now functional. Courtesy Musclecar Review Magazine.

The scoops were functional in '69, feeding a hyperactive 400 cid monster. 1,256 Stage Is were built for the '69 model year. Courtesy Musclecar Review Magazine.

The GS 400's regular equipment included all-vinyl seats, a deluxe steering wheel and carpeting.

The GS 400 had an independent ball-joint front suspension, coil springs and hydraulic shock absorbers front and rear.

DRIVETRAIN DATA

	California GS (Std.) GS 350 (Std.)	GS 400 (Std.)	Riviera Gran Sport (Std.)
Cyl:	V-8	V-8	V-8
Bore (in):	3.80	4.19	4.18
Stroke (in):	3.85	3.64	3.9
CID:	340	401	430
Carbs.:	1 4-bbl	1 4-bbl	1 4-bbl
Make:	Rochester	Rochester	Rochester
Model:	4MV	4MV	4MV
Comp.:	10.25	10.25	10.25
Max. BHP:	280	340	360
@ RPM:	4600	5000	5000
Torque ft-lb:	375	440	475
@ RPM:	3200	3200	3200

TRANSMISSIONS

California GS
Std: Turbo Hydra-matic Automatic
Opt: 3-speed Turbo Hydra-matic Column or Console-Mounted Automatic, 3-speed Floor-Mounted Manual, 4-speed Floor-Mounted Manual

GS 350
Std: 3-speed Column-Mounted Manual
Opt: 3-speed Turbo Hydra-matic Column or Console-Mounted Automatic,
3-speed Floor-Mounted Manual,
4-speed Floor-Mounted Manual

GS 400
Std: 3-speed Floor-Mounted Manual
Opt: 4-speed Consolette or Floor-Mounted Manual, 3-speed Column-Mounted Turbo Hydra-matic Automatic (Console-Mounted with bucket seat option)

Riviera Gran Sport
Std: 3-speed Turbo Hydra-matic Column-Mounted Automatic
Opt: 3-speed Turbo Hydra-matic Console-Mounted Automatic

REAR AXLE RATIOS
California GS, GS 350:
Std: 3.31
Opt: NA

GS 400:
Std: 3.55 (man), 3.07 (auto)
Opt: NA

Riviera Gran Sport:
Std: 3.42
Opt: NA

EXTERIOR DATA
California GS, GS 350:

	coupe
Length (in):	200.7
Width (in):	75.6
Height (in):	53.5
Wheelbase (in):	112
Weight (lb):	3406

(con't next page)

EXTERIOR DATA *(con't.)*

GS 400:

	sports coupe	convertible
Length (in):	200.7	200.7
Width (in):	75.6	75.6
Height (in):	53	53.7
Wheelbase (in):	112	112
Weight (lb):	3549	3594

Riviera Gran Sport:

	sports coupe
Length (in):	215.2
Width (in):	79.2
Height (in):	53.2
Wheelbase (in):	119
Weight (lb):	4199

FACTORY BASE PRICE DATA

Model	Sports Coupe	Convertible
California GS	$ NA	$ —
GS 350	2980	—

	Sports Coupe	Convertible
GS 400	3181	3325
Riviera Gran Sport	4834	—

POPULAR FACTORY OPTIONS

Interior: Seven-position tilt wheel; AM radio; AM/FM radio; AM/FM radio with stereo tape; Strato bucket seats on specific models; Map light on rear view mirror; Center console with bucket seats (GS 350 and GS 400 when equipped with Turbo Hydra-matic transmission); Four-way power seat.

Exterior: Vinyl top; Five-spoke chrome sport wheels; Protective body side moldings (full-size models); Trailering packages.

Miscellaneous: Air conditioning, $376 (intermediate-size models), $437 (full-size models); Power windows; Electric window defogger (Riviera); Power door locks; Power steering; Power brakes; Automatic Climate Control (full-size).

Chrome styled steel wheels gave the the GS 400 a visual lift. 1969 wheels are 14 x 6 inch. Courtesy Musclecar Review Magazine.

The GS 455 Stage I was the most powerful of Buick's performance packages offered in 1970. It developed 360 hp at 4600 rpm and included a high-lift cam, low-restriction dual exhausts, heavy-duty valve springs and cooling system and functional hood scoops.

1970 Buick

In the 1970 model year, Buick introduced its largest engine to date, a 455 cid V-8. This engine was used in the new GS 455, which replaced the GS 400, the new GSX and the Riviera. The GS 350, which was now simply called the GS, also received a more powerful engine. It still displaced 350 cubic inches but its brake horsepower had been increased. The California GS did not survive into the 1970 model year. A restyling created the most muscular GS yet, bulging at the seams and riding on 15-inch chrome styled steel wheels. Though the 1970 model year's production total was a healthy 665,501 cars manufactured, the calender year saw a drop in Buick's production to 459,931, mainly due to a strike by the United Auto Workers against GM.

GS

The GS had a hot new shape. But its engine was modified considerably so that it produced 315 horsepower at 4800 rpm and 410 ft-lb torque at 3200 rpm. Its performance features included dual exhausts, a fully synchronized three-speed transmission, full flow oil filter, heavyduty spring and shock absorbers and a semi-closed cooling system. A textured black grille and hood scoops on the panel above the grille, gave this model a muscular appearance. The GS emblem appeared on the left hand grille, front fenders and deck.

GS 455

This was truly a muscular Buick! The new 455 cid engine produced an impressive 350 hp at 4600 rpm and a whopping 510 ft-lb torque at 2800 rpm. No other engine, except the much larger Cadillac, produced more torque than this; furthermore, no engine, including the Cadillac, developed its maximum torque at a rpm lower than 2800. For the muscle car enthusiast, the Stage I equipment was still available. It included a high-lift camshaft, a special four-barrel carburetor, Posi-Traction differential and low-restriction dual exhausts that increased brake horsepower to 360. The Stage I logo appeared in place of the 455 emblem, located on the left-hand grille and the front fenders. A GS monogram appeared on the deck lid. *Car Life* tested one of

A 3-speed manual transmission was standard on the GS 455 Stage I. The Turbo Hydra-matic and a 4-speed were available.

The Stage I performance package was available with both the GS 455 (as in pictured model) and the mid-year GSX model.

the first GS 455's 0 to 60 time at 6.5 seconds and its top speed at 129.5 mph; it also noted that the GS 455 was a good car to "take home to mother, or to the dragstrip on grudge night."

GSX

During the 1970 model year, Buick introduced the limited edition GSX. This model was technically a GS 455 with a $1,196 equipment option. Though only 678 were built that year, Buick introduced it with much fanfare, calling it "A brand-new brand of Buick." The 1970 GSX included such goodies as a hood-mounted tachometer with variable lighting control, G60 x 15 tires on seven-inch wide chrome-plated wheels, molded plastic front and rear spoilers, twin exterior mirrors, a four-speed manual transmission with a Hurst linkage, front disc brakes, heavy-duty suspension and black vinyl bucket seats. The GSX option was available for both the standard 350 hp V-8 and the mighty Stage I engine. The GSX has become one of the most sought after muscle cars because of its superior blend of styling, performance and very limited production numbers.

RIVIERA GRAN SPORT

A new grille was featured on the 1970 Riviera and exposed headlights were re-introduced. Otherwise there were few changes made to the body of the Riviera, though it did gain 17 pounds. The biggest news for the Riviera was the introduction of the potent 455 cid V-8 engine into its full-sized body. The engine added considerable pep to the Riviera. *Mechanix Illustrated* clocked its top speed at over 125 mph and its 0 to 60 time at 7.9 seconds. This year the Gran Sport option consisted of a heavy-duty suspension, positive traction differential, H78 x 15 fiberglass belted white sidewall tires and the GS monogram on the front

fenders and instrument panel. Despite the increase in the performance of the Riviera, production was down by approximately 30% to 37,336.

VIN NUMBERS

Vehicle Identification Number: 4( )( )( )( )0( )100001
Explanation:
First five digits: Same as model number
First digit: GM line number: 4 = Buick
Second digit: Series number: 9 = Riviera
Second digit: Series number: 6 = GS 455
Second digit: Series number: 3 = Special
Third digit: Model/engine number:
  GS = 4
  GS 455 = 6
  Riviera = 4
Fourth & fifth digit: Body type number:
  Convertible = 67
  2-dr Sports Coupe (Riviera) = 87
  2-dr Sports Coupe (GS) = 37
Sixth digit: Last digit of model year = 0
Seventh symbol: Letter indicating assembly plant
Eighth to thirteenth digit:
Sequential production number

PRODUCTION TOTALS

Model	Total Units	Percent
GS	9,948	
GS 455	10,148	
GSX	678	
Riviera	37,336	
Gran Sport opt.	NA	

Stage I ornamentation could be found on the radiator grille, front fender, rear deck lid and on the door trim panel.

The GSX was Buick's meanest looking offering yet. It included a hood-mounted tachometer and two rear-view sports mirrors.

DRIVETRAIN DATA

	GS	GSX GS 455	GSX GS 455 Stage I
	(Std.)	(Std.)	(Opt.)
Cyl:	V-8	V-8	V-8
Bore (in):	3.80	4.31	4.31
Stroke (in):	3.85	3.9	3.9
CID:	350	455	455
Carbs.:	1 4-bbl	1 4-bbl	1 4-bbl
Make:	Rochester	Rochester	Rochester
Model:	4MV	4MV	4MV
Comp.:	10.25	10.0	10.5
Max. BHP:	315	350	360
@ RPM:	4800	4600	4600
Torque ft-lb:	410	510	510
@ RPM:	3200	2800	2800

	Riviera Gran Sport
	(Std.)
Cyl:	V-8
Bore (in):	4.31
Stroke (in):	3.9
CID:	455
Carbs.:	1 4-bbl
Make:	Rochester
Model:	4MV
Comp.:	10.0
Max. BHP:	370
@ RPM:	4600
Torque ft-lb:	510
@ RPM:	2800

TRANSMISSIONS

GS
Std: 3-speed Column-Mounted Manual
Opt: 3-speed Turbo Hydra-matic Column or Console-Mounted Automatic, 3-speed Floor-Mounted Manual (bucket seats required), 4-speed Floor-Mounted Manual

GS 455
Std: 3-speed Column-Mounted Manual
Opt: 3-speed Column-Mounted Turbo Hydra-matic Automatic (Console-Mounted with bucket seat option), 4-speed Consolette or Floor-Mounted Manual

GSX
Std: 4-speed Floor-Mounted Manual
Opt: 3-speed Turbo Hydra-matic Automatic

Riviera Gran Sport
Std: 3-speed Turbo Hydra-matic Column-Mounted Automatic
Opt: NA

REAR AXLE RATIOS

GS:
Std: 3.23
Opt: 3.42

GS 455, GSX:
Std: 3.42 (man), 2.93 (auto)
Opt: 3.64, 3.42

GS 455 and GSX Stage I:
Std: 3.64
Opt: NA

(con't. next page)

A 4-speed manual transmission, synchronized in all forward speeds was standard on the limited-edition GSX.

The new-for-'70 GSX was available only in Yellow and White.

REAR AXLE RATIOS *(con't.)*
Riviera Gran Sport:
Std: 3.42
Opt: NA

EXTERIOR DATA
GS:

	Coupe
Length (in):	202.2
Width (in):	77.3
Height (in):	53
Wheelbase (in):	112
Weight (lb):	3434

GS 455, GSX:

	Sports Coupe	Convertible
Length (in):	202.2	202.2
Width (in):	77.3	77.3
Height (in):	53	53.3
Wheelbase (in):	112	112
Weight (lb):	3562	3619

Riviera Gran Sport:

	Sports Coupe
Length (in):	216
Width (in):	80
Height (in):	53.2
Wheelbase (in):	119
Weight (lb):	4216

FACTORY BASE PRICE DATA

Model	Sports Coupe	Convertible
GS	$ 3098	$ —
GS 455	3283	3469
GSX	4479	4665
Riviera Gran Sport	4986	—

Buick's ram air system wasn't as flashy as some of the others, but subtlety was as much a part of the GS character as its incredible performance. Courtesy Musclecar Review Magazine.

POPULAR FACTORY OPTIONS

Interior: AM radio; AM/FM radio; Stereo tape player; Tilt steering wheel; Strato bench seats (Riviera); Console with shifter (Riviera); Consoles (bucket seats on GS, GS 455); Rearview mirror map light; Rim-mounted horn control; Four-way or Six-way power seat control.

Exterior: Vinyl top covering; Five-spoke chromed wheels; Cornering lights (full-size); Soft-ray tinted glass; Remote control outside rear view mirror.

Miscellaneous: Air conditioning; Power steering; Power brakes; Power windows; Automatic Climate Control (full-size); Automatic level control; Electric door locks; Tow Master trailering package; Electric trunk release.

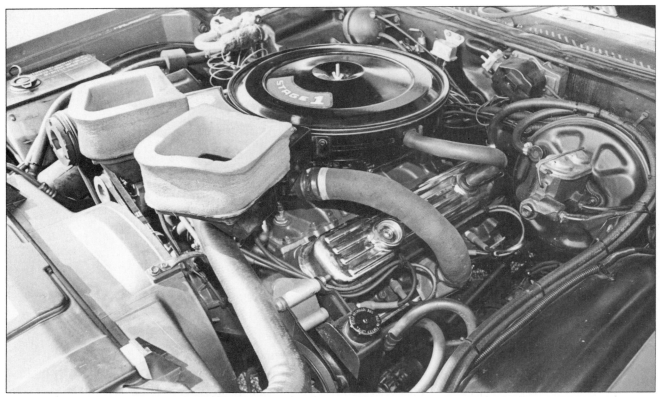

Under the GS 455's hood — one of GM's strongest muscle cars — the air cleaner was about the only visible clue to the power within. For its conventional engineering, its output was phenomenal. Just ask the man who raced one. Courtesy Musclecar Review Magazine.

The GS interior was attractive and well-laid out. The aluminum-spoked steering wheel helped foster a performance image. Shifter was either a column-mounted stalk, manual on the floor or console-mounted "upside down U" for automatics. Courtesy Musclecar Review Magazine.

The Gran Sport Buicks were simply called GSs in 1970. The 455 option could be distinguished from the other GSs by the addition of the number "455" under the GS monogram on the door side panel and the front grille.

1971 Buick

1971 saw the decline of the muscle in the Gran Sport. Due to federal government emissions regulations, horsepower was lowered in both the 350 cid and the 455 cid engine as were the compression ratios, allowing Buicks to run on low or no-lead fuel. Exhaust valves were nickel-plated for greater durability using unleaded gasoline. Though production of Buicks was up in 1971, production of GS's dropped to a total of 9,170. The GSX became an appearance option only. The GS 455 and its Stage I option became options for the GS, no longer separate models. *MaxTrac*, a device designed to enhance performance on slippery surfaces, was added to the list of options for various Buicks. The Riviera received one of its most controversial styling changes that year — a rear end that swept down to a point, dubbed a *boattail*. This feature had not been seen on a car produced by a major manufacturer since the thirties and there were those who felt that it shouldn't have been seen again.

GS

The GS 455 and the GS were combined and became just the GS. The same engines were available, but the 350 cid V-8's horsepower was lowered to 260 hp. The 455 was available as an optional engine and could be had with a Stage I upgrade. But the horsepower of these engines was also lowered to 315 and 345 hp respectively. The GSX appearance package was still available. It consisted of special hood paint, accent striping and GSX emblems. Production of the GS nose-dived 55% in 1971 both because of lower horsepower and because of the general waning interest in muscle cars. The GS still had its muscular appearance, with blacked-out grilles and bright trim and wheelhouse mouldings. Dual functional hood scoops remained on the deck lid. The *World Car Catalog* rated the 260 hp engine's top speed at 110 mph, down 7 mph from the previous year.

RIVIERA GRAN SPORT

In 1971, the Riviera received a new longer body with a controversial new boattail. Its overall length was stretched to 218 inches and it rode on a new chassis with a 122-inch wheelbase. It's new design and lowered engine output did not help its sales — production of the Riviera dropped to its lowest in any model year to date. Only 33,810 cars were produced, dropping it to the fourth most popular Buick. The 455 cid engine, modified to meet federal emissions standards, lost 40 hp from the previous year, falling to 330 in the Gran Sport. The compression ratio was also reduced to a mild 8.5:1. The Gran Sport option consisted of a chrome air cleaner top linked to a specially calibrated Turbo Hydra-matic transmission, heavy-duty suspension, Posi-Traction differential, H78 x 15 bias-belted whitewall tires and the Riviera GS monogram on the front fenders and the instrument panel. *Mechanix Illustrated* clocked the Riviera's 0 to 60 time at 8.1 seconds and its maximum speed at 120 mph — a definite drop in performance.

VIN NUMBERS
Vehicle Identification Number: 4( )( )( )( )1( )100001
Explanation:
First five digits: Same as model number
First digit: GM line number: 4 = Buick
Second digit: Series number: 9 = Riviera
Second digit: Series number: 3 = Special
Third digit: Model/engine number:
  GS = 4
  Riviera = 4
Fourth & fifth digit: Body type number:
  Convertible = 67
  2-dr Sports Coupe (Riviera) = 87
  2-dr Sports Coupe (GS) = 37
Sixth digit: Last digit of model year = 1
Seventh symbol: Letter indicating assembly plant
Eighth to thirteenth digit:
Sequential production number

PRODUCTION TOTALS

Model	Total Units	Percent
GS	9,170	
Riviera	33,810	
Gran Sport opt.	NA	

DRIVETRAIN DATA

	GS (Std.)	GS (Opt.)	Stage I (Opt.)
Cyl:	V-8	V-8	V-8
Bore (in):	3.80	3.80	4.31
Stroke (in):	3.85	3.85	3.9
CID:	350	455	455
Carbs.:	1 4-bbl	1 4-bbl	1 4-bbl
Make:	Rochester	Rochester	Rochester
Model:	4MV	4MV	4MV
Comp.:	8.5	8.5	8.5
Max. BHP:	260	315	345
@ RPM:	4600	4400	5000
Torque ft-lb:	360	450	460
@ RPM:	3000	2800	3000

	Riviera Gran Sport (Std.)
Cyl:	V-8
Bore (in):	4.31
Stroke (in):	3.9
CID:	455
Carbs.:	1 4-bbl
Make:	Rochester
Model:	4MV
Comp.:	8.5
Max. BHP:	330
@ RPM:	4600
Torque ft-lb:	455
@ RPM:	2800

TRANSMISSIONS
GS
Std: 3-speed Column-Mounted Manual
Opt: 3-speed Turbo Hydra-matic Column or Console-Mounted Automatic (bucket seat option required for Console-Mounted), 4-speed Floor-Mounted Manual

Riviera Gran Sport
Std: 3-speed Turbo Hydra-matic Column-Mounted Automatic
Opt: NA

Due to stricter emission regulations, horsepower was reduced on the GS. This GS with a 455 was now rated at 315 hp.

REAR AXLE RATIOS
GS:
Std: 3.08
Opt: NA

GS (455 cid, 315 hp):
Std: 3.08 (man), 3.42 (auto)
Opt: 3.42

GS Stage I:
Std: 3.42
Opt: NA

Riviera Gran Sport:
Std: 2.93
Opt: NA

EXTERIOR DATA
GS

	sports coupe	convertible
Length (in):	203.2	203.2
Width (in):	77.3	77.3
Height (in):	53.5	53.9
Wheelbase (in):	112	112
Weight (lb):	3461	3497

Riviera Gran Sport:

	sports coupe
Length (in):	217.4
Width (in):	89.9
Height (in):	54

Wheelbase (in):   122
Weight (lb):   4325

FACTORY BASE PRICE DATA

Model	Sports Coupe	Convertible
GS*	$ 3666	$ 3857
Riviera Gran Sport	5453	—

*Prices are for the 350 cid GS

POPULAR FACTORY OPTIONS
Interior: Tilt steering wheel; Strato bucket seats; AM radio; AM/FM radio; AM/FM stereo; Console (with bucket seats); Six-way power seats; Sport mirrors (GS); Instrument panel gauges (GS); Hood-mounted tachometer (GS); Custom interior trim (Riviera); Special sport steering wheel; Rallye steering wheel (GS).

Exterior: Vinyl top; Chrome five-spoke wheels; Cornering lights; Bumper guards (except Riviera); Protective body side moldings (except Riviera); GSX equipment for GS including: body side stripes, black hood panels, GSX grille emblem, body color headlamp bezels, black rocker moldings and rear spoiler; Front Spoiler (GS); Remote outside rear view mirror.

Miscellaneous: Air conditioning; Power windows; Speed alert control; Automatic Climate Control; Rear window defogger; Electric trunk release; Power door locks; Child safety seat; Intermittent wipers; Auto level control.

Dual exhausts, functional air scoops, a Full-Flow oil filter and a semi-closed cooling system helped the GS maintain its muscle.

The 1972 Buick GS was the last to be based on the Skylark. For 1973, the GS was based on the Century. Courtesy Musclecar Review Magazine.

1972 Buick

Strict government regulations were having their effect on the car industry. In 1972, Buick, at a new-car-introduction, showed two shiny new Buicks with their front fenders caved in. This was to demonstrate that Buick had met federal crash barrier standards before the 1973 deadline. The auto writers were duly impressed at Buick's safety features. More stringent emissions standards, however, had a negative impact on Buick's high performance cars. Engineers were under the onus of designing engines that met the strict standards without losing too much performance; but this was a losing battle — horsepower was down for all of Buick's high performance engines and consequently GS sales suffered with only 8,575 cars produced that year. As a result, Buick decided that 1972 would be the last year the Gran Sport, based on the Skylark, would be offered. The Buick Rivera's popularity also declined in 1972, only 33,810 were produced that year, the fewest built in any model year to date. A sizeable price increase and the unpopular boattail design probably accounted for this

decline. Federal emission standards also lowered the Rivera's performance.

GS

There were few styling changes on the 1972 GS. The GS Sport Coupe and convertible continued to be offered. Again, the standard engine was the 350 cid and the optional engine was the 455 cid, with or without the Stage I option. But this year, strict government regulations continued to take their toll on the GS's performance. Horsepower was down to 195 hp on the 350, 225 hp on the 455, and 270 hp on the Stage I engine. *Mechanix Illustrated* recorded the standard GS's 0 to 60 time at 9.9 seconds and its top speed at 105 plus; the muscle car of a few years ago clearly was losing its muscle. Nevertheless, the Gran Sport series ended its production in 1972 with over 105,000 of these magnificent cars built in its eight year run.

RIVIERA GRAN SPORT

The Riviera's performance also suffered under the tighter emissions control regulations. The Riviera's horsepower was reduced to 250 hp, though the Gran Sport option, with its dual exhausts, did increase the engine's output to 260 hp. Top speed for the Riviera Gran Sport was rated at 112 mph by *World Cars* (formerly *World Car Catalog*). In 1972 the Gran Sport option included the dual exhausts, mentioned previously, Posi-Traction differential, an engine tuned instrument panel insert and GS monograms on the front fenders and instrument panel. Only 1% of all the Rivieras produced in 1971 were without air conditioniong, yet air conditioning was still considered an option. The Riviera's price was reduced by about $100 in order to promote sales. This strategy had some effect—Riviera's sales stopped their downward slide, and remained at about the same level as the previous year.

VIN NUMBERS

Vehicle Identification Number: 4( )( )( )( )2( )100001
Explanation:
First five digits: Same as model number
First digit: GM line number: 4 = Buick

Second digit: Series number: 9 = Riviera
Second digit: Series number: 3 = Special
Third digit: Model/engine number:
  GS = 4
  Riviera = 4
Fourth & fifth digit: Body type number:
  Convertible = 67
  2-dr Sports Coupe (Riviera) = 87
  2-dr Sports Coupe (GS) = 37
Sixth digit: Last digit of model year = 2
Seventh symbol: Letter indicating assembly plant
Eighth to thirteenth digit:
Sequential production number

PRODUCTION TOTALS

Model	Total Units	Percent
GS	8,575	
Riviera	33,728	
Gran Sport opt.	NA	

In addition to the convertible, a Sun Coupe option was offered on the Skylark line. Built by the American Sunroof Company, the sliding fabric top was operated by a crank in the middle of the top. Today, the Sun Coupe Buicks are seldom seen and considered quite valuable. Courtesy Musclecar Review Magazine.

DRIVETRAIN DATA

	GS (Std.)	GS (Opt.)	Stage I (Opt.)
Cyl:	V-8	V-8	V-8
Bore (in):	3.80	4.31	4.31
Stroke (in):	3.85	3.9	3.9
CID:	350	455	455
Carbs.:	1 4-bbl	1 4-bbl	1 4-bbl
Make:	Rochester	Rochester	Rochester
Model:	4MV	4MV	4MV
Comp.:	8.5	8.5	8.5
Max. BHP:	195	225	270
@ RPM:	4000	4000	4400
Torque ft-lb:	290	360	390
@ RPM:	2800	2600	3000

	Riviera Gran Sport (Std.)
Cyl:	V-8
Bore (in):	4.31
Stroke (in):	3.9
CID:	455
Carbs.:	1 4-bbl
Make:	Rochester
Model:	4MV
Comp.:	8.5
Max. BHP:	260
@ RPM:	4400
Torque ft-lb:	380
@ RPM:	2800

TRANSMISSIONS
GS
Std: 3-speed Column-Mounted Manual
Opt: 3-speed Turbo Hydra-matic Column or Console-Mounted Automatic (bucket seat option required for Console-Mounted), 4-speed Floor-Mounted Manual

Riviera Gran Sport
Std: 3-speed Turbo Hydra-matic Column-Mounted Automatic
Opt: NA

REAR AXLE RATIOS
GS:
Std: 3.08
Opt: NA

GS (455 cid, 315 hp):
Std: 3.08 (man), 3.42 (auto)
Opt: 3.42

GS Stage I:
Std: 3.42
Opt: NA

Riviera Gran Sport:
Std: 2.93
Opt: NA

EXTERIOR DATA
GS

	sports coupe	convertible
Length (in):	203.2	203.3
Width (in):	76.8	76.8
Height (in):	53.5	53.8
Wheelbase (in):	112	112
Weight (lb):	3471	3525

Riviera Gran Sport:

	sports coupe
Length (in):	217.3
Width (in):	79.5
Height (in):	54
Wheelbase (in):	122
Weight (lb):	4343

The interior on the '72 was virtually unchanged from the earlier models — same great bucket seat comfort with plenty of additional goodies on the option list. Courtesy Musclecar Review Magazine.

The mighty Stage 1 was still on the option list, though horsepower for the big 455 was listed as 270 @ 4400 rpm SAE net. The ram air system was still standard on Stage 1s, though the driver's side breather intake was smaller than the passenger's side. This is a 1972 engine with a '70-'71 breather. Courtesy Musclecar Review Magazine.

FACTORY BASE PRICE DATA

Model	Sports Coupe	Convertible
GS*	$ 3225	$ 3525
Riviera Gran Sport	5349	—

*Prices are for the 350 cid GS

POPULAR FACTORY OPTIONS

Interior: AM radio; AM/FM radio; AM/FM radio with stereo and tape player; Center console (in Riviera, bucket seats required); Child safety seat; Custom seat and shoulder belts; Mirror map light; Electric clock; Tilt steering wheel (standard on Riviera).

Exterior: Front light monitors; Remote control outside rear view mirror (standard in Riviera); Soft-ray tinted glass; Cornering lights; Five-spoke chrome sport wheels.

Miscellaneous: Protective impact strips; Steel panel sun roof, electrically operated (only on Riviera); Climate control; Automatic climate control; Power windows; Electric trunk release; Rear window defroster; Power tailgate window; Speed alert; Trailer towing packages; Automatic level control.

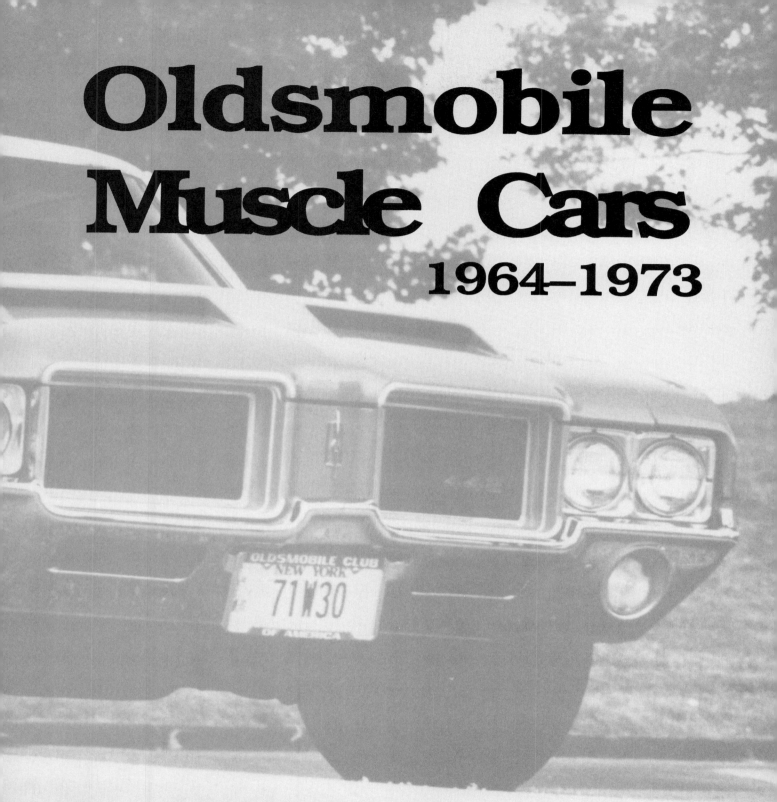

Oldsmobile
Muscle Cars
1964–1973

Oldsmobile in the Muscle Car Era

It is difficult for anyone living today to realize that there was a time when Oldsmobile was not a significant presence in the auto industry. In the early years of this Century, though, Oldsmobile's fame far out-ran its impact. Despite its claims to being America's oldest existing car maker (dating back to 1897), despite Ransom E. Olds' celebrated curved dash runabout of 1901 (America's first mass-produced automobile), and despite being glorified in one of the hit songs of the period ("Come Ride With Me Lucille In My Merry Oldsmobile" — a song that was still a standard in the post-World War II era), Oldsmobile never actually managed to sell large numbers of cars until the 1930s. Its sales appeal began to soar in 1934 when GM management repositioned it from the upper end of the market down to a more affordable slot just above Pontiac.

Oldsmobile's reputation was really built, however, in the 1930s and 1940s by a series of engineering triumphs that earned the division a name for being the "engineering" division of GM, i.e., the one to try important developments first. During 1929-30 with its short-lived Viking line, Olds was the first automaker to successfully cast a V-8 engine in one unit. Before that, V-8 engines were commonly cast in as many as nine pieces, rendering them enormously expensive to produce. If the Viking V-8 was not ultimately successful as either an engine or a car line, it represented genuine breakthrough technology. In 1937, Olds offered GM's first semi-automatic transmission and, in 1940, the industry's first true automatic: Hydramatic. Throughout the 1930s and 1940s,

Oldsmobiles were powered by six- and eight-cylinder L-head engines dating from 1928. In 1949, Olds shared with Cadillac the honor of building the industry's first lightweight, high-compression V-8: the famous Rocket engine. This engine was to transform Olds power-plant engineering from uninspired to state-of-the-art virtually overnight. So successful was the Rocket engine, that it formed the basis for all Olds-built V-8s from that point until the division stopped building V-8s in the 1980s. (It even formed the basis of the notorious Olds diesel — but the less said about that the better!) Olds also pioneered the two-door hardtop body style in the middle of 1949 with its first Holiday model on the big 98 platform. The Holiday name was used for years thereafter on all Oldsmobile hardtops.

Olds can also claim some credit for devising the muscle car concept, at least in embryonic form. When the new Rocket V-8 was installed in Oldsmobile's small A-body car — the body it shared at the low-end of its price spectrum with Chevrolet and Pontiac — to create the Olds 88 series in 1950, history was made. The Olds 88 and Super 88 quickly earned a reputation or being the hottest cars on the market in their time. Nothing could touch them at the price — certainly not the stovebolt-six Chevys and straight-eight Pontiacs — and Olds began to clean up on the stock car circuit. In fact, the Olds 88's only serious racing competition in the early 1950s was the Hudson Hornet. When Hudson folded as an independent automaker in 1954, Olds was the car to beat on the racing circuit once again. As late as 1959, Lee Petty won the Daytona 500 in an Olds. Furthermore, at least one interesting racing development at Olds made it to the nation's showrooms. This was the tri-carb J-2 engine option of 1957, which lasted into the 1958 model run.

That Olds was an engineer's company in the 1950s and 1960s is clearly indicated by the personnel in charge. Jack F. "Smilin' Jack" Wolfram served as chief engineer from 1944-51, the years during which the Rocket V-8 was developed. From 1951 until forced to retire due to ill health in 1964, he was general manager. Harold N. Metzel, who had served under Wolfram as chief engineer from 1951, was named to succeed him again in 1964. Metzel, in turn, was succeeded as general manager in 1969 by John B. Beltz, who had followed him into the chief engineering slot in 1964. In the light of the quality of its leadership, it is not surprising that Oldsmobile produced a string of solidly engineered cars throughout the 1950s and into the 1960s.

Olds did not, however, choose to parlay its racing successes of the early 1950s into a status as the high performance division at GM. Why it did not is something of a mystery, although GM's recurring discouragement of factory racing participation during this period peaking with the infamous AMA (Automobile Manufacturer's Association) racing ban of 1957 may have been a factor. (The ban didn't seem to stop Chevrolet and Pontiac, though, who carried on clandestine racing activities unbeknownst to GM executives.)

A more significant contributing factor, however, was Oldsmobile's general trend toward building cars at the top end of the medium-priced field. This trend could be looked upon as going back to its roots, in a sense. By 1965, Olds was offering some remarkably luxurious cars in the 98 series, featuring real wood trim, folding tray tables for back seat passengers, and other amenities that were seldom seen on recent American cars at any price.

Olds had not forgotten its sporting heritage entirely, though. There were attempts along the way to build "sporty" cars, usually of a luxurious nature. These included the semi-custom Fiesta convertible of 1953 and the limited-production Starfire series beginning in 1961. In 1962 and 1963, Olds offered a limited edition coupe on the compact F-85 platform that featured America's first modern, turbocharged engine (yet another derivative of the ever versatile Rocket V-8).

The *Jetfire*, as it was designated, set few sales charts on fire and was not a notable success, at least not in the marketing sense. The Jetfire was, however, yet another indication that advanced engineering was alive and well (although somewhat subdued) in Lansing.

As is noted in the Pontiac section of this book, Olds can even claim indirect credit for the car that started the muscle car revolution in the 1960s: the Pontiac GTO. According to the GM system at that time, certain engines were considered "small car" engines, while other engines were considered "big car" engines.

The new Olds 330 cubic-inch V-8 (yes, a derivative of the 1949 Rocket V-8) was supposed to be a small car powerplant. Oldsmobile's decision to offer it in the 1964 full-size Jetstar was one of the factors that got Pontiac engineers thinking seriously about mixing engines and platforms. The result was a decision to put Pontiac's "big car" 389 V-8 in the 1964 "small car" LeMans—the GTO. But, what goes around, comes around.

The sudden success of the Pontiac GTO clearly made an impact on the folks at Olds, because the mid-year Olds 4-4-2 was the first response from any sister GM division to the unexpected Pontiac challenge. The 4-4-2 designation signified: four-speed transmission, four-barrel carburetion and dual exhausts. Subsequently, an automatic was offered and differed carb set-ups were used, but the name remained unchanged.

The man behind the 4-4-2, if a single individual can be credited, was John Beltz. Beltz was not only chief engineer during the heyday of the 4-4-2, he was widely credited with being the main impetus behind the program (although general manager and former chief engineer Metzel cannot have raised too many objections). Dennis Casteele, who has written authoritatively about Oldsmobiles over the years and was a practicing automotive journalist in the early 1970s, recalls:

"John Beltz was an [auto] writer's dream come true. Here was a guy who knew cars inside and out and absolutely loved to talk about them. I remember one afternoon conversation with him that covered everything from curved dash Oldsmobiles to Ferraris. By 1969, Beltz had gone the traditional Olds management route from chief engineer to general manager. He most certainly was on a rather rapid path which would have led to the GM hierarchy as either president or board chairman. In 1972, I joined the Oldsmobile public relations staff and my lone regret was that earlier that year John Beltz had died."

Other key figures in the history of the 4-4-2 include Robert Dorshimer, who followed Beltz as chief engineer in 1969, and Dale "General Dale" Smith, who guided Olds' racing and high performance efforts within the engineering staff. Key designers in the 1960s who guided 4-4-2 styling included Stanley Wilen, head of the Olds Studio at GM Design, and David North.

Of major interest, as well, is the part played by George Hurst. Hurst, famed for the precision shifter mechanisms that bore his name, was a central figure in the muscle car era. Hardly a single machine worth remembering from any manufacturer failed to use his shifters. The first of what was to be a series of Hurst/Olds conversions was done by Hurst for his own use in 1968. It soon became a limited edition model marketed by Olds through Olds dealers. The color scheme was Peruvian silver and black. Power was produced by a special 390 hp, 455 cubic-inch Rocket V-8 that was fitted with, among other things, special heads and crankshaft, a high-overlap camshaft, and a performance modified Turbo Hydra-matic with a Hurst Dual-Gate shifter. Not your usual 4-4-2!

For 1969, a gold-and-white edition was offered. None were listed for 1970 or 1971, but, for 1972, a gold-and-white Hurst/Olds was the official pace car for the Indianapolis 500 and similar cars could be bought through your friendly neighborhood Olds dealer. The engine was still a 455, but emission and fuel standards had reduced performance by an alarming degree.

Hurst/Olds models of similar description were built and sold through Olds dealers in 1973, 1974, 1975, 1979, 1983 and 1984. The later models were cosmetically handsome and fairly decent performance cars for their day, but nothing like the fire-breathing H/Os — or, even the standard 4-4-2s — built during the height of the muscle car era.

The 4-4-2 was the longest-lived GM muscle car. Perhaps most important, the Olds-built 4-4-2 muscle cars from 1964 to 1970 were considered by most observers at the time to be the most refined such vehicles to come from any GM division, perhaps from any manufacturer. They weren't necessarily the fastest in straight-line acceleration (usually the rather simplistic yardstick used to compare muscle cars), but they were generally the most satisfying overall.

Introduced in mid-1964 as a response to the popular GTO, the 4-4-2 option was a tough street performer that offered as much balanced performance as could be obtained from any showroom stock car of the era.

1964 Oldsmobile

Sales of Oldsmobiles continued to climb. Over 548,915 cars were sold in 1964, making Oldsmobile sixth in the automobile sales race. In former years the traditional full-size models dominated Oldsmobile production; but now mid-size models, such as the F-85, were making a definite impact on the Olds' market. In fact over 165,000 F-85's were sold in the 1964 model year. Then, in the latter part of the 1964 model year, Oldsmobile introduced the 4-4-2 option, which was to be Oldsmobile's most enduring and popular performance package.

F-85 4-4-2

In late-1964 Oldsmobile quietly introduced the 4-4-2 option for the F-85/Cutlass. In fact its introduction was so quiet that only a single dealer sheet and lone factory photo accompanied its debut. The 4-4-2 was basically a performance package largely put together from the list of various options already available to police departments. In the rare

factory literature, Olds called the 4-4-2 option "A hot new number...Police needed it — Olds Built it — Pursuit proved it." The 4-4-2 got its name from the 4-barrel carburetor, 4-speed manual transmission and 2 (dual) exhausts that were at the heart of the option. Also included in the 4-4-2 package were heavy-duty shocks, springs and rear stabilizer bar, a dual-snorkel air cleaner and premium quality rod and main bearings. The car was powered by a 330 cid, 310 hp Rocket V-8. The 4-4-2 option was available on all the F-85/Cutlass V-8 models except for the station wagon. Because of its late introduction and lack of promotion, only 2,999 4-4-2's were produced in 1964. But, despite these inauspicious beginnings, the 4-4-2 would become one of the most popular muscle cars of the supercar era.

VIN NUMBERS

Vehicle Identification Number: 8( )4( )001001 and up
Explanation:
First digit: Number of cylinders = 8
Second digit: Series number: 0 = Standard
Second digit: Series number: 1 = Deluxe
Second digit: Series number: 2 = Cutlass

(con't. next page)

The Sports Coupe, one of nine F-85 models offered in 1964, featured new styling for a clean, sharp image.

With new advances in performance, the F-85 had come a long way since the little aluminum-engined unit first hit the scene.

VIN NUMBERS *(con't.)*

Third digit: Last digit of model year = 4
Last six digits: Sequential production number
Body Code Numbers:
F-85 Cutlass Holiday Coupe = 3237
F-85 Cutlass Sports Coupe = 3227
F-85 Cutlass convertible = 3267
F-85 Deluxe sedan = 3169
F-85 Standard Club Coupe = 3027
F-85 Standard sedan = 3069

PRODUCTION TOTALS

Model	Total Units	Percent
F-85	120,211	
4-4-2 opt.	2,999	2

DRIVETRAIN DATA

	4-4-2 (Std.)
Cyl:	V-8
Bore (in):	3.94
Stroke (in):	3.39
CID:	330
Carbs.:	1 4-bbl
Make:	Rochester
Model:	4GC
Comp.:	10.25
Max. BHP:	310
@ RPM:	5200
Torque ft-lb:	355
@ RPM:	3600

TRANSMISSIONS
4-4-2
Std: 4-speed Floor-Mounted Manual
Opt: None

REAR AXLE RATIOS
4-4-2
Std: 3.23
Opt: 2.78, 3.23, 3.08

EXTERIOR DATA
4-4-2

	Cutlass coupe	Cutlass hardtop	Cutlass convertible
Length (in):	203	203	203
Width (in):	73.8	73.8	73.8
Height (in):	54	54	54
Wheelbase (in):	115	115	115
Weight (lb):	3141	3180	3263

	Deluxe sedan	Standard coupe	Standard sedan
Length (in):	203	203	203
Width (in):	73.8	73.8	73.8
Height (in):	54	54	54
Wheelbase (in):	115	115	115
Weight (lb):	3140	3068	3096

The F-85 Cutlass Hardtop Coupe was powered by a 330 cid, ultra-high compression version of the Jetfire Rocket engine, which delivered an impressive 290 horsepower.

FACTORY BASE PRICE DATA

Model	Coupe	Sedan	Hardtop	Convertible
4-4-2 Cutlass	$ 2769	$ —	$ 2909	$ 3109
4-4-2 Deluxe	—	2702	—	—
4-4-2 Standard	2540	2594	—	—

POPULAR FACTORY OPTIONS

Interior: Clock, $16; Console; Padded instrument panel; Backup lights; Glareproof mirror; Bench power seat; Left bucket power seat; AM/FM radio, $150; Pushbutton radio, $66; Bi-Phonic radio speaker system; Front seat belts; Front and rear seat belts; Deluxe steering wheel; Custom steering wheel; Tilt steering wheel, $44.

Exterior: Tinted glass, $43; Tinted windshield glass only; Outside mirror, $4; Outside remote control mirror; Wheel discs; DeLuxe wheel discs; Simulated wire wheels; Windshield washer and two-speed wipers; Power antenna, $26.

Miscellaneous: Air conditioning, $351; Cruise control, $91; Anti-spin differential; Power brakes, $42; Power steering, $97; Power windows; Superlift rear shock absorbers; Rear window defroster, $21; Remote trunk lid release, $10.

The first 4-4-2 was cleanly styled. Though Oldsmobile did not aggressively promote the 4-4-2 in '64, high-performance cars would figure heavily in sales as the decade worn on. Wire wheel covers were optional. Courtesy Musclecar Review Magazine

New for 1965, the high performance 4-4-2 Cutlass convertible featured a 400 cubic-inch engine with a 4-barrel carburetor and 2 exhausts. Only 3,468 such convertibles were built.

1965 Oldsmobile

In 1965 Oldsmobile maintained its sixth place in automobile sales, producing 591,701 cars. The F-85 continued to keep its important position in Olds' total sales. 1965 also brought more advertising for the 4-4-2 option. No longer was it an unknown to all but a few car enthusiasts; this year it was advertised with the same vigor as were the other Oldsmobile models.

F-85 4-4-2

The 4-4-2 was enthusiastically promoted in 1965; sales correspondingly rose to 25,003. Furthermore the 4-4-2 option was greatly enhanced. The engine now displaced 400 cubic inches; its horsepower output rose to 345 hp and its torque was increased to 440 ft-lbs. Although the name remained the same, the designation of the numbers, "4-4-2" changed. The first "4" of 4-4-2 now referred to the 400 cid engine rather than the 4-barrel carburetor. The second "4" referred to the 4-barrel carburetor. The "2" still referred

to the dual exhausts. The 4-4-2's special heavy-duty equipment included front and rear shock absorbers, front and rear springs, radiator, propeller shaft, front engine mountings, clutch with synchromesh transmission, battery, front and rear stabilizer bar and fat tires. In 1965 the 4-4-2 option was no longer available on four-door sedans, but it could be ordered on the F-85 Club Coupe, Cutlass Sport Coupe, Cutlass Holiday Coupe or the Cutlass Convertible. The 4-4-2 was easily identifiable. Its emblem could be found on the front, the rear and the sculptured side panels, and a special grille further distinguished it. The 4-4-2 was widely acclaimed. *Hot Rod* concluded that "Emphatically, the 4-4-2 remained one of the most likeable machines we have ever had the pleasure to drive." *Motor Trend* said the 4-4-2 proved "that Detroit can build cars that perform, handle and stop, without sacrificing road comfort."

VIN NUMBERS

Vehicle Identification Number: 3(   )5( )100001 and up
Explanation:
First digit: GM line number: 3 = Oldsmobile
Second to fifth digit: Body number:

This F-85 Deluxe 4-door sedan featured a Jetfire Rocket V-8 engine and 4-speed synchromesh transmission.

With dual exhausts ready to blow away the competition, the stylish 4-4-2 Cutlass convertible was priced at $3,139.

F-85 Cutlass Sports Coupe = 3827
F-85 Cutlass Holiday Coupe = 3837
F-85 Cutlass Convertible = 3867
F-85 Standard Club Coupe = 3427
Sixth digit: Last digit of model year = 5
Seventh digit: Letter indicating assembly plant
Last six digits: Sequential production number

PRODUCTION TOTALS

Model	Total Units	Percent
F-85	162,407	
4-4-2 opt.	25,003	15

DRIVETRAIN DATA

	4-4-2
	(Std.)
Cyl:	V-8
Bore (in):	4
Stroke (in):	3.98
CID:	400
Carbs.:	1 4-bbl
Make:	Rochester
Model:	4GC
Comp.:	10.25
Max. BHP:	345
@ RPM:	4800
Torque ft-lb:	440
@ RPM:	3200

TRANSMISSIONS
4-4-2
Std: 3-speed Column-Mounted Manual
Opt: 4-speed Floor-Mounted Manual, 2-Speed Jetaway Column-Mounted Automatic

REAR AXLE RATIOS
4-4-2
Std: 3.23 (man), 3.08 (auto)
Opt: 3.08, 3.23 (auto), 3.55, 2.78, 3.90

EXTERIOR DATA
4-4-2

	Cutlass coupe	Cutlass hardtop	Cutlass convertible
Length (in):	204.3	204.3	204.3
Width (in):	74.4	74.4	74.4
Height (in):	54	54	54
Wheelbase (in):	115	115	115
Weight (lb):	3221	3245	3338

	Standard coupe
Length (in):	204.3
Width (in):	74.4
Height (in):	54
Wheelbase (in):	115
Weight (lb):	3146

FACTORY BASE PRICE DATA

Model	Coupe	Hardtop	Convertible
4-4-2 Cutlass	$ 2799	$ 2940	$ 3139
4-4-2 Standard	2605	—	—

POPULAR FACTORY OPTIONS
Interior: Electric clock, $16; Console; Glareproof mirror; Pushbutton radio, $66; Bi-Phonic radio speakers, $16; Front & rear retractable or non-retractable seat belts; Custom steering wheel; Tilt steering wheel, $43.

(con't. next page)

New interior schemes for the Cutlass convertible included bucket seats, center console, brushed aluminum instrument panel and an optional performance gauge. A Jetaway automatic or four-speed synchromesh transmission were available at an extra cost.

POPULAR FACTORY OPTIONS *(con't.)*

Exterior: Tinted glass, $31; Tinted windshield glass only; Backup lights; Outside mirror, $5; Outside remote control mirror; Wheel discs; DeLuxe wheel discs; Simulated wire wheels; Windshield washer and 2-speed wipers; Rear window defogger, $22.

Miscellaneous: Air conditioning, $351; Cruise control, $91; Anti-spin differential; Pedal-Ease power brakes, $43; Left bucket power seat; Roto-Matic power steering, $97; Power windows; Superlift rear shock absorbers; Three-speed transmission; Automatic transmission; Remote trunk lid release, $11.

Powered by an engine tuned up to 350 horsepower, the Cutlass 4-4-2 featured many performance options for 1966.

1966 Oldsmobile

1966 was an exciting year for Oldsmobile. Over 600,000 cars were produced, thrusting Olds into fourth place in the auto industry. It was also the year that Olds introduced the revolutionary front-wheel-drive Toronado. More than half of Oldsmobile's factory literature was devoted to the Toronado. Though much of the buying public's attention went to this new car, the 4-4-2 maintained its popularity and sales remained healthy, though down slightly from the year before because of greater competition from other muscle cars, such as the hot Pontiac GTO.

F-85 4-4-2

The Oldsmobile 4-4-2 had a new look in 1966. A very pronounced hump came up over the rear wheels. The C-pillars extended rearward like sails while the rear glass was inset. Though stylistically it made for an attractive car, it hindered rear visibility. Inside, the engine had been tuned up; its output was now 350 hp, up 5 from the previous year

and its compression ratio was increased to 10.5:1. Additionally, this year Oldsmobile offered a new performance option for the 4-4-2 package. The L69 option, as it was called, was designed for the real muscle car enthusiast. A three two-barrelled carburetion setup raised the official (and underrated) horsepower of the 4-4-2 by 10 hp to 360 hp. A host of other options were available including five transmissions and eight rear axle ratios. Though the 4-4-2 could hold its own with any of the other muscle cars on a straight run, what really distinguished it from the others and endeared it to its owners was its exceptional handling. And it was no wonder! Included in 4-4-2's handling equipment were stiffer heavy-duty four-coil springs, thicker front and rear sway bars, high performance axle, wide rims and redline nylon cord tires. The 4-4-2 logo was strategically placed on the front grille, the rear end, and the side panels. As interest in the muscle car market became increasingly widespread, Olds broke with tradition and published a separate sales publication entitled "Looking for Action," solely devoted to the 4-4-2. Oldsmobile advertised the 4-4-2 performance option in its factory literature as the "Anti-boredom machine...the sweetest, neatest, completest anti-boredom bundle on rubber!"

In 1966, Olds was on a roll with increased performance throughout the line, as was the case with this F-85 Deluxe four-door sedan powered by a 330 cubic-inch, 320 hp V-8.

The 4-4-2 logo was strategically placed on the deck lid lip, as well as the front grille and the side panels.

VIN NUMBERS

Vehicle Identification Number: 3(　)6(　)100001 and up

Explanation:

First digit: GM line number: 3 = Oldsmobile

Second to fifth digit: Body number:

   F-85 Deluxe Holiday Hardtop = 3617
   F-85 Cutlass Sports Coupe = 3807
   F-85 Cutlass Holiday Coupe = 3817
   F-85 Cutlass Convertible = 3867
   F-85 Standard Club Coupe = 3407

Sixth digit: Last digit of model year = 6

Seventh digit: Letter indicating assembly plant

Last six digits: Sequential production number

PRODUCTION TOTALS

Model	Total Units	Percent
F-85 & Cutlass	97,563	
4-4-2 opt.	21,997	23

DRIVETRAIN DATA

	4-4-2 (Std.)	4-4-2 (Opt.)
Cyl:	V-8	V-8
Bore (in):	4	4
Stroke (in):	3.975	3.975
CID:	400	400
Carbs.:	1 4-bbl	3 2-bbl
Make:	Rochester	Rochester
Model:	4MV	2GC
Comp.:	10.50	10.50
Max. BHP:	350	360
@ RPM:	5000	5000
Torque ft-lb:	440	440
@ RPM:	3600	3600

TRANSMISSIONS

4-4-2

Std: 3-speed Column-Mounted Manual

Opt: 3-speed Floor-Mounted Hurst Manual with Hurst Shifter, 4-speed Hurst Floor-Mounted Manual Close-Ratio with Hurst Shifter, 4-speed Hurst Floor-Mounted Manual Wide-Ratio with Hurst Shifter, 2-Speed Jetaway Column-Mounted Automatic

REAR AXLE RATIOS

4-4-2

Std: 3.23 (3-sp man, auto), 3.55 (4-sp man)
Opt: 3.55 (3-sp man, auto), 3.90 (4-sp man, auto)

EXTERIOR DATA

4-4-2

	Cutlass coupe	Cutlass hardtop	Cutlass convertible
Length (in):	204.2	204.2	204.2
Width (in):	75.4	75.4	75.4
Height (in):	53.6	53.6	53.6
Wheelbase (in):	115	115	115
Weight (lb):	3219	3243	3349

	Deluxe hardtop	Standard coupe
Length (in):	204.2	204.2
Width (in):	75.4	75.4

(con't. next page)

Olds advertising proclaimed, "No look-alike, the swinging new Olds 4-4-2 is a dandy with a demeanor all its own. No go-alike, either...with a 400-cube V-8, 4-barrel carb."

EXTERIOR DATA *(con't.)*

	Deluxe hardtop	Standard coupe
Height (in):	53.6	53.6
Wheelbase (in):	115	115
Weight (lb):	3272	3153

FACTORY BASE PRICE DATA

Model	Coupe	Hardtop	Convertible
4-4-2 Cutlass	$ 2786	$ 2883	$ 3118
4-4-2 Cutlass opt.	2889	3036	3231
4-4-2 Deluxe	—	2769	—
4-4-2 Deluxe opt.	—	2883	—
4-4-2 Standard	2603	—	—
4-4-2 Standard opt.	2868	—	—

POPULAR FACTORY OPTIONS

Interior: Electric clock, $16; Console, $75; Head rests, $31; Glareproof mirror; Left bucket power seat, $70; AM/FM radio, $147; Pushbutton radio, $64; Bi-Phonic radio speaker system, $15; Power windows, $105; Custom steering wheel; Tilt steering wheel, $42; Tachometer, $52.

Exterior: Tinted glass, $30; Tinted windshield glass only, $20; Outside mirror; Outside remote control mirror; Remote trunk lid release, $12; Wheel discs; Deluxe wheel discs; Simulated wire wheels, $69; Windshield washer and 2-speed wipers.

Miscellaneous: Air conditioning, $343; Cruise control, $42; Anti-spin differential, $42; Tri-carb engine, $266; Pedal-Ease power brakes, $41; Roto-Matic power steering, $95; Superlift rear shock absorbers; Four-speed wide-ratio transmission, $184; Jetaway automatic special duty transmission, $153.

Oldsmobile called the 4-4-2 "The road car/rally machine in street clothing!" Painted striping, a louvered hood, twin pipes and red-line tires gave the 4-4-2 its sporty look; the standard 400 cid Rocket V-8 gave this option its go!

1967 Oldsmobile

In 1967, Oldsmobile dropped a couple of slots in the automobile sales race. 551,932 cars were sold, down by almost 50,000 from the year before. But sales of the 4-4-2 improved to nearly 25,000, despite that this performance package was only available on the higher-priced Cutlass Supreme. The 4-4-2 was definately holding its own in the increasingly competitive supercar market. Though other manufacturers were introducing monster engines for their intermediate-sized muscle cars, 4-4-2's design, style and power made it the performance favorite of many supercar enthusiasts.

CUTLASS SUPREME 4-4-2

The 4-4-2 option was only available on the well-trimmed Cutlass Supreme Sports Coupe, Holiday Coupe and convertible. Thus the 4-4-2 owner not only got the performance he expected, but the style and comfort in which to enjoy it. Additionally, the 4-4-2 was trimmed with special

fender paint and a louvered hood for added style. In 1967 Oldsmobile, in an attempt to respond to the special interests of various buyers, offered two options for the 4-4-2. The Turnpike Cruising package, option L66, was designed for those who were not only interested in how fast their car went, but also in how far it went on a tank of gasoline. It was sort of a detuned 4-4-2 engineered for long range cruising, consisting of a 300 hp Rocket 400 cid V-8 with a fuel efficient two-barrel carburetor. The other option offered, which replaced the tri-carb option of the previous year, was known as the "force-air induction system" or W30 option. Built for those interested purely in speed and high performance, it increased the 4-4-2's horsepower by 10 to 360 hp. Included in this package were a special fan shroud, air duct, special camshaft and heavy-duty valve springs as well as chrome valve covers and a chrome air cleaner. To allow room for the air ducts and to offer better weight distribution, the battery was moved to the trunk. *Motor Trend* measured the 4-4-2's 0 to 60 time at 7.1 seconds and *World Car* reported its maximum speed at 122 mph. The Cutlass Supreme 4-4-2 was given increased advertising and promotional support. Oldsmobile called it the "Swashbuckler of the Oldsmobile line."

VIN NUMBERS

Vehicle Identification Number: 3( )7( )100001 and up

Explanation:

First digit: GM line number: 3 = Oldsmobile

Second to fifth digit: Body number:

    F-85 Cutlass Supreme Sports Coupe = 3807

    F-85 Cutlass Supreme Holiday Coupe = 3817

    F-85 Cutlass Supreme Convertible = 3867

Sixth digit: Last digit of model year = 7

Seventh digit: Letter indicating assembly plant

Last six digits: Sequential production number

PRODUCTION TOTALS

Model	Total Units	Percent
Cutlass Supreme	87,928	
4-4-2 opt.	24,829	29

DRIVETRAIN DATA

	4-4-2 (Std.)	4-4-2 W30 (Opt.)	4-4-2 Turnpike (Opt.)
Cyl:	V-8	V-8	V-8
Bore (in):	4	4	4
Stroke (in):	3.975	3.975	3.975
CID:	400	400	400
Carbs.:	1 4-bbl	1 4-bbl	1 2-bbl
Make:	Rochester	Rochester	Rochester
Model:	4MV	4MV	2GC
Comp.:	10.50	10.50	10.50
Max. BHP:	350	360	300
@ RPM:	5000	5000	460
Torque ft-lb:	440	440	425
@ RPM:	3600	3600	2600

TRANSMISSIONS

4-4-2

Std: 3-speed Floor-Mounted Manual with Hurst Shifter, Opt: 4-speed Floor-Mounted Manual Close-Ratio with Hurst Shifter, 4-speed Floor-Mounted Manual Wide-Ratio with Hurst Shifter, 2-speed Turbo Hydra-matic Column-Mounted Automatic (Console-Mounted available)

REAR AXLE RATIOS

4-4-2

Std: 3.08 (auto), 3.23 (3-sp man), 3.55 (4-sp wide man), 3.90 (4-sp close man)

Opt: 3.23 (auto, 4-sp wide man), 3.42, 3.55, 3.90 (3-sp man, auto), 3.91 (4-sp wide man)

EXTERIOR DATA

4-4-2

	Cutlass Supreme Holiday Coupe	Cutlass Supreme Sports Coupe	Cutlass Supreme Convertible
Length (in):	204.2	204.2	204.2
Width (in):	76	76	76
Height (in):	54.4	54.4	54.4
Wheelbase (in):	115	115	115
Weight (lb):	3469	3452	3575

FACTORY BASE PRICE DATA

Model	Holiday Coupe	Sports Coupe	Convertible
4-4-2 Cutlass Supreme	$ 3015	$ 2878	$ 3210
Turnpike Cruising	3157	3020	3352
W-30 Option	3048	2911	3243

POPULAR FACTORY OPTIONS

Interior: Console; Cruise control, $44; Anti-spin differential, $42; Air-induction engine, $34; Turnpike cruising engine, $142; Head rests; Left bucket power seat, $70; Power windows, $100; Pushbutton radio, $64; AM/FM radio, $134; Bi-Phonic radio speaker system, $17; Rally Pac (clock & tachometer), $84; Tilt steering wheel, $42.

Exterior: Tinted glass, Tinted windshield glass only; Transistorized ignition, $100; Outside remote control mirror; Vinyl roof, $84; Simulated wire wheels, $70; Super stock wheels, $88.

Miscellaneous: Air conditioning, $343; Pedal-Ease power brakes, $42; Front disc power brakes, $104; Roto-Matic power steering, $95; Rear window defroster, $21; Superlift rear shock absorbers; Four-speed wide-ratio transmission; Turbo Hydra-matic transmission, $237; Remote trunk lid release, $13.

By an overwhelming margin, the hardtop coupe was the most popular 4-4-2: 16,998 hardtops were produced.

The muscle car enthusiast was right at home in the buckets and console interior of the '67 4-4-2. This droptop is equipped with air conditioning. Courtesy Musclecar Review Magazine.

Corporate policy put a 400 cubic inch limit on A-body intermediates and Olds went right to the edge with its 400 4-barrel V-8. Horsepower was a healthy 350 @ 5000 rpm. Courtesy Musclecar Review Magazine

Oldsmobile pulled a fast one with its W30, hiding outside air intakes above and below the turn signal. Courtesy Musclecar Review Magazine

The 4-4-2 finally came into its own in 1968. Oldsmobile made it a new series and designated it as "the top of the F-85 line." Dual exhausts with outlets through rear bumper cutouts and bold 4-4-2 emblems made this car easy to identify.

1968 Oldsmobile

Sales totals of 607,382 enabled Oldsmobile to maintain its sixth place standing in the automobile sales competition. Notwithstanding, 4-4-2 sales increased dramatically, up by 35% from the previous year. 1968 was a milestone year for the 4-4-2 not only because of its terrific sales, but also because it finally got the recognition it deserved. No longer was it merely an option for the F-85/Cutlass series, but was finally accorded the status of being a separate series.

4-4-2

The 4-4-2 received a new body in 1968. The wheelbase was shortened by 3 inches to 112-inches and new sheetmetal was used. Hood louvers, painted stripes and a black mesh grille with the 4-4-2 ornamentation distinguished it from its mild-mannered kin. By far the most popular of the 4-4-2's produced in 1968 was the hardtop coupe. Over 24,000 were produced, while only 4,282 Sports Coupes and 5,142 convertibles were made. Although the standard engine and

the Force Air induction engine underwent quite a bit of change, their horsepower output (cars equipped with the Turbo Hydra-matic transmission had a slightly lower horsepower), torque and compression ratio remained the same. The big change was in the bore and stroke; contrary to postwar practice, the stroke had been increased so that it was larger than the bore. The Turnpike Cruising version of the 4-4-2 was still available, though it had been tuned down a bit more so that its output was lowered to 290 hp. Its top speed as recorded by *World Car* was a respectable 116 mph. The 360 hp engine's top speed measured at a hefty 123 mph. Oldsmobile recognized the increasing importance of the youth performance car market and geared their advertising accordingly. Their sales literature showed young adventurous men and women dressed in various sporting outfits standing next to a 4-4-2. This was superimposed on an action scene, such as a woman galloping on a horse or a man skydiving or skiing. The text accompanying this scene would refer to the youthfulness of the 4-4-2. One advertisement read, "4-4-2 is the Youngmobile for the purist." Throughout this sales literature words such as, "youth, pizzazz, chic," etc. were repeated. The message was clear. The 4-4-2 was the car for today's action-oriented youth.

A modified 455 Rocket V-8 engine, fitted with special heads, camshaft and crankshaft was the standard on the Hurst/Olds.

A 4-speed close or wide ratio manual transmission, a Hurst shifter and a Sports steering wheel were optional on the 4-4-2.

HURST/OLDS

One of the most exciting developments in 1968 was the introduction of the Hurst/Olds. The prototype Hurst/Olds was designed as a one-off car by Jack "Doc" Watson for George Hurst. Doc Watson convinced Oldsmobile management to produce a limited run to add excitement to the rest of the Olds lineup. It obviously did, because the '68 Hurst/Olds sold out immediately. It came as either a sports coupe or hardtop coupe. The top-of-the-line Oldsmobile A-Body was powered by a special 390 hp, 455 cid Rocket V-8, fitted with special heads, camshaft and crankshaft. A modified Turbo Hydra-matic transmission with a Hurst Dual-Gate shifter was standard, as well as oversized Goodyear polyglass tires, front disc brakes, heavy-duty suspension components and a high capacity cooling system. The Hurst/Olds, in keeping with its distinctive style, came only in silver and black; it had special interior trim and H/O emblems. This car was for the enthusiast who cared about both luxury and performance. *Hurst Heritage* timed its 0 to 60 speed at 6.5 seconds and its quarter-mile time and speed at 108.17 mph in 12.97 seconds. Though only 515 Hurst/Olds were produced, it would soon become one of the most desirable muscle cars around.

VIN NUMBERS

Vehicle Identification Number: 3( )8( )100001 and up
Explanation:
First digit: GM line number: 3 = Oldsmobile
Second to fifth digit: Body number:
   Hardtop Coupe = 4487
   Sports Coupe = 4477
   Convertible = 4467
Sixth digit: Last digit of model year = 8

Seventh digit: Letter indicating assembly plant
Last six digits: Sequential production number

PRODUCTION TOTALS

Model	Total Units	Percent
4-4-2	33,607	
Hurst/Olds	515	2

DRIVETRAIN DATA

	4-4-2 (Std.)	4-4-2 Automatic (Opt.)	4-4-2 W30 Force Air (Opt.)
Cyl:	V-8	V-8	V-8
Bore (in):	3.87	3.87	3.87
Stroke (in):	4.25	4.25	4.25
CID:	400	400	400
Carbs.:	1 4-bbl	1 4-bbl	1 4-bbl
Make:	Rochester	Rochester	Rochester
Model:	4MV	4MV	4MV
Comp.:	10.50	10.50	10.50
Max. BHP:	350	325	360
@ RPM:	4800	4800	5400
Torque ft-lb:	440	440	440
@ RPM:	3200	3200	3600

	4-4-2 Turnpike (Opt.)	Hurst/ Olds (Opt.)
Cyl:	V-8	V-8
Bore (in):	3.87	4.125
Stroke (in):	4.25	4.25

(con't. next page)

"What are those funny things under the bumper?" asked the ad. Copy like this was written by and for car enthusiasts. Courtesy Musclecar Review Magazine.

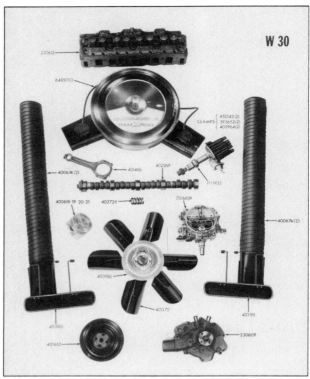

Those funny things under the bumper were force air induction tubes, part of the potent W30 package, which included the special high performance equipment shown here. Courtesy Musclecar Review Magazine.

DRIVETRAIN DATA *(con't.)*

	4-4-2 Turnpike *(Opt.)*	Hurst/ Olds *(Opt.)*
CID:	400	455
Carbs.:	1 2-bbl	1 4-bbl
Make:	Rochester	Rochester
Model:	2CG	4MV
Comp.:	9.0	10.25
Max. BHP:	290	390
@ RPM:	4600	5000
Torque ft-lb:	425	500
@ RPM:	2400	3200

TRANSMISSIONS
4-4-2
Std: 3-speed Heavy-Duty Floor-Mounted Manual with Hurst Shifter

Opt: 4-speed Floor-Mounted Manual Close-Ratio with Hurst Shifter, 4-speed Floor-Mounted Manual Wide- Ratio with Hurst Shifter, 2-speed Turbo Hydra-matic Column-Mounted Automatic (Console-Mounted available)

Hurst/Olds
Std: Modified Turbo Hydra-matic Automatic with Hurst Dual Gate Shifter

Opt: NA

REAR AXLE RATIOS
4-4-2 (Turnpike Cruising, 290 hp)
Std: 2.56
Opt: 2.78, 3.08

4-4-2 (Std. Automatic, 325 hp)
Std: 3.08
Opt: 3.31, 3.42, 3.91, 4.33, 4.66

4-4-2 (Std. 350 hp)
Std: 3.23 (3-sp man), 3.42 (4-sp wide man), 3.91 (4-sp close man)
Opt: 3.08 (3-sp man, 4-sp wide man), 3.23 (4-sp wide man), 3.42 (3-sp man, 4-sp close man), 3.91 (3-sp man, 4-sp close man)

4-4-2 (W30 Force-Air 360 hp)
Std: 4.33 (man), 3.42 (auto)
Opt: 3.42 (man), 3.91 (man), 4.33 (man), 4.66 (man)

Hurst/Olds
Std: 3.91
Opt: 3.08

EXTERIOR DATA
4-4-2

	4-4-2 Coupe	4-4-2 Hardtop	4-4-2 Convertible
Length (in):	201.6	201.6	201.6
Width (in):	76.2	76.2	76.2
Height (in):	52.8	52.8	52.8
Wheelbase (in):	112	112	112
Weight (lb):	3502	3512	3580

(con't. next page)

Oldsmobile's advertising was aimed towards young adventurous people. The message was clear: if you are the kind of person who likes exciting things, the 4-4-2 will be sure to satisfy your needs for adventure and performance.

EXTERIOR DATA *(con't.)*

	Hurst/Olds Coupe	Hurst/Olds Hardtop
Length (in):	201.6	201.6
Width (in):	76.6	76.6
Height (in):	52.8	52.8
Wheelbase (in):	112	112
Weight (lb):	3575	3603

FACTORY BASE PRICE DATA

Model	Coupe	Hardtop	Convertible
4-4-2	$ 3063	$ 3127	$ 3341
Turnpike Cruising	3300	3364	3578
Forced-Air Option	3326	3400	3604
Hurst/Olds	4224	4288	

POPULAR FACTORY OPTIONS

Interior: Console; Head rests; Left bucket power seat, $70; Power windows, $100; Pushbutton radio, $70; AM/FM radio, $134; Rear speaker radio, $13; Rally Pac (clock & tachometer), $84; Custom steering wheel; Tilt steering wheel, $42; Stereo tape player, $134.

Exterior: Tinted glass; Tinted windshield glass only; Outside remote control mirror, $12; Vinyl roof, $95; Wheel discs; Deluxe wheel discs; Simulated wire wheels, $89; Super stock wheels, $88.

Miscellaneous: Air conditioning, $360; Cruise control, $50; Anti-spin differential, $42; High voltage ignition, $100; Pedal-Ease power brakes, $42; Front disc power brakes, $104; Roto-Matic power steering, $95; Rear window defroster, $21; Superlift rear shock absorbers; Four-speed wide-ratio transmission, $184; Four-speed close-ratio transmission, $184; Turbo Hydra-matic transmission, $237; Remote trunk lid release, $14.

The high-performance 4-4-2 became even more distinctive in 1969. Hood paint and rally striping replaced the previous side rally striping and the grille was split in the middle by a wide divider with the 4-4-2 emblem centered on it.

1969 Oldsmobile

In 1969 Oldsmobile edged its way into fifth place in automobile sales ratings, selling 655,241 cars. The Hurst/Olds was a stronger seller this year; production was up by 75% (of course only 515 were produced the previous year). This year Oldsmobile offered a host of "W" options for high performance. The W31 was available for the F-85/Cutlass and the W30 (force-air induction) and the new W32 were offered for the 4-4-2. Sales of 4-4-2 were down by 22% this year. But this figure is a bit misleading since the W31 F-85/Cutlass, which many felt should be grouped with the 4-4-2's, was sold to the same market as the 4-4-2 but was not included in their sales figures. As sales of the 4-4-2 and the number of high performance options increased, so did the amount of advertising support. 1969 also saw the introduction of the new Olds' spokesman, Dr. Oldsmobile and "his performance committee." Resembling a tall Sonny Bono, Dr. Oldsmobile promised that the high performance Olds would let you "Make your escape from the ordinary."

4-4-2

The 4-4-2 was again available in three styles: the hardtop, the coupe and the convertible. Again the hardtop was by far the most popular model. The biggest change in styling that year was the grille, which was split in the center with a wide divider on which 4-4-2 appeared in large chrome numerals. Standard equipment for the 4-4-2 included a special 400 cid Rocket V-8 engine, 70 amp-hour battery, dual exhausts, hood stripes, Strato bucket seats, heavy-duty suspension and red-stripe wide oval tires. The W30 consisted of a forced-air induction package, which fed a 400 cid, 360 hp Rocket V-8, an anti-spin rear axle and a heavy-duty radiator. Externally, special hood striping and W30 front fender decals set it apart from the pack; subtle air scoops beneath the bumpers further distinguished it. The Turnpike Cruising option was phased out, but a new option, the W32 was available. It was a modified version of the force-air induction car that was slightly less fidgety on the street. Mandatory options for the W32 were the anti-spin rear axle, a heavy-duty radiator and a special Turbo Hydra-matic transmission. Its horsepower was rated by various sources at 350 hp or 360 hp. Oldsmobile advertised that the 4-4-2 "Makes everything else look tame" and its ratings certainly

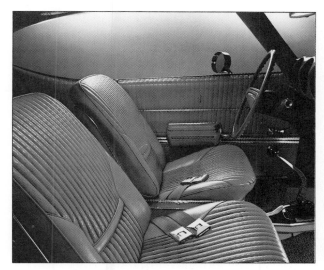

Strato-bucket seats were standard on the 4-4-2. A Hurst shifter and a sports console were optional.

The W31 engine included a special QuadraJet carburetor, force-air induction and a heavy-duty engine fan clutch.

didn't dispute this. *World Car* recorded the standard 4-4-2's top speed at 122 mph and the W30 4-4-2's at 123 mph.

F-85/CUTLASS *W31*

The W31 performance package or, as Olds called it, the "Junior Super Car," was only available on the F-85 Sports Coupe and the Cutlass Supreme Sports Coupe, Holiday Coupe (hardtop) and convertible. It was a force-air version of the 350 cid, 325 hp small-block V-8 motor with a special QuadraJet carburetor, special valves and camshaft and a heavy-duty engine fan clutch. Mandatory options included an anti-spin rear axle, a heavy-duty radiator and a dual exhaust system. W31 front fender decals enabled the world to know what kind of machine it was. A three-speed Hurst floor shifter was standard on the W31, but a four-speed Hurst floor shifter with either a wide or close ratio and a Turbo Hydra-matic automatic were available. Olds promoted the W31 as the car for those who are "ready to operate a mini-priced, maxi-powered machine."

HURST/OLDS

Though sales of the limited edition Hurst/Olds increased by a large percentage from the previous year, still only 906 were produced that year, making it a choice for only a few elite muscle car buyers. The base colors of the H/O were changed to a regal gold and white. The engine was again the 455 cid Rocket V-8, but this year it turned out 380 hp, down 10 from the year before. Other features included a modified Turbo Hydra-matic transmission, Hurst Dual-Gate shifter, Goodyear Polyglas tires on seven-inch rims and a spoiler mounted on the rear deck. Oldsmobile promoted the H/O as the ultimate muscle car: it "snarls softly and carries a big stick.... Some people insist that the H/O on the hood scoop

stands for Hairy Olds." The Hurst/Olds performance was remarkable. Its 0 to 60 time was recorded by *Hurst Heritage* at 7 seconds flat and it accelerated on a standing quarter-mile to 101.28 mph in 13.98 seconds.

VIN NUMBERS

Vehicle Identification Number: 3( )9( )100001 and up
Explanation:
First digit: GM line number: 3 = Oldsmobile
Second to fifth digit: Body number:
    4-4-2 Hardtop Coupe = 4487
    4-4-2 Sports Coupe = 4477
    4-4-2 Convertible = 4467
    Cutlass S Hardtop Coupe = 3687
    Cutlass S Sports Coupe = 3677
    Cutlass S convertible = 3667
    F-85 Sports Coupe = 3277
Sixth digit: Last digit of model year = 9
Seventh digit: Letter indicating assembly plant
Last six digits: Sequential production number

PRODUCTION TOTALS

Model	Total Units	Percent
4-4-2	26,357	
W-30 opt.	1389	5
W-32 opt.	297	1
Hurst/Olds	914	5
Cutlass S	90,675	
W-31 opt.	701	8
F-85	5,541	
W-31 opt.	212	4

Oldsmobile claimed that the 4-4-2 "makes everything else look tame." The Special 400 Rocket V-8 engine confirmed it.

A force-air induction system was still available on the 4-4-2. The W30 option raised the 4-4-2's output to 360 hp. Courtesy Musclecar Review Magazine.

DRIVETRAIN DATA

	4-4-2 (Std.)	4-4-2 Automatic (Std.)	4-4-2 W30 (Opt.)
Cyl:	V-8	V-8	V-8
Bore (in):	3.87	3.87	3.87
Stroke (in):	4.25	4.25	4.25
CID:	400	400	400
Carbs.:	1 4-bbl	1 4-bbl	1 4-bbl
Make:	Rochester	Rochester	Rochester
Model:	4MV	4MV	4MV
Comp.:	10.50	10.50	10.50
Max. BHP:	350	325	360
@ RPM:	4800	4600	5400
Torque ft-lb:	440	440	400
@ RPM:	3200	3000	3600

	4-4-2 W32 (Opt.)	Cutlass/F-85 W31 (Opt.)	Hurst/ Olds (Std.)
Cyl:	V-8	V-8	V-8
Bore (in):	3.87	4.057	4.125
Stroke (in):	4.25	3.39	4.25
CID:	400	350	455
Carbs.:	1 4-bbl	1 4-bbl	1 4-bbl
Make:	Rochester	Rochester	Rochester
Model:	4MV	4MV	4MV
Comp.:	10.25	10.5	10.5
Max. BHP:	350	325	380
@ RPM:	4800	5600	5000
Torque ft-lb:	440	360	500
@ RPM:	3200	3600	3200

TRANSMISSIONS

4-4-2 Std. & W30
Std: 3-speed Floor-Mounted Manual with Hurst Shifter
Opt: 4-speed Floor-Mounted Manual Close-Ratio with Hurst Shifter, 4-speed Floor-Mounted Manual Wide-Ratio with Hurst Shifter, 2-speed Turbo Hydra-matic Column-Mounted Automatic (Console-Mounted available)

4-4-2 W32
Std: Special Turbo Hydra-matic Automatic
Opt: NA

F-85/Cutlass S W31
Std: 3-speed Floor-Mounted Manual with Hurst Shifter
Opt: 4-speed Floor-Mounted Manual Close-Ratio with Hurst Shifter, 4-speed Floor-Mounted Manual Wide-Ratio with Hurst Shifter, 2-speed Turbo Hydra-matic Column-Mounted Automatic (Console-Mounted available)

Hurst/Olds
Std: Modified Turbo Hydra-matic Automatic with Hurst Dual-Gate shifter
Opt: 4-speed Floor-Mounted Manual Wide-Ratio, 4-speed Floor Mounted Close-Ratio

REAR AXLE RATIOS

4-4-2 (Std, 350 hp)
Std: 3.23 (3-sp man), 3.42 (4-sp wide man), 3.91 (4-sp close man)
Opt: 2.56 (3-sp man), 2.78 (3-sp man), 3.08 (3-sp man, 4-sp wide man), 3.23 (4-sp wide man), 3.42 (3-sp man,

(con't. next page)

It "snarls softly and carries a big stick...." The Hurst/Olds came with a Hurst Dual Gate shifter and console, a modified Turbo Hydramatic transmission, a force-air induction system and was powered by a 455 cid modified Rocket V-8.

REAR AXLE RATIOS *(con't.)*
4-sp close man), 3.91 (3-sp man), 4.33 (3-sp man, 4-sp close man), 4.66 (3-sp man, 4-sp close man)

4-4-2 (Std. Automatic, 325 hp)
Std: 2.78, 3.08 (with air conditioning)
Opt: 3.23, 3.42, 3.91, 4.33, 4.66

4-4-2 (W-30, 360 hp)
Std: 3.42 (4-sp wide man, auto), 4.33 (4-sp close man)
Opt: 2.73 (4-sp wide man), 3.08 (4-sp wide man), 3.23 (4-sp wide man), 3.42 (4-sp close man), 3.91, 4.33, 4.66

4-4-2 (W-32, 360 hp)
Std: 3.42
Opt: 3.91, 4.33, 4.66

F-85/Cutlass S (W-31, 325 hp)*
Std: 3.91 (3-sp man, 4-sp wide man), 4.33 (4-sp close man)
Opt: 3.42, 3.91 (4-sp close man), 4.33 (3-sp man, 4-sp wide man), 4.66
Rear axle ratio for automatic is not available

Hurst/Olds
Std: 3.42
Opt: 3.91, 3.23

EXTERIOR DATA
4-4-2

	4-4-2 Coupe	4-4-2 Hardtop	4-4-2 Convertible
Length (in):	201.9	201.9	201.9
Width (in):	76.2	76.2	76.2
Height (in):	52.8	52.8	52.8
Wheelbase (in):	112	112	112
Weight (lb):	3502	3512	3580

	Cutlass S Coupe	Cutlass S Hardtop	Cutlass S Convertible
Length (in):	201.9	201.9	201.9
Width (in):	76.2	76.2	76.2
Height (in):	52.8	52.8	52.8
Wheelbase (in):	112	112	112
Weight (lb):	3293	3316	3386

(con't. next page)

Top speed on the 4-4-2 with the 360 hp Rocket V-8 was recorded by World Car *at 123 mph. But performance did not add up to good gas mileage —* World Car *measured it at 11.3 mpg (combined) for the same engine.*

EXTERIOR DATA *(con't.)*

	F-85 Sports Coupe	Hurst/Olds Hardtop
Length (in):	201.9	201.9
Width (in):	76.2	76.2
Height (in):	52.8	52.8
Wheelbase (in):	112	112
Weight (lb):	3285	3716

FACTORY BASE PRICE DATA

Model	Coupe	Hardtop	Convertible
4-4-2	$ 3141	$ 3204	$ 3395
W-30	3404	3467	3658
W-32	3183	3246	3437
Cutlass S W-31	3103	3166	3420
F-85 W-31	2983	—	—
Hurst/Olds	—	3670	—

POPULAR FACTORY OPTIONS

Interior: Electric clock, $17; Console, $61; Left bucket power seat, $74; Power windows, $105; Pushbutton radio, $61; AM/FM radio, $134; AM/FM stereo radio, $238; Rear speaker radio, $17; Rally Pac (clock & tachometer), $85; Deluxe front & rear seat belts; Front shoulder straps seat belts; Rear shoulder straps seat belts; Deluxe steering wheel; Custom steering wheel; Tilt steering wheel, $45; Tape player, $134.

Exterior: Tinted Glass, $39; Tinted windshield glass only, $26; Outside remote control mirror, $11; Vinyl roof, $100; Wheel discs; Deluxe wheel discs; Simulated wire wheels; Super Stock I wheels, $73; Super Stock II wheels, $74.

Miscellaneous: Air conditioning, $376; Cruise control, $58; Anti-spin differential, $42; Power brakes, $42; Front disc power brakes, $64; Power door locks, $45; Power steering, $100; Rear window defroster, $22; Superlift rear shock absorbers, $42; Heavy-duty rear suspension; Four-speed wide-ratio transmission, $185; Four-speed close-ratio transmission, $184; Turbo Hydra-matic transmission, $227; Remote trunk lid release, $15.

The 4-4-2 equipped with the W30 was easily distinguishable by the air scoops on the hood. Additionally it had a special air cleaner, aluminum intake manifold, special body stripes, sports mirrors and a lightweight body insulation package.

1970 Oldsmobile

1970 was probably the ultimate year for Oldsmobile's high performance cars and the last year of relatively unrestrained catering to the muscle car market. For the first time in a decade an Oldsmobile, the 4-4-2 convertible, paced America's most famous auto race — the Indianapolis 500. Though this honor enhanced Olds' muscle car reputation, the supercar market was on the decline. One major factor contributing to this was the exorbitant insurance rates muscle car owners now had to pay. Oldsmobile was aware of this and tried to design a muscle car that had enough zip to satisfy customers, but not enough to warrant huge insurance premiums. Out of this effort came the Rallye 350, an option for the Cutlass Supreme and the F-85. Though it had lower horsepower ratings than the 4-4-2's, it looked more like a performance car than any other Olds. The Hurst/Olds was dropped in 1970, but would reappear two years later. Oldsmobile still maintained its fifth place standing in 1970, selling 569,444 cars.

4-4-2

The 4-4-2 was still offered in three styles: the Sports Coupe, hardtop and convertible. Again the hardtop far outsold the other styles, but the convertible was also quite popular this year — perhaps because of its status as the official pace car of the Indianapolis 500. A new, unique grille made of vertical black rectangles was virtually the only external change made on the 4-4-2, but inside, it received the more powerful 455 cid engine featured in the Hurst/Olds of the previous two years. Two versions were available, the standard 365 hp engine and the W-30 option's 370 hp forced-air engine. In addition to its powerful engine, the W30 had a special air cleaner, aluminum intake manifold, special body stripes, sports mirrors and a lightweight body insulation package. This year Olds called the 4-4-2's suspension package the Rallye-Sports system. It included heavy-duty springs (front and rear), shocks, stabilizer bars and rear suspension lower control arms, as well as heavy-duty driveshaft motor mounts and seven- inch wide rims fitted with G-70 x 14 whitewall wide oval tires. The W32 option was no longer available on the 4-4-2, though it was still offered on the Cutlass Supreme.

Olds muscle wasn't confined to the 4-4-2 as this W31 F-85 coupe demonstrates. The W31 package consisted of a 325-hp 350 V-8, aluminum intake manifolds, a heavy-duty clutch, disc brakes, special striping and W31 emblems. Courtesy Musclecar Review Magazine.

The 4-4-2 was available in three models, the Holiday Coupe, Sports Coupe and convertible of which 2,933 were produced.

F-85/Cutlass W31

The potent W31 performance package was still available on the Cutlass S and F-85. This year it consisted of a force-air induction 325 hp, 350 cid small-block V-8 engine with aluminum intake manifolds, heavy-duty clutch, disc brakes, special hood and paint stripes and external W31 emblems. A new lightweight fiberglass hood with functional scoops and big hood stripes topped off this powerhouse. The W31 continued to be one of "Dr. Oldsmobile's W Machines."

Rallye 350

The biggest news of 1970 was the introduction of the Rallye 350 option for the F-85 and Cutlass S, "Oldsmobile's challenge to 1970's mid-year intermediate competition." This was a single year Olds offering. Even if Oldsmobile had not heavily promoted the Rallye 350, not too many people would have missed it—it was available only in bright (some say very bright!) Sebring Yellow. Even the front and rear bumpers were painted yellow, and if that wasn't enough color for you, orange and black trim completed the package. And, of course, the 7-inch wide Super Stock wheels were not left out; they, too, were painted yellow. Mandatory options for the Rallye 350 included the 350 cid, 310 hp V-8 engine, Rallye-Sports suspension, Force-Air fiberglass hood, dual sport mirrors and the sport steering wheel. The Rallye 350 was conceived by Hurst and built by Oldsmobile, though Hurst was given no credit. This product package was designed for the customer who wanted to identify with the "performance look" while still having a more conventional engine and powertrain. While the concept looked good on paper, the Rallye 350 was not as successful as Olds had hoped it would be—only 3,547 were produced and it was dropped from Olds' lineup the following year.

VIN NUMBERS

Vehicle Identification Number: 3( )0( )100001 and up
Explanation:
First digit: GM line number: 3 = Oldsmobile
Second to fifth digit: Body number:
  4-4-2 Hardtop Coupe = 4487
  4-4-2 Sports Coupe = 4477
  4-4-2 Convertible = 4467
  Cutlass S Hardtop Coupe = 3687
  Cutlass S Sports Coupe = 3677
  F-85 Sport Coupe = 3277
Sixth digit: Last digit of model year = 0
Seventh digit: Letter indicating assembly plant
Last six digits: Sequential production number

PRODUCTION TOTALS

Model	Total Units	Percent
4-4-2	19,330	
W30 opt.	3,100	16
Cutlass S	99,255	
W31 opt.	1,145	1
Rallye 350 opt.	2,527	3
F-85	8,274	
W31 opt.	207	3
Rallye 350	1,020	12

DRIVETRAIN DATA

	4-4-2	4-4-2 W30	Cutlass/F-85 Rallye 350
	(Std.)	(Opt.)	(Opt.)
Cyl:	V-8	V-8	V-8
Bore (in):	4.125	4.125	4.057
Stroke (in):	4.25	4.25	3.385

(con't. next page)

Olds called the 4-4-2's suspension system the Rallye-Sports System. It included heavy-duty springs, shocks, front and rear stabilizer bars, rear suspension lower control arms, a heavy-duty driveshaft, motor mounts and 7-inch wide rims fitted with G-70 x 14 tires.

DRIVETRAIN DATA *(con't.)*

CID:	455	455	350
Carbs.:	1 4-bbl	1 4-bbl	1 4-bbl
Make:	Rochester	Rochester	Rochester
Model:	4MV	4MV	4MV
Comp.:	10.25	10.50	10.25
Max. BHP:	365	370	310
@ RPM:	5000	5200	4200
Torque ft-lb:	500	500	490
@ RPM:	3200	3600	2400

Cutlass/F-85
W31
(Opt.)

Cyl:	V-8
Bore (in):	4.057
Stroke (in):	3.385
CID:	350
Carbs.:	1 4-bbl
Make:	Rochester
Model:	4MV

Comp.:	10.50
Max. BHP:	325
@ RPM:	5400
Torque ft-lb:	360
@ RPM:	3600

TRANSMISSIONS

4-4-2 Std. & W30

Std: 3-speed Floor-Mounted Manual with Hurst Shifter
Opt: 4-speed Floor-Mounted Manual Close-Ratio with Hurst Shifter, 4-speed Floor-Mounted Manual Wide- Ratio with Hurst Shifter, 3-speed Turbo Hydra-matic Column-Mounted Automatic (Console-Mounted available)

4-4-2 W30

Std: 3-speed Floor-Mounted Manual Close-Ratio with Hurst Shifter
Opt: 3-speed Turbo Hydra-matic Column-Mounted Automatic (Console-Mounted available), 4-speed Floor-Mounted Manual Close-Ratio with Hurst Shifter, 4-speed Floor-Mounted Manual Wide-Ratio with Hurst Shifter

(con't. next page)

The W31 package was available on the Cutlass S and F-85 only. It included all the equipment listed for the W30, but in place of the 455 V-8 was a 350 force-air engine. "W31" emblems on the front fenders and special striping along the body sides identified it.

TRANSMISSIONS *(con't.)*
4-speed Floor-Mounted Manual Wide-Ratio with Hurst Shifter

F-85/Cutlass W31
Std: 3-speed Floor-Mounted Manual with Hurst Shifter
Opt: 4-speed Floor-Mounted Manual Close-Ratio with Hurst Shifter, 4-speed Floor-Mounted Manual Wide-Ratio with Hurst Shifter, 3-speed Turbo Hydra-matic Column-Mounted Automatic (Console-Mounted available), Hurst Dual-Gate Shifter Console-Mounted

Rallye 350
Std: 3-speed Floor-Mounted Manual with Hurst Shifter
Opt: 4-speed Floor-Mounted Manual Close-Ratio with Hurst Shifter, 4-speed Floor-Mounted Manual Wide-Ratio with Hurst Shifter, 3-speed Turbo Hydra-matic Column-Mounted Automatic (Console-Mounted available)

REAR AXLE RATIOS
4-4-2 (Std, 365 hp)
Std: 3.08 Opt: 2.56 (3-sp man), 2.78 (auto), 3.23 (auto), 3.42 (3-sp man, auto)

4-4-2 (W30, 370 hp)
Std: 3.23
Opt: 3.42 (auto), 3.91

F-85/Cutlass (W-31, 325 hp)
Std: 3.91
Opt: 3.42

Rallye 350
Std: 3.23 (man), 3.42 (auto)
Opt: 3.42, 3.91

EXTERIOR DATA
4-4-2

	4-4-2 Coupe	4-4-2 Hardtop	4-4-2 Convertible
Length (in):	203.2	203.2	203.2
Width (in):	76.2	76.2	76.2
Height (in):	52.8	52.8	52.8
Wheelbase (in):	112	112	112
Weight (lb):	3667	3713	3740

(con't. next page)

EXTERIOR DATA (con't.)

	Cutlass S Coupe	Cutlass S Hardtop	F-85 Coupe
Length (in):	203.2	203.2	203.2
Width (in):	76.2	76.2	76.2
Height (in):	52.8	52.8	52.8
Wheelbase (in):	112	112	112
Weight (lb):	3440	3451	3411

FACTORY BASE PRICE DATA

Model	Coupe	Hardtop	Convertible
4-4-2	$ 3312	$ 3376	$ 3567
4-4-2 W-30	3682	3746	3937
Cutlass S W-31	3493	3556	—
Cutlass S Rally 350	3283	3346	—
F-85 W-31	3373	—	—
F-85 Rally 350	3163	—	—

POPULAR FACTORY OPTIONS

Interior: Electric clock, $17; Sports console, $61; Dual gate console, $77; Power door locks, $48; Left bucket power seat, $74; Power windows, $105; Pushbutton radio, $69; AM/FM radio, $134; AM/FM stereo radio, $238; Rear speaker radio, $17; Rally Pac (clock & tachometer), $84; Deluxe front & rear seat belts, $11; Shoulder straps front seat belts, $23; Shoulder straps rear seat belts, $26; Custom steering wheel; $16; Tilt steering wheel, $45; Tape player, $134.

Exterior: Tinted glass, $39; Tinted windshield glass only, $26; Fiberglass hood, $158; Special paint hood, $11; Outside remote control mirror, $10; Trunk lid spoiler, $74; Vinyl roof, $102; Simulated wire wheels,

The W30's engine included a high-overlap cam, a lightweight aluminum intake manifold, and a power-saving clutch fan.

$74; Super Stock I wheels, $91; Super Stock II wheels, $74.

Miscellaneous: Air conditioning, $376; Aluminum axle carrier, $158; Cruise control, $58; Anti-spin differential, $42; Front disc brakes, $64; Vari-Ratio power steering, $105; Rear window defogger, $26; Superlift rear shock absorbers, $42; Four-speed wide- ratio transmission, $184; Four-speed close-ratio transmission, $184; Turbo Hydra-matic transmission, $227; Floor-mounted three-speed transmission, $84; Remote trunk lid release, $15.

The Rallye 350 was almost the 1970 Hurst Olds. Introduced in February 1970, the Rallye 350 sported a super loud Sebring Yellow paint job and matching urethane coated bumpers. Courtesy Musclecar Review Magazine.

Despite increasing pressure from emission regulations, the 4-4-2 with the W30 option still managed to put out 300 hp net or 350 hp gross. This was down only 10 hp from the previous year, even though the compression ratio had been reduced to 8.5:1.

1971 Oldsmobile

The year 1971 marked the beginning of the decline of the muscle car era. Federal emissions regulations and increased safety standards took their toll on all muscle cars, including the Olds. Horsepower ratings were down for all the muscle cars. Yet federal regulations were not the only cause of these lowered ratings; in fact much of ratings' decline can be traced to the new system for determining horsepower. Ratings had been taken from the engine with no power-robbing items attached; beginning in 1971 they were taken at the flywheel with all accessories (water pump, alternator, etc.) attached. This new system of determining net horsepower was probably more accurate than the previous method; furthermore, it may have soothed some insurance companies' fear of high-powered cars. Olds' high performance offerings for 1971 were much slimmer than in the previous couple of years. The W31 option was dropped from the high performance list, as was the Rallye 350 option. The 4-4-2 was only offered in two styles: the ever-popular hardtop and the convertible. Over-

all, the Cutlass/F-85 intermediate group was becoming more popular in Olds' model mix. The sales situation at Olds was depressed that year, and the decline of the muscle car market only made things worse. Oldsmobile division dropped into sixth place, selling only 550,314 cars, down considerably from 1970.

4-4-2

The 4-4-2 was still powered by the large 455 cid engine. But in order to meet federal emissions standards, Olds was forced to lower horsepower. Thus horsepower on the standard 4-4-2 dropped to 270 net (340 gross) and on the W30 it fell to 300 net (350 gross). But the 4-4-2 still handled beautifully, largely because of its Rallye suspension system. Single white-stripe, wide oval tires mounted on seven-inch rims, dual exhausts, special emblems and stripes and strato bucket seats all contributed to the 4-4-2's special style. The W30 option included the forced-air induction 455 cid engine, as well as a heavy-duty air cleaner, aluminum intake manifold, sports mirrors, body stripes and special W-car emblems. *World Car* measured the standard 4-4-2 and the W30's top speed at 119 mph and 120 mph, not quite as good as in previous years, but still impressive.

The Sport Coupe was discontinued for the 4-4-2 in 1971 and only 1,304 convertibles were produced. This one is equipped with the W30 option and included a lightweight fiberglass hood with functional air scoops and chromed hood pins.

Despite its capacity for performance, production of the 4-4-2 was down to 7,589, as overall interest in supercars declined.

VIN NUMBERS

Vehicle Identification Number: 3(   )1( )100001 and up
Explanation:
First digit: GM line number: 3 = Oldsmobile
Second to fifth digit: Body number:
   4-4-2 Hardtop Coupe = 4487
   4-4-2 Convertible = 4467
Sixth digit: Last digit of model year = 1
Seventh digit: Letter indicating assembly plant
Last six digits: Sequential production number

PRODUCTION TOTALS

Model	Total Units	Percent
4-4-2	7,589	

DRIVETRAIN DATA

	4-4-2 (Std.)	4-4-2 W30 (Opt.)
Cyl:	V-8	V-8
Bore (in):	4.125	4.125
Stroke (in):	4.25	4.25
CID:	455	455
Carbs.:	1 4-bbl	1 4-bbl

Make:	Rochester	Rochester
Model:	4MC	4MC
Comp.:	8.5	8.5
Max. BHP:	270	300
@ RPM:	4600	4700
Torque ft-lb:	370	410
@ RPM:	3200	3200

TRANSMISSIONS
4-4-2 Std. & W30
Std: 3-speed Floor-Mounted Manual with Hurst Shifter
Opt: 4-speed Floor-Mounted Manual Close-Ratio with Hurst Shifter, 4-speed Floor-Mounted Manual Wide-Ratio with Hurst Shifter, 3-speed Turbo Hydra-matic Column-Mounted Automatic (Console-Mounted available)

REAR AXLE RATIOS
4-4-2 (Std. & W30)
Std: 3.23 (3-sp man, auto), 3.42 (4-sp man)
Opt: 3.73

EXTERIOR DATA
4-4-2

	4-4-2 Hardtop	4-4-2 Convertible
Length (in):	203.6	203.6
Width (in):	76.8	76.8

(con't. next page)

The 1971 4-4-2 was offered as either a convertible or a hardtop coupe. Strato Bucket seats, a wide louvered hood, heavy-duty wheels and super-wide bias-ply glass-belted tires with white stripes were standard. Courtesy Musclecar Review Magazine.

EXTERIOR DATA *(con't.)*

Height (in):	52.9	53.2
Wheelbase (in):	112	112
Weight (lb):	3688	3731

FACTORY BASE PRICE DATA

Model	Hardtop	Convertible
4-4-2	$ 3552	$ 3743
4-4-2 W-30	3899	4090

POPULAR FACTORY OPTIONS

Interior: Electric clock, $19; Sports console, $77; Cruise control, $63; Anti-spin differential, $44; Power door locks, $47; Left bucket power seat, $79; Power windows, $116; Pushbutton radio, $75; AM/FM radio, $139; AM/FM stereo radio, $239; Rear speaker radio, $19; Rally Pac (clock & tachometer) $84; Custom steering wheel, $32; Tilt steering wheel, $45; Stereo tape player, $134.

Exterior: Tinted glass, $43; Tinted windshield glass only, $31; Outside remote control mirror, $13; Left & right mirrors, $22; Trunk lid spoiler, $73; Vinyl roof, $102; Super Stock I wheels, $91.

Miscellaneous: Air conditioning, $408; Aluminum axle carrier, $26; Front disc power brakes, $69; Vari-Ratio power steering, $116; Rear window defogger, $63; Superlift rear shock absorbers, $42; Four-speed wide-ratio transmission, $195; Four-speed close-ratio transmission, $238; Turbo Hydra-matic transmission, $243; Remote trunk lid release, $15.

The "4-4-2" emblem was moved to the grille's right side.

In 1972 the Hurst/Olds reappeared as a limited production model. Oldsmobile wrote that its purpose was "To provide true, all-around performance through better engine response, handling, braking, driver comfort, styling, exclusivity and lasting value."

1972 Oldsmobile

Olds' sales rose dramatically in 1972. Having sold 749,018 cars, Oldsmobile climbed into third place, knocking its long-time GM rival, Pontiac, out of its traditional niche. The 4-4-2 did not fare as well as Oldsmobiles other models. It lost its status as a separate model and became merely a handling and appearance package. The good news was that Olds reintroduced Hurst/Olds into its performance camp and was again given the honors of having an Olds model, the Hurst/Olds as a pace setter for the Indianapolis 500.

Cutlass/Cutlass S/Cutlass Supreme 4-4-2

For 1972 the 4-4-2 option was available on selected Cutlass, Cutlass S and Cutlass Supreme models. It consisted of a heavy-duty suspension, heavy-duty wheels, special paint striping on the hood and body and hood louvers. A special 4-4-2 grille and 4-4-2 numbers in strategic locations made sure that everyone would know what kind of car you were

driving. The W-30 performance package was still available for those who wanted more than style. Included in it was a high-performance forced-air induction Rocket 455 cid V-8, a high-performance camshaft, a heavy-duty radiator, a fiberglass hood with functional air scoops and chromed tie-downs, and an anti-spin rear axle.

Hurst/Olds

The Hurst/Olds was again a limited production model, based on the Cutlass Supreme; only 629 were built in 1972. It was designed to "provide true, all-around performance through better engine response, handling, braking, driver comfort, styling, exclusivity and lasting value." Its engine was the hefty 455 cid and it included a host of performance and appearance equipment such as the Rallye suspension, power disc brakes, a 3.23 rear axle ratio, custom gold striping, black accents and an antique gold vinyl roof. The Hurst/Olds was only available in Cameo White; with its gold and black accents, the muscle car enthusiast enjoyed its great performance in style. Quite a few fancy options were available, including an electric sun roof, a Hurst digital performance computer, security alarm system, and an Indianapolis 500 pace car replica decal set.

The Hurst/Olds came only in Cameo White; it had black accents and custom gold striping.

A Hurst Electric Sun Roof with a wind deflector and a W30 High-Performance engine were optional on the Hurst/Olds.

VIN NUMBERS

Vehicle Identification Number: 3( )( )( )2( )100001 and up

Explanation:

First digit: GM line number: 3 = Oldsmobile

Second digit: Letter indicating line:
  Cutlass = F
  Cutlass S = G
  Cutlass Supreme = J

Third and fourth digit: Last two digits of body number:
  Cutlass Hardtop = 87
  Cutlass S Hardtop = 87
  Cutlass S Sports Coupe = 77
  Cutlass Supreme Convertible = 67

Sixth digit: Last digit of model year = 2

Seventh digit: Letter indicating assembly plant

Last six digits: Sequential production number

PRODUCTION TOTALS

Model	Total Units	Percent
Cutlass	37,790	
4-4-2 opt.	751	2
Cutlass S	82,602	
4-4-2 opt	7,923	10
Cutlass Supreme	11,571	
4-4-2 opt.	1,171	10
Hurst/Olds Hardtop	499	
Hurst/Olds Convertible	130	

DRIVETRAIN DATA

	Cutlass, S, Supreme L-32 (Std.)	Cutlass, S, Supreme L-34 (Opt.)	Cutlass, S, Supreme L-75 (Opt.)
Cyl:	V-8	V-8	V-8
Bore (in):	4.057	4.057	4.125
Stroke (in):	3.385	3.385	4.25
CID:	350	350	455
Carbs.:	1 2-bbl	1 4-bbl	1 4-bbl
Make:	Rochester	Rochester	Rochester
Model:	2CG	4MC	4MC
Comp.:	8.5	8.5	8.5
Max. BHP:	160	180	250
@ RPM:	4000	4000	4200
Torque ft-lb:	275	275	370
@ RPM:	2400	2800	2800

	Hurst/ Olds (Std.)	All Models W-30 (Opt.)
Cyl:	V-8	V-8
Bore (in):	4.125	4.125
Stroke (in):	4.25	4.25
CID:	455	455
Carbs.:	1 4-bbl	1 4-bbl
Make:	Rochester	Rochester
Model:	4MC	4MC
Comp.:	10.5	8.5
Max. BHP:	300	300
@ RPM:	4700	4700
Torque ft-lb:	370	410
@ RPM:	2800	3200

TRANSMISSIONS

Cutlass, S, Supreme

Std: 3-speed Column-Mounted Manual

Opt: 4-speed Floor-Mounted Manual Wide-Ratio, 2-speed Turbo Hydra-matic Column-Mounted Automatic (available with 350 cid engine), 3-speed Turbo Hydra-

TRANSMISSIONS *(cont.)*
matic Column-Mounted Automatic (available with 455 cid engine)

Hurst/Olds
Std: Turbo Hydra-matic Automatic with Hurst Dual-Gate Shifter
Opt: NA

REAR AXLE RATIOS
Cutlass
Std: 3.23 (3-sp man, auto), 3.42 (4-sp man)
Opt: 3.73, 3.08

Hurst/Olds
Std: 3.42
Opt: 3.23

EXTERIOR DATA
4-4-2

	Cutlass Hardtop	Cutlass S Coupe	Cutlass S Hardtop
Length (in):	203.6	203.6	203.6
Width (in):	76.8	76.8	76.8
Height (in):	52.9	52.9	52.9
Wheelbase (in):	112	112	112
Weight (lb):	3379	3387	3404

	Cutlass Supreme Convertible
Length (in):	203.6
Width (in):	76.8
Height (in):	53.5
heelbase (in):	112
Weight (lb):	3528

FACTORY BASE PRICE DATA

Model	Coupe	Hardtop	Convertible
Cutlass	$ —	$ 2973	$ —
Cutlass S	3027	3087	—
Cutlass Supreme	—	—	3433
Hurst/Olds	—	3659	4005

Note: The W-30 option cost between $599 to $722 depending on the series it was fitted on.

POPULAR FACTORY OPTIONS
Interior: Electric clock, $18; Sports console, $75; Dual gate console; Power door locks, $46; Left bucket power seat, $77; Power windows, $113; Pushbutton radio, $73; AM/FM radio, $135; AM/FM stereo radio, $233; Rear speaker radio, $18; Rally Pac (clock & tachometer), $82; Custom steering wheel, $31; Tilt steering wheel, $44; Tape player, $130.

Exterior: Tinted glass, $42; Tinted windshield glass only, $29; Outside remote control mirror, $12; Left & right mirrors, $22; Vinyl roof, $99; Wire wheel discs, $113; Super Stock wheels, $72.

Miscellaneous: Air conditioning, $397; Aluminum axle carrier; Cruise control, $62; Anti-spin differential, $43; 180 hp engine, $46; 270 hp engine, $183; Front disc power brakes, $68; Vari-Ratio power steering, $113; Rear window defogger, $62; Superlift rear shock absorbers; Four-speed wide-ratio transmission, $190; Turbo Hydra-matic transmission, $215, Remote trunk lid release, $14.

The prototype Hurst/Olds, shown here, had extended C-pillars not used on production models. Goodyear G60-14 Polysteel radials were the OEM tires, replacing the Goodrich T/A Radials used on the prototype.

The 1973 4-4-2 was officially called an Appearance and Handling Package. The W30, the dual intake forced-air hood, the Sports Console — the "hot-car" items were no longer available. The 4-4-2 was barely mentioned in the sales literature of that year.

1973 Oldsmobile

Olds held onto its third place standings in 1973 with an all-time high of 853,793. The Cutlass models underwent dramatic styling changes; the popularity of the new Cutlass was one of the factors contributing to Olds' tremendous sales growth. The 4-4-2 was still purely a handling and appearance option as it had been in the previous year. Additionally, a new Salon package was offered on the Cutlass S and Cutlass Supreme models. It was a mild attempt at making a touring sedan. Included in this package were special suspension components tuned to a new type of steel-belted radial tires. The Hurst/Olds limited edition model was available again this year. It was the hottest performance car Olds offered that year and it was also one of the most handsome.

Cutlass/Cutlass S 4-4-2

As the demand for high performance cars increasingly waned, the 4-4-2 option was limited to even fewer models in 1973; it was only available on the Cutlass and Cutlass S coupes. Its handling and appearance features included various body side and deck lid stripes, a special louvered hood and grille and the FE-2 heavy-duty Rallye suspension package. It was listed as option W-29, the only "W" prefix option listed for 1973. Cost was $121. on the Cutlass models and $58. on the Cutlass S. Two 350 cid and 455 cid engines were available with the 4-4-2 option. The W30 engine was dropped from the lineup. Again, horsepower was down because of tighter federal pollution standards. *Car and Driver* rated the 180 hp engine's top speed at 110 mph and the 250 hp engine's at 115 mph.

Hurst/Olds

The Hurst/Olds was the only true performance car built by Oldsmobile in 1973. Olds called it the car "designed and built exclusively for the man in motion." It was based on the striking new Cutlass S but was decked out in Cameo White or Ebony Black with gold stripes. The blacked-out taillight bezels and grille, and its white vinyl roof with opera windows gave it added class. Standard equipment included a Hurst Dual-Gate Shifter, Super Stock III wheels in Hurst

Included in the Cutlass's 1973 restyling was a new instrument panel aimed at "improved serviceability." The major components of the panel were removeable for easy repairs.

Gold and Ebony Black, custom chrome tailpipes, swivel seats, power disc brakes and the Rallye suspension. A digital tachometer, Hurst Loc/Lugs, a security alarm system and super air shocks could be ordered at an extra cost. The Hurst/Olds was powered by the 455 cid V-8 engine, which was detuned to produce "just" 250 hp due to federal emissions controls and the energy crisis.

VIN NUMBERS

Vehicle Identification Number: 3( )3( )100001 and up
Explanation:
First digit: GM line number: 3 = Oldsmobile
Second digit: Letter indicating line:
  Cutlass = F
  Cutlass S = G
Third and fourth digit: Last two digits of body number:
  Cutlass Colonnade Coupe = 37
  Cutlass S Colonnade Coupe = 37
Sixth digit: Last digit of model year = 3
Seventh digit: Letter indicating assembly plant
Last six digits: Sequential production number

PRODUCTION TOTALS

Model	Total Units	Percent
Cutlass	22,002	
4-4-2 opt.	360	1.6
Cutlass S	77,558	
4-4-2 opt.	9,777	12
Hurst Olds	1,097	

DRIVETRAIN DATA

	Cutlass, Cutlass S, Cutlass S (Std.)	Cutlass, Cutlass S (Opt.)	Hurst/ Olds (Opt.) Cutlass S (Std.)
Cyl:	V-8	V-8	V-8
Bore (in):	4.057	4.125	4.125
Stroke (in):	3.385	4.250	4.25
CID:	350	455	455
Carbs.:	1 4-bbl	1 4-bbl	1 4-bbl
Make:	Rochester	Rochester	Rochester
Model:	4MC	4MC	4MC

(con't. next page)

Oldsmobile billed the 1973 Hurst/Olds as the car, "For the particular individual who values true automotive excellence." The 455 cid L77 engine, which featured a special camshaft and a special transmission with a high stall speed torque converter, was optional.

DRIVETRAIN DATA *(con't.)*

Comp.:	8.5	8.5	8.5
Max. BHP:	180	250	250
@ RPM:	3800	4000	4000
Torque ft-lb:	275	370	370
@ RPM:	2800	2100	2100

TRANSMISSIONS

Cutlass, S, Supreme
Std: 3-speed Column-Mounted Manual
Opt: 4-speed Floor-Mounted Manual Wide-Ratio with Hurst Shifter, 3-speed Turbo Hydra-matic Column-Mounted Automatic

Hurst/Olds
Std: Turbo Hydra-matic Automatic with Hurst Dual-Gate Shifter
Opt: NA

REAR AXLE RATIOS

Cutlass, Cutlass S (350 cid, 180 hp)
Std: 3.23 (man), 2.73 (auto)
Opt: 3.08

Cutlass, Cutlass S (455 cid, 250 hp)
Std: 3.23 (man), 2.73 (auto)
Opt: 3.08

Hurst/Olds
Std: 3.23, 3.08 (with air conditioning)
Opt: NA

EXTERIOR DATA
4-4-2

	Cutlass Coupe	Cutlass S Coupe	Hurst/Olds Hardtop
Length (in):	207	207	207
Width (in):	76.5	76.5	76.5
Height (in):	53.3	53.3	53.3
Wheelbase (in):	112	112	112
Weight (lb):	3713	3721	NA

FACTORY BASE PRICE DATA

Model	Coupe
Cutlass 4-4-2	$ 3124
Cutlass S 4-4-2	3166
Hurst/Olds	3743

POPULAR FACTORY OPTIONS

Interior: Electric clock, $18; Sports console, $59; Instrument gauges, $31; Power door locks, $46; Power windows, $75; Pushbutton radio, $65; Pushbutton radio & tape; AM/FM radio, $135; AM/FM stereo radio, $233; AM/FM stereo radio & tape, $363; Rear speaker radio, $18.
Exterior: Bumper guards; Bumper rubber strips; Tinted

(con't. next page)

This year the Hurst/Olds came in either Ebony Black or Cameo White with gold stripes and body accents. Its appearance equipment included twin sport mirrors, a landau style half-roof, Super Stock wheels, special ornamentation and unique rear quarter windows.

POPULAR FACTORY OPTIONS *(con't.)*
glass, $42; Tinted windshield glass only, $30; Outside remote control mirror, $12; Left & right mirrors, $22; Custom steering wheel, $31; Tilt steering wheel, $45; Vinyl roof, $99; Wheel discs, $50; Wire wheel discs, $26; Super Stock II wheels, $72; Super Stock III wheels, $72.

Miscellaneous: Air conditioning, $397; Cruise control, $62; Anti-spin differential, $43; 250 hp engine, $137; Front disc power brakes, $46; Power steering, $113; Rear window defogger, $62; Superlift rear shock absorbers, $41; Four-speed wide-ratio transmission, $190; Turbo Hydra-matic transmission, $215; Remote trunk lid release, $14.

HP AUTOMOTIVE BOOKS

HANDBOOK SERIES

Auto Electrical Handbook
Auto Math Handbook
Baja Bugs & Buggies
Brake Handbook
Camaro Restoration Handbook
Clutch & Flywheel Handbook
Metal Fabricator's Handbook
Mustang Restoration Handbook
Off-Roader's Handbook
Paint & Body Handbook
Sheet Metal Handbook
Small Trucks
Street Rodder's Handbook
Turbochargers
Turbo Hydra-Matic 350
Welder's Handbook

CARBURETORS

Holley 4150
Holley Carburetors & Manifolds
Rochester Carburetors
Weber Carburetors

PERFORMANCE SERIES

How to Hot Rod Big-Block Chevys
How to Hot Rod Small-Block Chevys
How to Hot Rod Small-Block Mopar Engines
How to Hot Rod VW Engines
How to Make Your Car Handle
Small-Block Chevy Performance Handbook

REBUILD SERIES

How to Rebuild Air-Cooled VW Engines
How to Rebuild Big-Block Chevys
How to Rebuild Big-Block Fords
How to Rebuild Small-Block Chevys
How to Rebuild Small-Block Fords
How to Rebuild Small-Block Mopars
How to Rebuild Your Ford V-8

SPECIAL INTEREST

Auto Repair Shams & Scams
Car Collector's Handbook
Fast Fords
Guide to GM Muscle Cars

Books are available from your local auto store, bookstore or order direct from publisher,
Price Stern Sloan, 11150 Olympic Boulevard, Suite 650, Los Angeles, CA 90064.
Call toll-free: 800/421-0892.